Organisation Design

Organisation Design

Re-defining complex systems

Nicolay Worren

Harlow, England • London • New York • Boston • San Francisco • Toronto • Sydney • Auckland • Singapore • Hong Kong
Tokyo • Seoul • Taipei • New Delhi • Cape Town • São Paulo • Mexico City • Madrid • Amsterdam • Munich • Paris • Milan

Pearson Education Limited
Edinburgh Gate
Harlow
Essex CM20 2JE
England

and Associated Companies throughout the world

Visit us on the World Wide Web at:
www.pearson.com/uk

First published 2012
© Pearson Education Limited 2012

ISBN: 978-0-273-73883-1

British Library Cataloguing-in-Publication Data
A catalogue record for this book is available from the British Library

Library of Congress Cataloging-in-Publication Data
Worren, Nicolay A. M., 1966–
    Organisation design : re-defining complex systems / Nicolay Worren.
        p. cm.
    Includes bibliographical references and index.
    ISBN 978-0-273-73883-1
 1. Delegation of authority. 2. Line and staff organization. 3. Hierarchies.
4. Workflow. 5. Personnel management. 6. Complex organizations. I. Title.
    HD50.W67 2012
    658.4'02—dc23
                                                        2011053137

10 9 8 7 6 5 4 3 2 1
16 15 14 13 12

Typeset in 9/13pt Stone Serif by 30
Printed and bound by Ashford Colour Press Ltd, Gosport

On the one hand, design creates nothing. By itself, design is an empty vessel waiting to be filled with people, meanings, and actions . . . it is a dead form that has no life or energy itself . . . Yet on the other hand, it creates everything since the organisational design will have a fundamental framing effect on people's expectations and perceptions, setting the context for the organising activity – the social construction of roles and relationships – through which structure is enacted.

Bate, Khan & Pye (2000)

Brief contents

Contents

Supporting resources

Visit **www.pearsoned.co.uk/worren** to find valuable online resources:

For instructors

- Complete, downloadable Instructor's Manual
- PowerPoint slides that can be downloaded and used for presentations

For more information please contact your local Pearson Education sales representative or visit **www.pearsoned.co.uk/worren**

About the author

Nicolay Worren is an independent consultant specialising in organisation design. He has led or participated in more than 20 organisation re-design projects for firms in several industry sectors, including oil services, financial services, retail and telecom. He holds a master's degree from McGill University and received his doctorate from Oxford University. Worren lives in Oslo, Norway.

He writes a blog: *www.organizationdesign.net.*

Acknowledgements

I have benefited from the ideas and suggestions from numerous people in writing this book. I would like to thank the following individuals, who have discussed ideas and concepts with me or provided feedback on drafts:

- Ron Sanchez, Copenhagen Business School
- Tido Eger, WCI Consulting
- Kjartan Pedersen, Aker Solutions
- Alexander Huun, DNB
- Anne Flagstad, Oslo University Hospital
- Tor Håvard Sekse, Aker Solutions
- Jan Svendsen, PA Consulting Group
- Thorvald Hærem, BI Norwegian Business School
- Karl Moore, McGill University
- Ali A. Yassine, University of Illinois
- Tyson R. Browning, Texas Christian University
- Nam P. Suh, former professor, MIT
- Tore Skeide, Storebrand
- Kerstin Kampen, Nav
- Terje Bjølseth, Petroleum Geo-Services
- Tor Kielland, BrightArch
- Thomas Kirsebom, Navigio
- Pål Erik Engelsgaard, JP Morgan
- Ken Shepard, Global Organization Design Society

- Carlos Henao, Conocimiento Aplicado
- Fernando Rubio, Universidad Politécnica de Madrid
- Paul Tolchinsky, European Organisation Design Forum

As a first time author, I feel very fortunate in being able to publish my book with an internationally renowned publisher such as Pearson Education. I am grateful to Gabrielle James, the acquisitions editor, for having supported the project from start to finish. I am also grateful for the advice I received from the anonymous reviewers appointed by Pearson Education.

The writing process has demanded a lot of time that would otherwise have been spent with the family. My gratitude goes to my wife, Maria and to our children, Alvaro, Joaquim, Catalina, Tomas and Julia, for their patience and understanding. I also wish to thank another member of my family, Edmund Båtvik, for his support.

Nicolay Worren

Publisher's acknowledgements

We are grateful to the following for permission to reproduce copyright material:

Figures

Figure 2.7 from 'A methodology based on theory of constraints' thinking processes for managing complexity in the supply chain', doctoral thesis, Technical University of Berlin (SerdarAsan, S., 2009) p. 51, Figure 3.7, http://opus.kobv.de/tuberlin/volltexte/2009/2406/pdf/serdar_asan_seyda.pdf; Figure 4.2 adapted from 'Matrix organization designs: how to combine functional and project forms', *Business Horizons*, February, pp. 29–40 (Galbraith, J., 1971), p. 37, Figure 3, copyright © 1971 Elsevier, with permission from Elsevier.

Tables

Table 6.2 adapted from 'Disorganization theory and disorganizational behavior: towards an etiology of messes', *Research in Organizational Behavior*, vol. 24, pp. 139–80 (Abrahamson, E. 2002), copyright © 2002 Elsevier, with permission from Elsevier.

Text

Case study on pp. 31–2 from Academy of Management Newsletter: Executive of the Year Award 2007, http://publications.aomonline.org/newsletter/index.php?option=com_content&task=view&id=97&Itemid=10025 http://meeting.aomonline.org/2007/downloads/podcasts/Distinguished_Executive_AG_Lafley_Speech.pdf

In some instances we have been unable to trace the owners of copyright material, and we would appreciate any information that would enable us to do so.

Preface

Purpose

This book is written at a time when the field of organisation design is experiencing a revival. Yet despite an increasing interest among both practitioners and scholars, there are only a handful of textbooks in this area, and – to my knowledge – none that has been published recently. Many of the existing textbooks are very broad and only include organisation design as one of several topics such as strategy, change management and organisation development. It is therefore my hope that this book will fill a gap and prove useful to those who want to learn more about this exciting field of research and practice.

The book aims to be:

- *focused* – in concentrating on the core elements of organisation design;
- *current* – in addressing key challenges facing organisational leaders today;
- *rigorous* – in advocating the use of systematic, data-based approaches; and
- *pragmatic* – in developing prescriptions for action.

Audience

This book is primarily intended for:

- *MBA and other master-level students;*
- *participants in executive education programmes;*
- *postgraduate students* who are in the process of identifying topics for their research projects; and
- *internal and external consultants* and *project managers* who assist leaders in (re-) designing organisations.

Although the book has been written to provide an integrated and complete treatment of the core elements of organisation design, it is also possible to use individual chapters and combine these with chapters from other books.

Approach

Organisation design is sometimes considered as the applied version of *organisational theory*. Unfortunately, organisational theory is a diverse and fragmented field with many competing paradigms. In addition, scholars in many other disciplines, including law and economics, strategic management, operations management, engineering, sociology and psychology – carry out research that may have a bearing on organisation design issues.

For a textbook to be focused, and reasonably coherent theoretically, one faces some choices as an author. The basic orientation that I have adopted has led me to include some theories and frameworks, while leaving out others. I realise that some readers may have a different view of the field. I still hope that they accept my choices as logical, given the aims of the book.

The approach taken in this book is mainly inspired by systems theory as defined by Russell Ackoff (Ackoff and Emery, 1972). Ackoff emphasised that the study of systems is a *transdisciplinary* undertaking. He defined systems as sets of interrelated elements. He argued that human systems are purposeful, that is, goal-seeking, and have some degree of autonomy in being able to select goals as well as the means by which to pursue them.

We may add that the elements in question are roles (or groups of roles, i.e., units) rather than individuals (Jaques, 1990). This differentiates organisation design from organisation behaviour, which focuses mainly on the individuals in the organisation, as opposed to the roles they hold.

Among systems theorists, there are some who place greater emphasis on learning about the nature of real-world systems, while others concentrate on developing methodologies to intervene in and change systems (Jackson, 2000).

My thinking on this issue has been influenced by Chris Argyris, who argued that it should be the goal of social scientists to produce knowledge that can help people change the status quo. As he said:

> The most powerful empirical tests for theories are provided when predictions are made about changing the universe, not simply describing it.

(Argyris, 2005, p. 424)

Argyris goes on to say that one must specify causal and testable propositions about how to create change in order to produce actionable knowledge. I attempt to heed this advice by deriving specific design propositions that can be used as a basis for both interventions and empirical research.

The common theme through the different chapters is *organisational complexity*. The key assumption is that it should be the goal to minimise complexity in organisation design, as complexity reduces the probability that a system will achieve all of its goals.

In selecting topics to cover, I have focused on topics that I deem to be core elements of the field. I have also prioritised those areas where I think the book can make a contribution. As an example, I do describe some change management aspects of organisational re-design in Chapter 3, but the issues that receive the most attention are those that are specifically related to the design process (particularly the early phases when the key structural choices are made). This in no way assumes that other aspects of change management are unimportant – they are, but in my judgement, they fall outside the core area of the field and have already been well covered in existing texts.

Key features

Chapter overviews. Every chapter begins with an overview that briefly describes the background and current situation with regard to the chapter topic, the key challenges, the questions that these challenges raise and the proposed solutions.

Extensive use of examples. Every chapter features one or more examples that are used to illustrate the key conceptual ideas of the chapter. For the most part, the examples are based directly on real cases, but in some cases hypothetical cases have been developed for pedagogical purposes (although these are always an aggregation of observations that have been made in real companies).

Tools and frameworks. There are numerous tables and illustrations that summarise and visualise the key concepts being discussed.

Case exercises. Every chapter ends with a case exercise that is suitable for group or classroom discussion. All of the issues that are described are based on observations in real companies, but the identities of the companies have been disguised.

Review questions. The review questions are intended to aid the reader both in remembering the content and in reflecting on the implications of the issues being discussed.

Design propositions. Every chapter includes a list of actionable principles that practitioners can use as the basis for interventions in organisations.

Research questions. Every chapter also contains a list of research questions that identify important areas for further research in the field.

Teaching aids. A slide set and suggested case solutions are available to lecturers adopting this textbook from *www.pearsoned.co.uk/worren*.

Chapter structure

This book contains eight chapters, which may be divided into three parts.

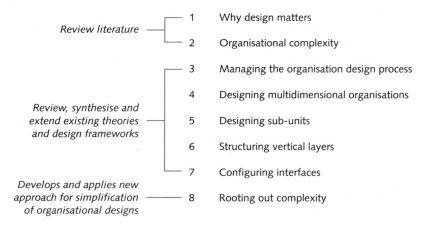

Chapters 1 and 2 review existing theory and research and thus provide the background for the subsequent chapters. Chapter 1 covers some key elements of organisational theory that have implications for organisational design in general. Chapter 2 focuses more specifically on theory and research related to organisational complexity.

Chapters 3 to 7 provide an in-depth discussion of the core elements of organisation design, beginning, in Chapter 3, by considering methodologies used for planning organisational re-design projects.

The subsequent chapters in this part roughly follow the sequence of an actual re-design project. As Russell Ackoff used to point out in his lectures, an architect draws the house (the whole), before he adds the rooms (the parts). In Chapter 4 we thus discuss various ways in which to design the overall structure of organisations. We proceed, in Chapter 5, by considering how sub-units are designed. We then look at the definition of roles and the placement of roles at different hierarchical layers in Chapter 6. Chapter 7 discusses how to improve interfaces, with the main emphasis on frameworks that are relevant once a sub-unit has been established.

Finally, Chapter 8 is slightly more experimental, in presenting a new approach aimed at identifying, analysing and simplifying complex organisational designs. The chapter is based on fairly detailed descriptions of five specific cases drawn from client engagements.

Your feedback

I welcome communication from readers. Readers may contact me directly or post a comment on my blog: *www.organizationdesign.net*.

References

Ackoff, R. L. and Emery, F. E. (1972). *On Purposeful Systems*. Chicago, IL: Aldine-Atherton.

Argyris, C. (2005). Actionable knowledge. In Tsoukas, H. and Knudsen, Ch. (eds), *Oxford Handbook of Organisation Theory*, pp. 423–52. New York: Oxford University Press.

Jackson, M. C. (2000). *Systems Approaches to Management*. London: Springer.

Jaques, E. (1990). *Creativity and Work*. Madison, CT: International Universities Press.

Chapter 1

Why design matters

Overview

Background

- Organisation design is part of every manager's job
- Empirical research confirms the potential impact of organisation design on the functioning and performance of organisations
- Three foundational concepts in the literature are hierarchical decomposition, strategy/structure alignment and coordination cost

Challenges

- Business schools have historically placed little emphasis on organisation design
- Management education has generally focused on *decision making* as opposed to the creation of decision alternatives (i.e., design)
- With the exception of some economics-based theories, academic research has generally failed to influence the actual design of organisations
- Well-known business 'gurus' have also downplayed the role of formal structure in creating effective organisations

Key question

- How can the discipline of organisation design be revitalised in order to ensure that it has a stronger impact on managerial practice – without losing academic rigour?

Proposed approach

- Reaffirm the strategic importance of design
- Adopt a 'design attitude' as a complement to the 'decision attitude'

- Use *organisational architecture* as the overarching concept
- Incorporate an explicit focus on purpose and functional requirements
- Develop prescriptive knowledge to bridge the gap between research and practice

Introduction

A project manager is recruited to the corporate staff of a large divisionalised firm to run a project charged with the implementation of a new IT system. During the first week in his new role, he discovers that there are three other IT projects, at the divisional level of the firm, that are configuring software solutions that will deliver the functionality that partly overlaps with the functionality that his project is supposed to deliver. He is pondering how the projects could be aligned and, as a first step, he draws a simple diagram that he intends to show to his manager to illustrate how the three projects interrelate.

The CEO of a national oil company asks his leadership team to consider how to organise its drilling teams. The company consists of several operating units, each responsible for the operations on a particular oil field. Each unit has its own drilling team, which is called on when new oil wells need to be drilled. Several members of the leadership team argue that this organisation is inefficient, as it is difficult to utilise capacity effectively across assets: at times, drilling teams in one unit have been idle while there have been insufficient resources to perform the work required in other units. The CEO challenges his team to come up with an alternative model.

A sales unit has grown to more than 25 people. The manager responsible for the unit feels that she spends too much time on administration and supervision of employees. She concludes that there needs to be two or three teams, each led by a manager who can be responsible for handling day-to-day responsibilities. However, she is not sure how to subdivide the unit. Should they be grouped according to geography, with one team for each main region, or by product, with one team for each main product category?

What these stories have in common is that they portray managers who, for various reasons, find themselves in the role of *organisational designers* attempting to make sense of, and improve, the functioning of complex organisations through the creation or adjustment of roles, processes and structures. This is also the topic of this book, which will review concepts and frameworks for re-designing complex organisations. This introductory chapter briefly introduces some key concepts that will serve as a foundation for the remaining chapters. It also reviews the status of organisation design – as a field of research and as a practical discipline – both its achievements, and some of its challenges and limitations. It then discusses how we can develop the field further to ensure that it provides research-based and useful knowledge that contributes to enhancing the effectiveness of organisations.

As the stories above suggest, organisation design is part of every manager's job. In fact, most managers are faced with organisation design challenges on an almost daily basis. Managers constantly design and re-design individual roles, define new projects (including their structure and reporting relationships) and contemplate better ways to coordinate organisational processes with multiple internal stakeholders. Periodically, they may also make more fundamental changes to the structure of sub-units or entire organisations, or participate in adapting and implementing high-level designs developed by others.

Many, if not most, professionals engage in design activities: engineers design products; architects design buildings; art directors design advertising campaigns. The main difference is the 'materials' with which one designs – in designing organisations, managers create, or re-define, *roles*, *processes* and *structures*. Unlike products, buildings and advertising campaigns, the outputs of organisation design processes are abstract and invisible artifacts (Kennedy, 2002). None the less, they are real enough for the people who work in the organisations that are being affected. Choices made during organisation design processes may to a large extent define people's roles and responsibilities, determine with whom they will collaborate, and either broaden or limit the career paths available to them.

Design is, as Romme (2003) formulated it, 'inquiry into systems that do not yet exist' (p. 558). The starting point is usually a problem or opportunity for which there is no self-evident solution, which triggers a process of search, aimed at identifying or developing a new solution that will work in the specific case with which one is confronted. For a manager, the problem or opportunity may have emerged as the result of external events (e.g., a merger) or may be the result of internal events (e.g., a decision to expand the business). The basic condition is that the manager, or a group of stakeholders, perceives that there is a potential for improvement, and initiates a design process to change the existing situation into a preferred one (Simon, 1996).

At times, *organisation design* and *organisation theory* are treated as synonymous. However, it may be useful to draw a distinction between the two. Organisation theory is essentially a *descriptive* field of study. Organisational theorists build theories to understand organisational functioning and carry out empirical research to test the validity of the theories (for example, examining whether the adoption of a certain corporate structure has an effect on the financial performance of firms). The term 'organisation design', on the other hand, more often refers to a body of *prescriptive* (or normative) knowledge – knowledge about what *one should do* in different situations in order to attain a given objective (Romme, 2003). The goal for many of those working in this field is to develop tools and frameworks that are *pragmatically valid* – that is, usable by practitioners attempting to create new organisations or re-design existing organisations (Worren et al., 1999).

Despite these differences, organisation design and organisation theory are certainly closely related. Indeed, there are several ideas developed by organisational theorists that have gained widespread acceptance, and that also inform organisation design methodology and practice. Below we will briefly review three concepts that are central to both organisation theory and organisation design: Hierarchical decomposition, coordination cost and fit or alignment (between strategy, environment and structure).

Foundational concepts

Hierarchical decomposition

In designing organisations, one sub-divides the organisation into, for example, divisions, work functions, departments, teams or roles. The basic process of dividing a system, composed of interacting elements, into units and sub-units is called *decomposition*. In this process, one decides which tasks, roles or processes should be grouped together in the same unit, thereby implicitly separating other tasks, roles and work functions. Depending on how far one decomposes the organisation, one also creates a hierarchical structure (Figure 1.1). One may choose to define a relatively flat structure (with many units at the same level, but few levels between the top and bottom) or may create a more pyramidal form (few units at the same level, but many levels between the top and bottom).

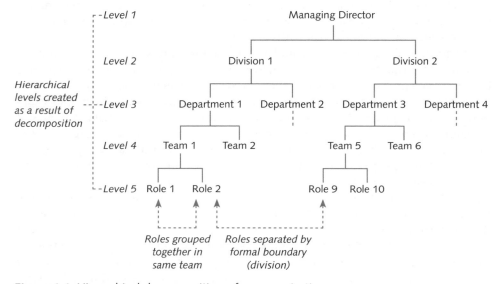

Figure 1.1 Hierarchical decomposition of an organisation

Decomposition creates several effects. The most immediate effect is *division of labour*, or specialisation. The basic idea of division of labour was first introduced by Smith (1776/1977), who described it as a key condition for increasing productivity. Smith explained that a worker who carries out one specific task repeatedly will likely develop greater skill, and perform the task faster, than a worker who switches between different tasks that they are not accustomed to performing. The same is true for sub-units of the organisation that focus on one functional area or one particular activity in a work process. Over time, specialisation allows the sub-unit to build up specialised knowledge pertaining to the specific functional area or activity in the work process for which it is responsible. It may also spur innovation, if the sub-unit has been granted the necessary operational autonomy to introduce changes to improve the performance of its work processes[1] (Sanchez, 1995; Jacobides, 2006).

There is another, related term used in the literature: *grouping* (e.g., Galbraith, 2001; Nadler and Tushman, 1997). Compared to the term decomposition, here one takes the 'bottom-up' perspective: instead of focusing on how one sub-divides a large systems into smaller parts, grouping involves the aggregation of parts (e.g., roles) that have already been defined into larger units. For example, one may define a set of roles, focused on, say, marketing, and decide that these should be grouped together in a new unit called 'the marketing department'. Another set of roles, related to sales, may be grouped together to form 'the sales department'.

Integration, on the other hand, is the task of developing relationships across the formal boundaries that separate the different sub-units that have been defined. For example, once you have decided that sales and marketing functions should be handled by two separate departments, the question becomes to what extent these two departments need to coordinate among themselves, and secondly, what 'coordination mechanisms' they should employ for this purpose. Coordination mechanisms range from unofficial means, such as informal meetings to exchange information, to the establishment of formal and structural linkages across sub-units. One may define a cross-functional process that ensures that information is shared and that work is coordinated across the two units; or one may alter the formal structure by having one manager oversee both units.

Aligning structure and strategy

There are many different ways of decomposing an organisation and many ways of integrating different sub-units. To understand the rationale guiding the decomposition of organisations, we first need to consider the relationship between the organisational structure and the firm's strategy. This relationship was first systematically studied by Chandler (1962), in his analysis of the historical development of large firms during the years 1850–1920. During this time period, new national and international markets emerged. In response to these external developments, some firms were able to grow rapidly in size by developing new products and scaling up their production facilities. Chandler observed that as firms adopted a diversification strategy, moving into new product or geographical areas, they moved from a functional to a multidivisional structure (Figure 1.2) (This observation was later supported by the empirical research carried out by Rumelt, 1974.) Unlike the more centralised functional structure, the multidivisional structure allowed relatively autonomous divisional executives to pursue growth within a given market segment, coordinated by a centralised executive office responsible for broad policies and coordination across the divisions. Chandler concluded that the multidivisional structure was a key innovation that simplified the management of diversity.

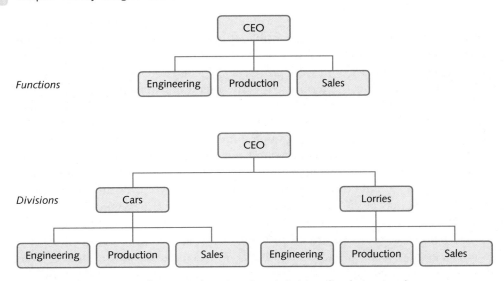

Figure 1.2 Comparison between functional and divisionalised structure[2]

The overall implication is that the structure of the organisation needs to be aligned with new strategies that are formed in response to changes in the business environment. This insight generated much research, particularly during the 1960s and 1970s. This line of research is referred to as *contingency theory* (for a review, see Donaldson, 2001). A key assumption is that high performing firms are those that find the right fit between the way the organisation is designed and the environmental contingencies it faces. For example, in stable, mature markets, consumers typically value reliable but low cost products. Firms in such market environments may thus succeed by focusing on efficient production. Work processes in these firms may be characterised by a high degree of formalisation (i.e., operating procedures that are documented and standardised). The formal structure may be relatively centralised and the responsibilities of different units and individual jobs may be both stable and clearly defined. More dynamic market environments, on the other hand, may require firms to innovate in order to provide new product features and/or adapt their strategies to respond to the actions of both existing competitors and new entrants. In such market environments, firms clearly need to develop internal flexibility to succeed; they need a capability to respond to changes introduced by new customer preferences, emerging technologies or competitor actions. Such firms typically require organisational structures that are easier to reconfigure. This may involve, among other things, allowing more autonomy to operating units (i.e., more decentralisation), use of temporary project teams, and more reliance on quick and informal communication to achieve coordination across units.[3]

◼ Coordination cost

A third, well-established principle is the concept of coordination cost.[4] This is a key criterion for guiding organisation design decisions, particularly more operational level decisions about grouping. This principle was first discussed in Gulick and Urwick (1937) but is more frequently attributed to Thompson (1967), who stated (p. 57):

> Under norms of rationality, organizations group positions to minimize coordination costs ...

> Organizations seek to place reciprocally interdependent positions tangent to one another, in a common group, which is (a) local and (b) conditionally autonomous.

In other words, when grouping people into units, managers seek to put the people who need to interact most frequently with each other (or most intensively) in the same sub-unit.[5] In most companies, accounting people are placed in one department, separate from other staff functions such as legal, communications, HR or procurement. In hospitals, doctors specialising in cardiology usually belong to the same department, whereas those who specialise in other disciplines, such as neurology or emergency medicine, belong to other departments. The IT consultants who configure software systems are normally placed in one team, while the consultants who plan and support implementation of the software system are placed in another.

The underlying assumption is that the cost of coordination is lower *within* than *across* a unit. In most cases, people who belong to the same unit coordinate effectively because they report to the same boss, pursue the same goals and priorities, share the same resources and usually work on the same physical premises. Over time, members of a sub-unit are likely to develop a shared culture, further facilitating collaboration. On the other hand, if one is dependent upon other units in performing one's work, it will require coordination with people who usually report to another manager, pursue different goals and priorities, work on a different site, and who may hold different norms and assumptions. It goes without saying then, that it is important to place the boundaries between units in the right places.

Key challenges facing the discipline

Although some organisation design concepts are by now well established, the discipline has, on the whole, exerted much less of an impact than one would expect. Today, several scholars concede that for a long period the field was marginalised as a result of a general neglect of the importance of design, combined with a lack of connection between theory and practice in management research and teaching.

Until recently, few business schools offered courses in organisation design as part of their undergraduate or MBA curriculums. The main focus has been on other subjects, such as corporate strategy, finance and organisational behaviour. More generally, Boland and Collopy (2004) contend that a 'decision attitude' has pre-vailed in management education. Case studies often portray managers facing a set of alternative courses of action from which a choice must be made. Similarly, manage-ment techniques such as net present value analysis seem to assume that it is easy to come up with alternatives to consider, but difficult to choose among them. Boland and Collopy argue that the decision attitude is useful in stable situations where the feasible alternatives are well known, but that a 'design attitude' is needed in more uncertain and demanding situations that require novel solutions.

As for research, despite the more than 40 years that have passed, Thompson's book dating from 1967 is still the most frequently cited book in the field (Heath and Staudenmayer, 2000). According to Jeffrey Pfeffer (1997), a leading management theo-rist, the key reason for this neglect is the general lack of interest in applied issues among business school faculty. A large number of studies are published each year on organisational issues, but most of these focus on testing existing theories rather than on resolving issues facing practising managers. The result is that managers rarely turn to academic research for guidance when considering how to design their organisa-tions (Rynes et al., 2002). Pfeffer notes that there are some lines of research, such as contingency theory, that initially focused on issues that were managerially relevant. However, even this research lost its relevance over time as it gradually employed more abstract, high-level theoretical constructs that were further removed from the 'design variables' that a manager can manipulate directly (see also Miller et al., 2009).

One possible cause of this problem is that traditional management research (par-ticularly that published in leading US journals) is modelled on the natural sciences, adopting rigorous, quantitative methods in describing organisational functioning. Bettis (1991) argued that this research paradigm only leads to *explanation*, not to meaningful *prescription*:

> What would we think for example, of medical schools whose research did not address the treatment of disease, or electrical engineering departments whose research did not aim at the improvement of integrated circuit design and manufacture, or law schools whose research did not address the interpretation of the U.S. Constitution by the courts?
>
> (Bettis, 1991, p. 317).

Bettis concluded that business schools should be modelled on other professional schools and that business school faculty to a greater extent should undertake 'prob-lem driven' as opposed to 'theory driven' research. He also argued that one needs to encourage the development of prescriptive implications based on the research, i.e., principles that managers can employ to re-design their organisations.

The lack of interest in organisation design has been releated to a more gen-eral scepticism toward 'structure' and toward hierarchical structures in particular. Hierarchies have been associated with a top-down, control-oriented management style (Leavitt, 2005). Indeed, a vast management literature has emerged since the 1950s that criticises (hierarchical) structure and advocates more informal and 'humane' ways of directing and coordinating work. Some of the best-known concepts include partici-pative management, transformational leadership, social networks and self-managing teams. The advent of modern information systems reinforced the impression that hierarchical structures would be supplanted by new and flatter organisational forms. (One of the effects of hierarchy is to regulate information flow. With modern information systems, information could be transferred at low cost; one of the key predictions by management theorists was thus that modern information systems would lead to a radical decentralisation of large hierarchies.) Well-known management gurus are among the most vocal opponents of (traditional) organisational designs. Tom Peters (2006) argued that the best companies are the most disorganised ones. Michael Hammer (2001), the originator of the term 're-engineering', stated in his 2001 book that the goal should be to create a 'structureless organization'.

Managers who are influenced by this rhethoric may underestimate the importance of the formal aspects of organising. Even if most managers accept that some structural forms are inappropriate in certain contexts, many have assumed that you can easily compensate for an inappropriate structure by encouraging informal collaboration across formal boundaries. For example, two product divisions that want to sell an integrated solution that includes both of the divisions' products may, instead of making any formal changes to their organisation, simply create an ad hoc project team charged with developing and selling the integrated solution to customers. Unfortunately, after having performed several studies on this subject, Hansen (2009) concluded that as many as two-thirds of all attempts at informal collaboration across formal organisational boundaries fail to produce a positive return. His conclusion is that managers often underestimate the cost of informal collaboration.

The story of Oticon, a Danish hearing aid manufacturer, is a case in point. In 1990, it introduced a radical new organisational form called the 'spaghetti organisation'. According to the then CEO, Lars Kolind, the new organisation should consist of 'knowledge centres . . . connected by a multitude of links in a non-hierarchical structure' (Foss, 2003, p. 333). The new organisation only consisted of two formal layers: a management group of 10 people, and the employees, working in temporary projects. The goal was to remove the need for management intervention and create a self-organising company. For example, employees could join whichever projects they wanted, and project managers were free to manage the projects as they wanted, once the project had been ratified in a management committee. Oticon was able to introduce several new products during the 1990s (such as in-the-ear hearing aids) and experienced increased growth and financial performance. It was hailed by Tom Peters – as well as several business magazines – as a prime example of a network-based, innovative company.[6] Just like Michael Hammer, the message seemed to be that 'Structure is out.'

A few years later, however, a Danish researcher, Nicolai Foss (2003), decided to examine the Oticon organisation in more detail. His version is quite different from the story about Oticon that had been created by business journalists and management gurus. First, he discovered that the organisational model was far from as decentralised as one was made to believe. In fact, the CEO, through his role as chairman of the so-called 'Projects and Products' committee, retained ultimate decision-making authority, as no project would receive funding without the committee's approval. However, the real problem appeared after a project had been ratified. It became clear that the committee could at any time halt, change or even shut down projects, and that this kind of intervention took place frequently. The result was frustration among project managers, who felt that their projects could be arbitrarily interrupted, and declining motivation among employees in general, because of the gap between the official rhetoric of delegation and the actual manner of governance in the firm. A second problem that Foss observed related to competition for employees. Managers had no guarantee that they could actually carry their projects through, because of the risk that key team members would leave and instead join other projects. Oticon gradually realised that the organisation was not working as intended and, starting in 1995, made several changes to the model including introducing a more layered organisation. As Foss dryly concludes: 'the spaghetti organization may have been beset by organizational costs that came to dominate the benefit aspects' (Foss, 2003, p. 332).

In fairness, we should note that even management gurus learn, and adjust their message accordingly. In a more recent article, Michael Hammer acknowledged that unclear accountability is a common cause of failure in process improvement efforts (Hammer, 2004). Since structure can basically be defined as an accountability hierarchy (a system for allocating roles and responsibilities), Hammer seems to concede that being structureless may not be such a good idea after all. Moreover, it should be emphasised that the moral of the Oticon case is not that we should stop experimenting with new ways of organising. Indeed, Oticon introduced a number of important concepts, which we should try to study and refine. Importantly, Nicolai Foss notes in his paper that the spaghetti organisation might have been a viable organisational form, had it been more carefully designed.

Even as traditional organisation theory has yielded less and less influence on managerial practice (Miller et al., 2009), and much of the rhetoric directed at managers has focused on other issues than design, there is one notable exception, namely *organisational economics* (Williamson, 1981; Jensen, 1983). As noted in Pfeffer (1997), economists have recently displayed an eagerness to take on topics traditionally left to psychologists and sociologists. Economic models and methods have been used to study such organisational issues as the effects of rewards and incentives on performance, the boundaries between firms and markets and the advantages and disadvantages of different organisational structures.

However, the import of economics-based models into organisation theory and the use of such models in providing guidance to managers is controversial. A number of well-known scholars have argued that these models are ill-suited as prescriptive frameworks (Ghoshal, 2005; Pfeffer, 1997; Davis et al., 1997). The economics-based models are based on somewhat pessimistic assumptions about human nature, as they assume that people are primarily driven by self-interest, and will act 'opportunistically', that is, seek to maximise their own 'utility function' rather than that of the organisation to which they belong. One concern is that the application of these ideas will lead to control-oriented management practices, where the main task is seen as using surveillance, monitoring and authority to curb opportunistic behaviour. There is also only mixed empirical support for many of the key predictions made in agency theory as well other economics-based organisational theories (Pfeffer, 1997; Ghoshal, 2005).

We may add that this perspective is of limited value in illuminating some of the more prosaic challenges that organisational designers must deal with. The organisational economics literature has focused on conflicts of interest between the principal and the agent, assuming the principal and agent are already known. If one were to apply this approach at a lower level in an organisation, the initial problem would probably be to define who the principals and the agents actually are. Organisational designers will frequently encounter situations where these roles are poorly defined or where the same individual plays the role of both agent and principal in different processes, or where the same agent is responsible for multiple and poorly coordinated principals.

The value of effective designs

Given the challenges described, there is a need to consider how the organisation design discipline can best adapt to stay relevant. How can we ensure that managers fully exploit the potential of effective design? How can we develop design knowledge that can be of help to those who seek to improve the effectiveness of their organisations? What can we do to generate more attention to organisation design among business school faculty?

In the following, some important developments are described that may contribute in revitalising the discipline: the adoption of a *design attitude*, the introduction of the term *architecture* as an overarching concept; a stronger focus on purpose and requirements in design methodologies; and the introduction of a new, solutions-oriented research paradigm that can improve the interface between research and practice. The first priority, however, should probably be to reaffirm the importance of the concept itself.

It is clear that organisation design decisions have a major impact on how an organisation functions and performs. The most obvious examples may be decisions regarding the vertical layering of organisations. Such decisions define the hierarchical structure – in particular, the number of vertical layers, which in turn determine the size of units and the span of control for each manager (the number of direct reports per manager) and the hierarchical placement of different functions and roles (for example, whether different staff functions are placed at the corporate level, or decentralised to the divisional level). The vertical structuring of a firm also has a direct impact on costs – a flatter organisation will have fewer managers (which usually are the more expensive resource). Indeed, one explanation for why organisations are pyramidal in shape is the fact that resources become more expensive the higher you go in the hierarchy.[7] Decisions regarding vertical structure may also have longer-term, more indirect effects on both work processes and individual jobs. Flat structures generally have smaller status differences and provide more autonomy for the individual worker. On the other hand, flat structures also require that managers spend more time resolving differences and coordinating the efforts of their many subordinates (Mintzberg, 1979). Flat structures also provide fewer ladders in the internal career paths available to employees (i.e., a reduced chance of promotion).

There are a number of empirical studies that evaluate the impact of organisational design on organisational functioning. Some studies have investigated the effects of grouping decisions. These studies generally show, as would be expected, that people belonging to the same formal unit communicate much more frequently with each other than with people in other units. For example, a study in Norwegian governmental ministries showed that 73 per cent of employees indicated that they interacted frequently (i.e., once or more per week) with colleagues within their own ministry; only 41 per cent indicated that they had frequent contact with employees belonging to other ministries (Egeberg, 1989).[8] A similar study from Germany concluded that conflicts over policy were more than twice as frequent in interactions across governmental departments as in interactions within a department (Scharpf, 1977, cited in Mintzberg, 1979).

It is also well documented that organisation design has an impact on individual motivation and productivity. Several studies have looked at sources of stress, and concluded that it is not only the work load or pace of work that create stress, but the design of the job itself (Wong et al., 2007). In particular, employees may experience stress due to role conflicts and role ambiguity, which in turn is related to the existence of (and nature of) interdependencies. Employees may be subject to conflicting expectations from different parties, or face uncertainty about with whom or what they need to coordinate. As we will consider in greater depth in the following chapters, these are typical symptoms of complex organisations, and reflect managerial decisions regarding the definition of individual roles, allocation of responsibility and grouping of functions.

There are also studies that consider the effect of organisation design choices on firm performance. A study of 244 manufacturing firms examined the relationship between organisational structure, lean manufacturing practices and plant performance (Nahm et al., 2003). The organisational variables that were considered were the nature of formalisation (the reliance upon written procedures), the number of layers in the hierarchy, the level of horizontal integration, locus of decision making and the level of communication. The study concluded that there were strong relationships between these organisational variables and the implementation of lean manufacturing practices, which in turn was positively related to plant performance (measured as sales growth, return on investment, market share gain and overall competitive position). More specifically, the study showed that the most successful firms in this sample had few hierarchical layers, combined with a high level of horizontal integration. The successful firms pushed decision making down the organisation, achieved fast, easy and abundant sharing of information, and encouraged creativity and learning among employees.

The most dramatic illustrations of the value of organisation design come from studies of horizontal integration. One study, published in a medical journal, investigated the outcomes over two decades for patients with a serious form of cancer (high-grade bone sarcoma) (Aksnes et al., 2006). Although the same basic medical techniques were available during the time period of the study (1980–99), the survival rate increased from 39 per cent to 53 per cent (the use of chemotherapy remained stable during the period, while the amputation rate decreased from 64 per cent to 23 per cent). The authors concluded that the improved survival rate was due to more effective use of existing medical techniques, which in turn was made possible by better organisation of the hospital's cancer treatment teams. During the period, the responsibility for treating this form of cancer was centralised (transferred to one institution) and new patient databases were introduced which allowed more systematic monitoring of the activities and outcomes of the cancer treatment programme. However, the most significant change, according to the authors,[9] was 'that *the specialists involved in cancer treatment were organised into multidisciplinary teams*, where all decisions regarding diagnosis and treatment were taken by the group as a whole.

Indeed, many crises and breakdowns have been attributed to a lack of effective integration. For example, the failure to prevent the 9/11 terrorist attacks has been partly blamed on an inability to share information across different US agencies responsible for security. During the months leading up to the attacks, several agencies were receiving frequent, but fragmentary reports about threats, including reports about an imminent attack in the US by terrorists associated with Al Qaeda. However, officials employed by the various agencies often failed to share information across the different US bodies and agencies responsible for law enforcement, intelligence and security. For example, it was known to FBI that potential terrorists were undergoing flight training in the United States, but this information was not passed on to the Federal Aviation Authorities, who issued a pilot's license to one of the terrorists. To investigate the facts and circumstances relating to the terrorist attacks, President Bush set up the 9/11 Commission. In its final report,[10] many of the recommendations centre on organisational changes required for more effective counterterrorism intelligence. The report points to 'structural barriers to performing joint intelligence work' (p. 408) and also laments the complexity of a system of 15 different agencies in intelligence gathering and analysis (including the FBI, CIA, Immigration authorities, Customs service, Federal Aviation Administration, National Security Agency, etc.). One of the key recommendations made was to establish a central body, led by a National Intelligence Director, to oversee the different agencies.

Table 1.1 summarises some hypothesised effects of organisation design decisions. In the table, the 'direct outcomes' are the immediate effects resulting from organisation design choices. For example, the number of layers, the number of sub-units, the size of units, etc. are direct consequences of decomposition and grouping decisions. The causal chain is somewhat longer for 'intermediary' outcomes, and for 'eventual outcomes' organisation design choices have an indirect impact on the outcomes listed, together with many other internal and external factors. As the examples above indicate, there does exist empirical support for many of the hypothesised effects indicated in the table, but future research will undoubtedly further our understanding of the nature and strength of the linkages between different design choices and organisational outcomes.

Table 1.1 Traditional focus areas of organisation design and some hypothesised effects

Key design activity	Description	Direct outcomes	Intermediary outcomes	Eventual outcomes
Decomposition and grouping	Sub-division of the organisation into lower level elements (divisions, departments, teams, etc.) or aggregation of lower level elements (e.g., roles/jobs) into higher order units (e.g., teams, departments, divisions)	• Number of layers (the degree to which an organisation has many versus few layers of management) • Specialisation/differentiation (the number of sub-units and the scope of their responsibilities) • Size of units and span of control (the number of people in each unit, and consequently the number of people reporting to each manager) • Locus of decision making (the degree to which decision-making authority is placed at a high versus low level in the organisational hierarchy) • Employee costs (cost arising from the number of employees and managers required at different levels of the organisation)	• Degree of alignment with strategy (the extent to which the organisation has the required capabilities, structures and processes to realise its strategic goals) • Structural coherence (the extent to which the different units have been defined in a consistent manner in order to minimise overlaps, gaps and goal conflicts) • Communication patterns (the extent to which people interact within versus between units) • Coordination costs (the costs associated with exchanging information and adjusting to actions of interdependent units) • Career paths (the vertical and horizontal career paths) • Role clarity (the extent to which the purpose and expectations of jobs are perceived as clear by the job holders) • Autonomy and authority (the degree to which jobs allow decision-making latitude) • Inter-unit conflict (the frequency and severity of conflicts between sub-units)	• Overall performance (the organisation's ability to attain its objectives and satisfy stakeholder expectations) • Productivity (the outputs produced in relation to the inputs expended) • Employee satisfaction (employee's level of satisfaction with their job)
Integration	Establishment of mechanisms to facilitate vertical and horizontal coordination	• Level of vertical and horizontal integration (the degree to which there has been defined formal or informal processes crossing the main vertical organisational boundaries)	As above, plus: • Information flow and knowledge transfer (the extent to which (and speed at which) information is actively shared across vertical and horizontal boundaries) • Resource utilisation and sharing (the degree to which resources are utilised across internal boundaries) • Joint value creation (the extent to which sub-units collaborate in creating new business opportunities) • Social networks (the extent of informal ties among members of different sub-units)	

The table is based on the relatively narrow definition of design as the decomposition and integration of formal structures. It is also based on the traditional conception of organisation design as an element of *strategy implementation* rather than *strategy formulation*, in other words, as a topic that one can attend to once the strategic goals have been set.

More recent theorising suggests that this conceptualisation may be too restrictive in some cases, in that design also influences the ability to *form* new strategies. Chandler's (1962) dictum was that 'structure follows strategy' and the contingency theorists similarly operationalised structure as the *dependent variable*, whereas the environment and strategy were defined as the *independent variables* (Mintzberg, 1979). Rather than adapting the structure to the strategy, however, successful firms also take their existing structure into account when choosing which strategy to pursue. This possibility was documented in a study of US pizza restaurants reported in Yin and Zajac (2004). The results show that franchised stores were more likely to pursue complex strategies that allowed them to capitalise on their flexibility and local responsiveness as semi-independent entities, whereas company-owned stores tended to pursue simpler strategies that emphasise predictability and control.

For firms facing dynamic environments, the very distinction between strategy and structure may itself become blurred. It is rarely feasible for top managers to create longer-term strategies if the environment is undergoing rapid change. And even if it were possible to strategise from the top, Roberts (2004) pointed out that by the time a new, long-term strategy could be communicated and the organisation restructured, the environment might have changed again. Management can set a broad strategic direction, but is reliant on the decisions taken at the various levels within the organisation in order to respond to on-going market developments. What management can do, however, is to create the right structure and processes to allow effective strategic decision making at lower levels of the organisation. In this sense, *strategy becomes a design for an adaptive organisational structure* (Haeckel, 1999).

Design attitude

During the last few years, several conferences and workshops on design have been held, suggesting an increasing interest in the concept among both practitioners and researchers. Some of these conferences have taken a broad view – considering design as a generic approach to problem solving, relevant to all fields of management. In contrast to the prevailing 'decision attitude', the goal of some key proponents, such as the group summoned by Boland and Collopy (2004), is to instil a 'design attitude', inspiring and energising new designs for products, services and processes that are both profitable and humanly satisfying.

What implications would follow from adopting a 'design attitude' in terms of how we think about the form and function of organisations? One key implication is probably that we need to consider how to conduct effective *design processes*.

Traditionally, considerable attention within organisation design has been focused on organisational *models*. Is a divisionalised structure better than a functional structure? Should companies adopt a market-based structure? Does a process-based structure offer a viable alternative to a functional organisation? The development and selection of the right organisational model certainly remain important issues. We need to develop better organisational models, ensure that this knowledge is disseminated to managers and learn from the experience of implementing the models.

However, the design processes in which organisational models are developed and selected are also important. Managers face a number of challenges in such processes:

How do we deal with multiple, conflicting requirements?

How do we create consensus for change among different internal stakeholders?

How do we ensure that the design process actually achieves its aim?

An improved understanding of design processes may make it possible to provide more effective tools and methods to support managers.

The challenges faced by managers are similar to those faced by practitioners in other 'design sciences', such as architecture and engineering. Whether one is designing a product, a building or an organisation, the task is similar. One must try to understand a system of multiple components, identify the requirements from different stakeholders, visualise possible solutions and create a blueprint for how the solution can be realised (Liedtka, 2000). Although the *content* is different, the *process* of design is similar across different fields.

For product designers, sketching and modelling are important tools when they try to visualise 'what might be'. In organisations, visual depictions of business processes and reporting structures are often thought of mainly as tools for communicating new designs to people who have not been part of the decision process. However, these are visual tools that potentially play a much more important role:

> The problem space that a manager deals with in her mind or in her computer is dependent upon the way she represents the situation that she faces. The first step in any problem-solving episode is representing the problem, and to a large extent, that representation has the solution hidden within it.

> (Boland and Collopy, 2004, p. 9)

In addition to helping a manager frame a problem, tools also play an important social role in enabling 'cognitive coordination', that is, helping to establish shared reference points among a diverse group of stakeholders in the design process (Werr et al., 1997). Sometimes, the choice of tools contributes to an unnecessary narrowing of the 'problem space'. Using an organisation chart as the main tool in a design process may create clarity with regard to the vertical structure and reporting lines, but may lead participants to ignore possibilities for improvements in terms of how units coordinate and integrate their efforts. The question is thus how we can develop effective tools to support design processes. This is an issue we shall return to repeatedly in the remaining chapters of this book.

Organisational architecture

In the literature, the term *organisational architecture* is increasingly used instead of the more traditional term *organisational structure*. The difference is not merely semantic. Organisational architecture refers to a wider set of characteristics than the term organisational structure (Gerstein, 1992). Organisational structure is usually defined as the formal reporting relationships that define roles and authority at different levels of the organisation. Architecture potentially encompasses other elements, such as processes used for governance and even informal means of coordinating and organising work (e.g., social networks and ad hoc commitments made among organisational members). The notion of architecture may also help us to see organisations, and the design process, from a different perspective. It encourages us to think about the process of building organisations, the fit between the organisation and its environment and the coherence of different design elements.

Gerstein (1992) reviewed the history of architecture and asked what lessons we could learn from physical architecture that would help us design more effective organisations. He noted, first of all, that *architecture is purposeful*. Architecture is defined as the art and science of creating structures or systems whose function fulfil an intended purpose. Similarly, one can view organisational architecture as the conceptual design of key roles, processes and structures intended to realise the firm's strategic intent and the requirements of key stakeholders. In other words, the process of organisation design must start with a fundamental understanding of the purposes to be served by the organisation.

We often think about designs as applying only to unique instances, such as a building (Kennedy, 2002). But organisational architectures can be adaptive and 'generative' platforms, that is, allow the firm to develop and grow by generating an infinite set of processes by replicating, scaling and reconfiguring a finite set of basic architectural elements. For example, a large manufacturing firm may create a blueprint for how to organise its plants that specifies how to design processes, roles and operating procedures at the plants. Creating such a blueprint is a vehicle for a firm to codify its internal best practices and create a platform for knowledge sharing. However, it may also help the firm expand, by reducing the time and cost that it takes to establish a new plant or re-design an existing plant. The blueprint may even be flexible enough to support a strategic move into another product area, even if it requires somewhat different machinery or manufacturing processes. In this sense, architecture is *future oriented*. An architect's building 'should preferably be ahead of its time when planned so that it will be in keeping with the times as long as it stands' (Rasmussen, 1991, cited in Gerstein, 1992, pp. 14–15).

Architectures should represent *unifying and coherent structures* (McDavid, 1999). As Stephen Haeckel (1999) pointed out, a collection of decisions that make local sense are unlikely to cohere into a purposeful organisational design. Different parts of the system must 'fit together'. If a firm does not, at a minimum, have some common principles and priorities, local decision makers will have no common frame or standard with which decision alternatives can be compared. A manufacturing firm not only needs to ensure that each plant works effectively, but that the different plants that it operates function effectively together in a manufacturing network.

This presents us with the apparent contradiction of *designing for autonomous action*. Architectures should enable coherency by providing a *context* for individual action and decision making rather than by dictating individual behaviour. Blueprints for how to organise a plant are likely to include certain mandatory elements (e.g., procedures for Health, Safety and Environment), but they may also contain many optional elements, intended primarily as a guide to decision making, as well as recommended practices that local plant managers are encouraged to develop further, based on the experience that they gain locally.

Axiomatic design theory

The fact that the design process is fairly generic may allow us to borrow tools and methods that are used for design in other professions. Within the engineering sciences, there is an approach called axiomatic design theory (Suh, 2001), which may be particularly suited to organisation design.

As already mentioned, some parts of the literature have focused on describing generic organisational models and have focused less strongly on why and how models are developed/adjusted to the unique requirements of an organisation. The assumption has perhaps been that by first considering the firm's overall strategy, one would have enough information to select the right organisational structure. Indeed, Galbraith (2001, p. 13) stated, 'Strategy establishes the goals and criteria for choosing among organisational forms.' However, the strategy is rarely specific enough to allow choices to be made about alternative organisational designs, particularly at lower levels of the organisation. It is not necessarily the case, either, that feasible decision alternatives even exist (Boland and Collopy, 2004). In such cases, the main challenge is not to choose among pre-existing alternatives, but to conceive of and develop new alternatives. The high-level organisational models presented in textbooks (including the present one) are, at best, ideas that can be further developed and adapted for the particular organisation that one is (re)designing. If we want to ensure the development of purposeful architectures, we need an approach that can help elucidate what the requirements are and ensure that a design is developed in a manner that maximises the chance that the requirements will be met.

In systems theory (Ackoff and Emery, 1972) one distinguishes between the *purpose* that a system is serving (why it exists), the *functions* that it is intended to perform (what it does), and the design parameters (how it is done). Axiomatic design theory (Suh, 2001) builds on this distinction by considering the relationship between functions and design parameters.

Articulating and agreeing on a purpose for the system to be designed is fundamental in all design activities, including the design of organisations. Stephen
Haeckel (1999) has called this the *reason for being* – managers must be able to explain
why the organisation (or a sub-unit) exists. Provided that a purpose has been
defined, it will be the starting point for identifying specific functions or *functional
requirements* (FRs) to the system. A function is *what* we want to achieve – a statement identifying a necessary characteristic or capability of a product (or system) for
it to have value or utility for the user (or for a group of stakeholders). Ideally, the FR
is phrased in a solution-neutral manner (usually starting out with a verb), to avoid
narrowing the space of possible solutions. For a car, a functional requirement may
be 'transport passengers'. In organisational designs, a functional requirement can
best be thought of as the purpose or desired outcomes produced by an entire organisation or by a sub-unit (for example, 'market and sell cars'), which in turn can be
operationalised as more specific requirements.

A *design parameter* specifies *how* we intend to satisfy a functional requirement. For
a product, a design parameter may be a physical component ('vehicle with engine'),
whereas it will be an organisational sub-unit, team or process in organisational
design (for example, 'sales department'). It may also be an individual role – if that
role performs a unique function in the organisation. Design parameters are usually
phrased using a noun to distinguish them from the functional requirements.

These concepts provide a refined understanding of how one may decompose an
organisation. The key proposition is that both functional requirements and design
parameters corresponding to each functional requirement should be explicitly
defined as part of the design process. As explained by Suh (2001), one starts in the
'what' domain and then moves to the 'how' domain (see Figure 1.3). Consider the
design of a life insurance company. The overall mission or strategic intent (Hamel
and Prahalad, 1989) may be stated as, for example, that of 'maximising profits by
offering life insurance products that provide security and protection for individuals
and their families'. We may adopt this mission statement as our top-level functional
requirement. We then proceed by determining the corresponding design parameter
('Life insurance company'). One then goes back to create the functional requirements at the next level. For an insurance company, there are typically four key
functional requirements. First, one must develop products that customers perceive as
attractive (one might add that the products should be attractive to the company as
well – a key challenge is to set a price (insurance premium) that is affordable, while
taking into account the insurer's risk, based on an assessment of the probability and
cost of a loss). Second, one must maximise premium income by maximising sales
of new insurance policies. (Here one might add that one should also ensure that
customers don't deflect once they have bought a policy.) Third, one must admin-
ister the pension plans and handle claims. Finally, one must maximise the return
on invested capital. (A key source of income for insurance companies is the profits
earned from investments funded by the income from the sales of insurance policies.)
Each of these requirements is satisfied by the definition of an organisational unit.[11]
This process of decomposing proceeds layer by layer until one has provided enough
information to implement the design.

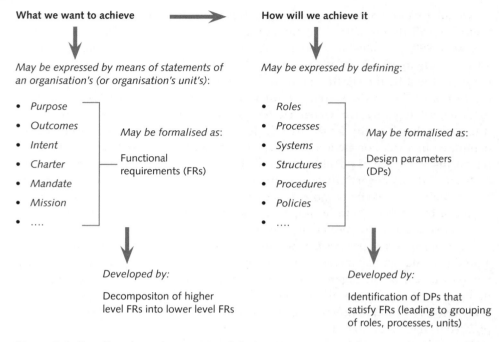

Figure 1.3 Functional requirements and design parameters and more commonly used terms to describe organisations

The design parameters listed in Figure 1.4 represent the structure of a traditional insurance company. However, several design options exist. One key factor is the extent to which an insurance company is vertically integrated (i.e., the extent to which it controls lower-level processes involved in the development and delivery of its products and services). There are insurance companies that do not have any internal sales units and that instead rely on intermediaries to distribute their products. There are even insurance companies that outsource the investment management process to competitors deemed to have superior capabilities in this area.

It is important to note that although design parameters, in principle, are formulated to satisfy functional requirements, the relationship is to some extent reciprocal in the sense that high-level design parameters will also have an influence on lower-level functional requirements. For example, if an insurance company defines a sales unit as a DP, it may, at a lower level, identify 'manage sales process' as an FR, whereas this will not be a relevant FR for a company that has chosen an intermediary channel to sell and distribute products. (Such companies may instead identify 'manage intermediaries' as a lower-level functional requirement.)

The *design hierarchy* created by decomposition is somewhat different from the term *hierarchical structure*. As Thompson (1967) pointed out, it is unfortunate that the term hierarchy is associated only with 'highness' and 'lowness' related to authority relationships. Although the chosen design will be translated into an organisational structure, which also represents a hierarchy of authority, axiomatic theory

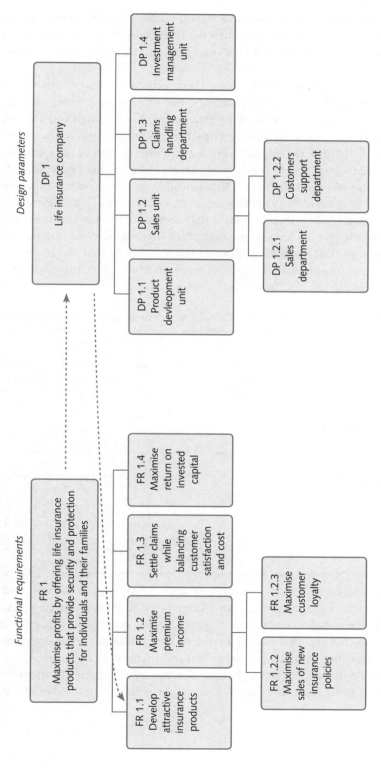

Figure 1.4 Decomposing FRs and DPs for the design of a life insurance company

is primarily about defining the *hierarchy of functionality* (Haeckel, 1999). Each level in a design hierarchy is not only higher than the level below, but also represents a more inclusive clustering, one that combines and integrates the functions of lower-level units.

There are several advantages to using these principles derived from axiomatic theory. By defining functional requirements, one orients the process toward objectives and desired outcomes. Second, by gradually decomposing both FRs and DPs, one creates a design hierarchy that links higher-level objectives to lower-level roles and processes.[12, 13] Third, the approach encourages the creation of coherent designs if one ensures that lower-level FRs collectively satisfy the FR at the higher level. Finally, by mapping the FRs against the DPs in a so-called design matrix (as illustrated in Table 1.2) one may evaluate the correspondence between FRs and DPS more systematically. The most obvious requirement is that there should exist DPs to satisfy every FR. The approach also encourages an analysis of dependencies among the different FRs and DPs to control the total number of FRs and ensure that the achievement of one FR does not compromise the achievement of other FRs (a topic which will be discussed in more detail in Chapter 2).

Table 1.2 Design matrix that maps functional requirements against design parameters

	Design parameters			
Functional requirements	Product development unit	Sales unit	Pensions and claims settlement unit	Investment management unit
Develop attractive insurance products	X			
Maximise premium income		X		
Administer client accounts and settlements			X	
Maximise return on managed funds				X

By abstracting key features from a specific design, the tools used in axiomatic design should facilitate effective communication between practitioners, and allow comparisons across organisations. For example, by mapping different insurance companies by means of a matrix as shown in Table 1.2, one would quickly be able to identify the key features of the design chosen by the different companies (provided that the information the matrices contain has been accurately recorded).

The PowerPoint presentations that are used in most organisations to describe structures and processes often fail to convey the underlying logic of the designs being presented. Different individuals may use slightly different formats for describing the same organisational characteristics (perhaps as a result of the relative ease with which graphical symbols can be created with today's software). Many presentations do not explicitly list the design criteria (why a given design was chosen), what the functional requirements of the organisation are (what it is supposed to do or what goals it is supposed to achieve), let alone how functional requirements map to the design parameters. Without such information it is difficult to systematically compare designs and share knowledge. In contrast, the mapping tools used in axiomatic design provide a standard 'vocabulary and grammar' for describing organisational functioning.

It is important to add that one will rarely have complete freedom in defining the design parameters. There will usually be a number of both internal and external constraints that reduce the number of design options available to managers. One type of external constraints is the laws and regulations that affect the industry. As an illustration, consider financial services. The financial services industry in most countries is already highly regulated, but following the finance crisis, even stronger regulation was proposed, some of which may affect the way financial institutions are organised. There is an international body – the Basel Committee on Banking Supervision – which develops guidelines and supervisory standards for banks that member states may adopt in statutory form. (In Europe, similar guidelines for insurance companies are developed as part of the Solvency initiative.) Some of the guidelines being developed affect organisation design directly, for example, by specifying the roles, processes and structure of the risk management function in financial institutions.

If there is more than one design parameter available for satisfying a functional requirement, on what grounds does one select the most appropriate DP? We will consider in detail in Chapter 3 how one selects and evaluates *design criteria* given the particular challenges that a particular organisation is facing. However, Suh (2001) maintains that there are also general design criteria (or axioms) that apply across different situations. One such criterion is *the probability of achieving the design goals* as expressed by the functional requirements.[14] One key consideration is whether the organisation in question has the necessary capability to implement the proposed design (or perform according to the principles implied by the design, once implemented). A proposed design may be adequate from a purely functional point of view, yet the current organisation may be incapable of implementing it. For example, there may be proposals that require significant improvements in the quality of internal processes or radical changes in the way different units relate to each other. One may therefore state as a general design criterion that, if faced with a choice between two or more sets of designs parameters that both address the functional requirements, one should select the set that is easiest to implement, given the current organisational capabilities. In Chapter 2, we will explore this issue further by considering the situation when there are multiple and conflicting functional requirements.

'Layers' of design parameters

We mentioned that roles, processes or structures are examples of organisational design parameters.[15] This topic deserves some more deliberation, as it goes to the heart of how we define organisation design. The term was traditionally defined somewhat narrowly, as the formal and semi-formal means used to divide labour and integrate the work of different roles and sub-units (cf. Table 1.1). More recently, the tendency is to employ very wide definitions of organisation design, and some practitioners and authors now include informal and emergent aspects or organisations, such as corporate culture, or individual level characteristics, such as attitudes and skills.

Yet as Mintzberg (1979) stated, design assumes discretion, that is, an ability to alter a system. This means that our definitional framework should only include parameters that a manager can actually manipulate. At the same time, it should be broad enough to include all of the relevant design parameters that are at a manager's disposal. Moreover, recognising that design activities may take place at many levels – from individual roles to the overall structure of large organisations – we should try to avoid restricting our definition to design parameters that are only applicable at one particular level.

Given these considerations, we would suggest that organisational design parameters can be conceptualised as five different 'layers' (Table 1.3). The first layer is the *Governance model*, which defines the formal roles, decision rights and accountabilities. The second layer is the *Operating model*, which decomposes the core activities of the organisation into units and processes. The third layer is the *Resource model*, which defines the principles and processes used to fund units and allocate resources. The fourth is the *Contracting model*, which specifies how a role or unit will interact with other roles or units to establish agreements and fulfil commitments. Finally, we also include a layer called the *Social network model*, to cover design parameters that are chosen to deliberately shape the social network and create ties between individuals, for example, in order to facilitate efficient knowledge sharing and coordination across two formally defined units. Together with the corresponding functional requirements, these five layers constitute an 'organisational architecture', that is, a complete design of an organisation.

These design parameters are relevant across hierarchical levels. For example, governance issues such as decision rights may be defined for an individual role or for a top management team. Key processes and interfaces may be defined for both a small sub-unit and a large division, and so on. Moreover, this framework is not only relevant for the design of roles and units when considered as elements in a vertical structure, but also for the definition of *cross-unit*, horizontal processes. In Chapter 7 we shall use the exact same categorisation in considering different types of interdependencies that emerge between different roles and units in an organisation.

Table 1.3 Layers of organisational design parameters

Design parameter	Examples
Governance model	• Formal reporting structure • Decision rights (decision-making authority of different levels/roles) and accountabilities • Decision bodies (management teams, steering groups, technology boards, etc.)
Operating model	• Work units and interfaces • Key processes
Resource model	• Designation of units as cost, revenue or profit centre • Principles for internal transactions (e.g., whether cost or market price is to be used) • How a sub-unit is to be funded
Contracting model	• Designation of units as either (internal) customer or (internal) supplier • Principles and processes to be used to establish and fulfil commitments toward other units
Social network model	• Network forums • Mentoring programme • Knowledge management system

Design-oriented research

A number of authors have recently developed proposals for how to bridge the gap between theory and practice in organisational studies and in management research more generally. There is generally broad agreement that business schools need to focus more strongly on producing managerially relevant research; on the other hand, there is also some uncertainty about the right approach to achieve this goal. Some scholars are concerned that the quest for relevance will reduce academic rigour, with the risk of producing findings that are incorrect, or promoting prescriptions that do not contribute to improved business performance (e.g., Markides, 2007). Vermeulen (2005) has proposed, however, that this challenge may be handled by asking research questions that are important to managers but investigate the questions by using conventional research methods.

Two Dutch professors, van Aken and Romme (2009), have described in more detail how such a research paradigm can be developed. They call their approach 'design-oriented' research. The purpose is to build a *solutions-oriented* science of management and thereby support design processes in which practitioners engage. For organisation design, this means improving how managers design organisations to increase performance or attain specified goals. An important aspect of design-oriented research is to formulate and test *design propositions* (also called Design rules). Design propositions are similar to descriptive, scientific hypotheses in terms of logical structure. However, unlike scientific hypotheses, which are descriptive, design propositions are prescriptive, that is, they contain rules for *how to achieve a given goal in a given situation* (see Table 1.4 for an example).

Table 1.4 Comparison between science and design mode of inquiry

	Science mode	Design mode
Purpose	Produce descriptive (general and objective) knowledge supported by data about cause-and-effect relationships	Guide action to change systems and produce *pragmatically valid* knowledge (knowledge that is actionable and open to testing)
General form	'If X, then Y' Or: 'X is positively or negatively related to Y'	'In Situation S, in order to achieve A, do B'
Example	The best performing organisations are those that are structured in a manner that maximises 'fit' with key contingencies	In developing and selecting a design, to ensure that the structure will maximise performance: • Identify key contingencies (external and internal) • Translate these into *functional requirements* • Identify design parameters that satisfy the functional requirements

The principles used in design-oriented research – together with the tools of axiomatic design – provide a framework for how practitioners (particularly consultants) could structure their methodologies. By expressing a methodology in the form of design propositions, one would facilitate a more cumulative knowledge building process, which would contribute to more effective prescriptive knowledge. It is essentially about using the real world as a laboratory. Organisation re-design projects are the experiments, whose outcomes are used to test and refine our design propositions, which in turn enable improvements in the design process. At the same time, the design propositions provide an interface to academic research (Romme, 2003). Design propositions should not only be grounded in managerial experience but reflect relevant academic knowledge. Scholars also have an important role to play in empirically validating the outcomes from applying the design propositions.

This book adopts this approach by identifying a set of propositions in each chapter. The design propositions serve three purposes. They are intended to capture the key points in each chapter. The intention has been to formulate the propositions at a level of specificity that will allow a manager or consultant to use them as a basis for design interventions. Finally, the intention has also been to formulate the propositions in a falsifiable manner, to allow others to build on this work by testing and refining the propositions. It is hoped that the majority of the propositions will survive such testing by allowing organisational designers to produce the intended consequences. However, it is also to be expected that some of the propositions will need to be revised, that new propositions will need to be added and that a few may be disproved altogether. A set of research questions is also identified; these summarise important theoretical issues that should be examined more closely in order to further our understanding of organisation design.

Conclusion

In designing organisations, managers determine how work is to be performed inside an organisation by defining roles, processes and formal authority relationships. In the literature, three key concepts used to explain organisation design are hierarchical composition, strategy and structure alignment (here we included contingency theory) and coordination cost.

Empirical research confirms the value of effective designs, and documents the risks associated with inappropriate designs. Yet the field of organisation design must also confront some challenges. Many leading business 'gurus' have dismissed the value of organisation design. Business schools have placed little emphasis on organisation design in their curriculums, and research within organisation theory has been neglecting organisation design issues. Many leading scholars today concede that academic research in the field has failed to make an influential contribution to practice. (The main exception being organisational economics, which has influenced choices made by organisations in the area of corporate governance.)

These challenges have created a debate about how the field can be revitalised. Six proposed responses to this challenge are discussed in this chapter. The first is to reaffirm the value of design – as defined in the classic texts in the field – by demonstrating its effects on key organisational outcomes. Second, we discussed the proposal that a different orientation, a 'design attitude', may be needed in terms of how we approach problem-solving processes in business, including those dealing with organisation design issues. Furthermore, in line with recent work in the field, the chapter proposes using *architecture* as the key concept. This implies that the mission of the organisation design discipline should be to help leaders develop organisational architectures that are *purposeful* and *future-oriented*, and which balance the need for *autonomous action* with the need for *system coherency*. To create purposeful architectures, it is necessary to link design parameters to functional requirements. It was shown, using an example of a life insurance company, how this may be done by utilising *axiomatic design principles*, originally developed for the engineering sciences. The chapter introduced five layers of organisational design parameters: the governance model; the operating model; the resource model; the contracting model; and the social network model. Finally, to create a more effective interface between research and practice, Romme (2003) recommended the adoption of a research paradigm focused on developing prescriptive knowledge based on the formulation *design propositions* that can be tested by practitioners in the field.

Design propositions

Objective *Create rigorous yet pragmatically valid knowledge about organisation design*

1.1 Re-orient design inquiry toward the goal of identifying architectures that are purposeful, future-oriented, unifying and coherent, yet allow autonomous action.

1.2 Adopt the design matrix as a tool to standardise the description of organisation design features.

1.3 Formulate prescriptive knowledge in the form of design propositions (actionable and testable hypotheses about interventions to achieve specific goals).

Objective *Create organisational architectures that enable the attainment of strategic goals*

1.4 Translate the purpose and goals of the organisation into explicit functional requirements.

1.5 Define design parameters corresponding to each functional requirement.

1.6 Decompose the functional requirements and design parameters (by iterating between FRs and DPs) until a realisable design has been defined.

1.7 If there is more than one design (i.e., more than one set of design parameters) that may satisfy the functional requirements, select the set that is simplest to implement, given the organisation's current capabilities.

Review questions

1 How does organisation design differ from the traditional conception of organisation theory?

2 Consider an organisation that you have been working for or with which you are familiar. How is it structured? What is the key criterion used for grouping? Have similar criteria been used to group units at different levels of the organisation?

3 What is the relationship between strategy and organisational structure?

4 How do organisation design choices influence organisational functioning?

5 What are the characteristics of (good) architecture that suggest how we can design more effective organisations?

6 How would you compare the coordination cost of two alternative organisational designs?

7   How would you formulate the key functional requirements for a university?

8   The chapter reviews some of the advantages of adopting a 'design attitude'. What are the limitations of a design attitude? Under what circumstances should designers instead adopt a 'decision attitude'?

Research questions

1   How does decomposition affect organisational functioning (cf. Jacobides, 2006)?

2   What are the causal paths linking organisational design choices, intermediary outcomes and eventual outcomes (e.g., financial performance)? What is the relative strength of these causal paths?

3   Do the general principles formulated by Thompson (1967) still hold under all circumstances?

4   How can coordination cost be quantified and measured?

5   What is the relative difference in coordination cost when comparing coordination *within* versus *across* organisational units?

6   How can prescriptive theory best be developed in order to ensure that is both relevant and rigorous?

Notes

1   Baldwin and Clark (2000) attributed the rapid innovations that have happened in the computer industry during the last three decades to the modularisation of both product and organisational structures (i.e., the creation of semi-independent sub-units within an overall architecture).

2   In the example shown in Figure 1.2, the divisions are based around product or product category; however, divisions may of course also be defined based on brand, geography, work process, technology, etc.

3   Although most scholars would probably support the overall tenet of contingency theory, there has been considerable debate about the specific linkage between environmental contingencies and organisational characteristics. At times, different researchers have presented diametrically opposed findings. See Donaldson (2001), Mintzberg (1979) and Pfeffer (1997) for detailed discussions.

4   It is interesting to note that coordination cost was implicitly a part of Chandler's analysis as well. One of his key insights was that a functional structure would lead to higher coordination cost than a multidivisional structure in a firm that pursues a diversification strategy, as functional departments such as sales and production would have to interact with a large number of other internal departments. He also mentioned other issues, however, such as the difficulty of monitoring performance in diversified, functional organisations.

5   Thompson described the grouping of 'positions', but of course, the same principle may also be relevant at higher levels. For example, executives of a large multinational company, consisting of various business units and subsidiaries, may seek to minimise coordination costs by grouping related business units and subsidiaries into divisions or business areas.

6   Peters has cited Oticon as a role model in several presentations and at the time of printing still referred to the company on his website: http://www.tompeters.com/col_entries.php?note=005384&year=1992.

7   Of course, in practice this issue is more complicated, as managers provide value by supervising employees and coordinating work processes. So the basic trade-off in terms of designing the vertical structure is the value versus the cost of management.

8   The introduction of new communication technologies such as e-mail has not changed these patterns. An extensive study of e-mail traffic in a large company concluded that, among several factors, being in the same organisational unit is the factor that most strongly affects the probability that two individuals will communicate with each other via e-mail (Kleinbaum, 2008).

9   This interpretation of the results was also emphasised in a presentation of the paper by one of the authors, 23 January 2008.

10   The report can be downloaded from the internet: http://www.gpoaccess.gov/911/pdf/fullreport.pdf.

11   Minimisation of cost is another possible functional requirement. In this case, it applies to all of the design parameters and may thus instead be treated separately, as a *constraint* (see Suh, 2001, and discussion below).

12   The ability to link higher- and lower-level objectives is an important feature in the axiomatic approach. A key shortcoming of many 'mission statements' is that they remain isolated, high-level statements that rarely are operationalised. In contrast, a design hierarchy developed according to the axiomatic approach is not terminated before one has developed a design that can be realised.

13   In the literature, it is common to distinguish between two types of design. The first is strategic design – top-down processes aimed at aligning the overall structure with the strategy, and usually focused only on defining the main units, key executive roles and their reporting relationships. Operational design, on the other hand, is the more frequent adjustments made to roles and structures within sub-units, often driven by process improvement initiatives with targets related to quality or cost. This distinction is also relevant here. Operational design is simply the specification of lower-level FRs and DPs.

14   Suh did not address the organisational design context specifically but the proposed generic design criterion described in the text is consistent with what he termed the 'information axiom' (Suh, 2001).

15   In axiomatic design theory, there is no formal restriction with regard to elements that may be considered a design parameter as long as they fulfil a function and can be manipulated by the designer. In the examples provided by Suh (2001) design parameters include both physical components and the effects produced by those components (e.g., steam).

Case study

Procter & Gamble's Organisation 2005 initiative

Procter & Gamble is a large US multinational corporation that manufactures a wide range of consumer goods. Procter & Gamble is known for having several 'billion dollar brands' that are sold on all continents, such as Ariel (laundry detergent), Braun (small appliances), Gillette (razors) and Pampers (nappies).

During the 1990s, the company's performance deteriorated. Many of the 30 product categories were losing market share and disappointing financial results led to a declining share price.

In 1998, a six-year restructuring plan was announced named Organisation 2005. The company's CEO, Durk Jager, resigned in June 2000, but the new CEO, A. G. Lafley, continued the implementation of the plan.

The restructuring involved a number of changes. Costs were reduced by a round of lay-offs and by business process improvements. Some units that were not deemed strategic were sold off.

Procter & Gamble had introduced a matrix organisation[1] in the US in 1987, and the matrix structure was extended to the rest of the world in 1995. Four regional presidents (North America, Latin America, Europe and Asia) had profit and loss responsibility. Global product category presidents also reported directly to the CEO and were responsible for global standardisation and product development. There was also a third, functional dimension (e.g., Research & Development).

As part of the restructuring, the matrix was dismantled. The company's operations were grouped into three global business units (Beauty & Grooming; Household Care, and Health and Well-Being) with each Global Business Unit further divided into Business Segments. The hierarchical structure was also simplified by reducing the number of management layers from 13 to 7.

Procter & Gamble's restructuring is now viewed as one of the most successful large-scale corporate transformations in recent history. Between 2000 and 2010, sales doubled, profits quadrupled and P&G's market value increased by more than $100 billion dollars.

A. G. Lafley received the 'Executive of the year award' in 2007 from the Academy of Management (the world's largest association of management scholars). In the speech he gave after receiving the award,[2] he provided an interesting glimpse into the thinking behind Procter & Gamble's reorganisation:

> We moved to a new organisational structure in the late '90s. It included global business unit profit centers, a global Market Development Organisation, and global Business Shared Services.

> There was a lot of confusion as we moved people into new roles and as critical factors like decision rights were ironed out. This confusion was another reason our business got into trouble in 2000.

> There was a lot of pressure to turn back the clock and abandon the new structure, but I resisted it. I believed the structure could become a source of competitive advantage because it played to P&G's strengths. I felt it would be difficult for competitors to duplicate. They lacked P&G's scale, which the structure leveraged.

But even more important, the structure was tailor-made for P&G's promote-from-within culture. Because we all grow up together and spend our careers together, we have high levels of trust and familiarity. We're very collaborative.

It's difficult to achieve the same level of trust and collaboration in organisations that are not primarily promote-from-within. As a result, we can take better advantage of our structure than other companies could do with a similar structure. This is an enormous advantage.

The power of the design is in the balance of independence and interdependence, of autonomy and collaboration. The problem with matrices is overlap, duplication, and friction. P&G's design reduces the overlap and the friction.

We're essentially running a number of highly focused companies that share common go-to-market operations: global shared services and corporate capability. We've made it possible for each business unit to maintain focus on its unique consumers, customers and competitors – yet still capture all the capability, knowledge and scale of a $76 billion global company.

The benefits of the structure are clearest in our go-to-market capability. We can commercialize a larger innovation pipeline on more leading brands, in more markets, with more trade partners, simultaneously, because of our structure.

Notes

1 A matrix structure essentially entails dual reporting lines (i.e., that employees or managers report to more than one boss). The matrix structure is described in more detail in Chapter 4 of this book. However, the discussion questions below do not presuppose a precise understanding of the structure that was adopted.

2 The entire speech is available online: http://publications.aomonline.org/newsletter/index.php?option=com_content&task=view&id=97&Itemid=10025.

Discussion questions

1 Based on this excerpt from his speech, how would you summarise Mr Lafley's views on the strategic importance of organisation design?

2 To what extent would you say that this case exemplifies the concept of *organisational architecture* described in the chapter?

References

Ackoff, R. L. and Emery, F. E. (1972). *On Purposeful Systems*. Chicago, IL: Aldine-Atherton.

Aksnes. H. H. et al. (2006). Management of high-grade bone sarcomas over two decades: the Norwegian Radium Hospital experience. *Acta Oncologica*, 45, 1, 38–46.

Baldwin, C. Y. and Clark, K. B. (2000). *Design Rules*, Vol. 1: *The Power of Modularity*. Cambridge, MA: MIT Press.

Bettis, R. (1991). Strategic management and the straightjacket: an editorial essay. *Organization Science*, 2, 315–19.

Boland, R. J. and Collopy, F. (2004). Design matters for management. In R. J. Boland and F. Collopy, *Managing as Designing*. Stanford, CA: Stanford Business Books.

Chandler, A. (1962). *Strategy and Structure: Chapters in the History of the Industrial Enterprise*. Cambridge, MA: MIT Press.

Davis, J. H., Schoorman, F. D. and Donaldson, L. (1997). Toward a stewardship theory of management. *Academy of Management Review*, 22, 20–47.

Donaldson, L. (2001). *The Contingency Theory of Organisations*. Thousand Oaks, CA: Sage.

Egeberg, M. (1989). Effekteravorganisasjonsendring i forvaltningen [The effects of reorganisations in government department and agencies, not translated]. In Egeberg, M. (ed.): *Institusjonspolitikk og forvaltningsutvikling. Bidrag til en anvendt statsvitenskap*. Oslo: Tano.

Foss, N. J. (2003). Selective intervention and internal hybrids: interpreting and learning from the rise and decline of the spaghetti organisation. *Organisational Science*, 4, 331–49.

Galbraith, J. (2001). *Designing Organisations: An Executive Guide to Strategy, Structure, and Process*. San Francisco, CA: Jossey-Bass.

Gerstein, M. S. (1992). From machine bureaucracies to networked organisations: An architectural journey. In D. A. Nadler, M. S. Gerstein, R. B. Shaw, and associates: *Organisational Architecture: Designs for Changing Organisations*. San Francisco, CA: Jossey-Bass.

Ghoshal, S. (2005). Bad management theories are destroying good management practices. *Academy of Management Learning and Education*, 4, 1, 75–91.

Gulick, L. and Urwick, L. (eds) (1937). *Papers on the Science of Administration*. New York: Institute of Public Administration.

Haeckel, S. H. (1999). *Adaptive Enterprise: Creating and Leading Sense-and-Respond Organisations*. Boston, MA: Harvard Business School Press.

Hamel, G. and Prahalad, C. K. (1989). Strategic intent. *Harvard Business Review*, 67, May/June, 63–76.

Hammer, M. (2001). *The Agenda: What Every Business Must Do To Dominate the Decade*. New York: Crown Business.

Hammer, M. (2004). Deep change. *Harvard Business Review*, 82, 4, 84–93.

Hansen, M. (2009). *Collaboration*. Boston, MA: Harvard Business School Press.

Heath, C. and Staudenmayer, N. (2000). Coordination neglect: how lay theories of organising complicate coordination in organisations. *Research in Organisational Behavior*, 22, 53–191.

Jacobides, M. G. (2006). The architecture and design of organisational capabilities. *Industrial and Corporate Change*, 15, 1, 151–71.

Jensen, M. C. (1983). Organisation theory and methodology. *Accounting Review*, 56, 319–38.

Kennedy, M. (2002). Management decisions versus design. Paper presented at the Frontiers of Management conference, Weatherhead School of Management, Case Western University, OH, 14–15 June.

Kleinbaum, A. M. (2008). The social structure of organisation: coordination in a large, multi-business firm. Unpublished doctoral dissertation, Harvard University, Cambridge, MA.

Leavitt, H. J. (2005). *Top Down: Why Hierarchies are Here to Stay and How to Manage them More Effectively*. Boston, MA: Harvard Business School Press.

Liedtka, J. (2000). In defense of strategy as design. *California Management Review*, 42, 8–30.

Markides, C. (2007). In search of ambidextrous professors. *Academy of Management Journal*, 50, 4, 762–8.

McDavid, D. W. (1999). A standard for architecture description. *IBM Systems Journal*, 38, 1, 12–31.

Miller, D., Greenwood, R. and Prakash, R. (2009). What happened to organization theory? *Journal of Management Inquiry*, 18, 4, 273–9.

Mintzberg, H. (1979). *The Structuring of Organisations*. Englewood Cliffs, NJ: Prentice-Hall.

Nadler, D. and Tushman, M. (1997). *Competing by Design: The Power of Organisational Architecture*. New York: Oxford University Press.

Nahm, A. Y., Vonderembse, M. A. and Koufteros, X. A. (2003). The impact of organisational structure on time-based manufacturing and plant performance. *Journal of Operations Management*, 21, 281–306.

Peters, T. (2006). *Re-imagine*. New York: DK Publishing.

Pfeffer, J. (1997). *New Directions for Organisation Theory: Problems and Prospects*. New York: Oxford University Press.

Roberts, J. (2004). *The Modern Firm. Organisational Design for Performance and Growth*. New York: Oxford University Press.

Romme, G. L. A. (2003). Making a difference: Organisation as design. *Organisation Science*, 14, 5, 558–73.

Rumelt, R. P. (1974). *Strategy, Structure, and Economic Performance*. Cambridge, MA: Harvard University Press.

Rynes, S. L., Colbert, A. E. and Brown, K. G. (2002). HR professionals' beliefs about effective human resource practices: Correspondence between research and practice. *Human Resource Management*, 41, 149–74.

Sanchez, R. (1995). Strategic flexibility in product competition. *Strategic Management Journal*, 16, 135–59.

Simon, H. A. (1996). *The sciences of the artificial*, 3rd edn. Cambridge, MA: MIT Press.

Smith, A. (1776/1977). *An Inquiry into the Nature and Causes of the Wealth of Nations*. Chicago, IL: University of Chicago Press.

Suh, N. P. (2001). *Axiomatic Design: Advances and Applications*. New York: Oxford University Press.

Thompson, J. D. (1967). *Organisations in Action*. New York: McGraw-Hill.

Van Aken, J. E. and Romme, A. G. L. (2009). Reinventing the future: adding design science to the repertoire of organisation and management studies. *Organisation Management Journal*, 6, 5–12.

Vermeulen, F. (2005). On rigor and relevance: fostering dialectic progress in management research. *Academy of Management Journal*, 48, 978–82.

Werr, A., Stjernberg, T. and Docherty, P. (1997) The functions of methods of change in management consulting. *Journal of Organisational Change Management*, 10, 4, 288–307.

Williamson, O. E. (1981). The economics of organisation: the transaction cost approach. *American Journal of Sociology*, 87, 548–77.

Wong, S., DeSanctis, G. and Staudenmayer, N. (2007). The relationship between task interdependency and role stress: a revisit of the job demands-control model. *Journal of Management Studies*, 44, 2, 284–303.

Worren N., Moore K. and Elliott R. (2002). When theories become tools: toward a framework for pragmatic validity. *Human Relations*, 55, 10, 1227–49.

Yin, X. and Zajac, E. J. (2004). The strategy/governance structure fit relationship: theory and evidence in franchising arrangements. *Strategic Management Journal*, 25, 365–83.

Chapter 2

Organisational complexity

Overview

Background

- Complexity is recognised by economists and management scholars as a key factor limiting the growth and profitability of large firms
- More recent studies have exposed the negative effects of internal complexity on strategy formation, process performance and individual productivity
- Indicators suggest that the level of complexity continues to increase in many organisations

Challenges

- Some theorists view *internal* complexity as an inevitable result of *external* complexity
- Managers may overlook factors that lead to the gradual build-up of complexity over time
- 'Business gurus' sometimes advocate management concepts that only lead to further complexity
- More rigorous methods to measure and manage complexity are lacking

Key question

- How can we develop a proactive agenda for managing and reducing organisational complexity?

Proposed approach

- Adopt a clear definitional framework to allow identification, measurement and analysis of complexity
- Identify the overall organisational strategy to manage, reduce or prevent complexity

Introduction

A multinational supplier of medical equipment chose to reorganise from a product-based to a process-based organisation. The key purpose was to increase process orientation by implementing a structure more aligned with its value chain. Whereas the old structure had three main divisions, each responsible for one product, the new structure comprised four global business lines: Product development, Operations (i.e., manufacturing), Marketing and Sales. Operations was further subdivided into two main dimensions (linked in a matrix structure): Production plants located in different countries on one axis, and common functions on the other (Supply chain, HR, Finance, etc.). The new structure led to some intricate reporting relationships. For example, the quality manager for a particular production plant no longer reported to the director of the plant, but to a manager in the so-called Supply chain unit, who would typically be located in a different country. There were indications that some managers were confused about the relationship between the formal reporting structure and the set of business processes that the company had defined. To explain the new structure, the company had distributed thick booklets with dozens of organisation charts, but none of the charts described how the new reporting relationships matched up with the processes. In interviews that were held one and a half years after the change, managers were asked whether the new structure had actually contributed to increased process orientation. One senior marketing manager remarked:

> We introduced a new structure 1½ years ago, we went from a divisional (product-based) structure to a process-based structure. . . but roles and responsibilities are still not clear. . . we spend way too much time in internal coordination between functions. . . we're still working in silos. . . then there are overlaps, for example, we have split marketing and sales into two functions. . . is it the sales director or the marketing director that should decide?

This example raises several important questions. Why do managers sometimes select organisational models that seem to increase, rather than decrease, complexity? What is the impact of complexity on performance? How does it affect the work of individual employees? Can we manage, reduce or even avoid complexity? These are the issues we will discuss in this chapter. We start by considering how the concept can be defined.

Simplicity versus complexity

In classical economics, one expected *scale economies* to provide important advantages to large firms. Larger scale means, among things, that a firm can achieve cost advantages: higher production volume means that major investments and overhead costs can be spread over more units, leading to lower average costs per unit (Barney, 1996). Larger firms may also gain market power and thus enjoy higher profitability due to reduced competition in the industry. However, economists also recognise that there are important *diseconomies of scale*, which lead to an increase of costs when firms grow too large. Economists include complexity among 'managerial diseconomies', that is, factors that impede effective control and operation of firms that become too large. One of the best-known proponents of this view is the 2009 Nobel Prize winner in economical sciences, Oliver Williamson, who developed the transaction cost approach. Transaction costs are the costs related to planning and monitoring task completion in an organisation, including the negotiation of agreements and the handling of disputes with internal and external parties. Williamson argued that transaction costs generally increase with size, mainly due to growing bureaucracy. As stated in Canbäck et al. (2006), 'Problems are solved by adding structure and the firm reaches a point at which the added structure costs more than the problems solved' (p. 34).

Generally speaking, economists have not defined complexity or related terms with any great precision, but a possible definition can be found in organisation theory. Organisational theorists traditionally viewed complexity as the increasing *differentiation* or variety brought about by increasing size. In empirical studies of complexity, one would thus count the number of elements in an organisation, such as the number of different products, technologies or processes, or, in terms of organisation design variables, the number of hierarchical levels and sub-units (Burton and Forsyth, 1986; see also Anderson, 1999; Ashmos et al., 2000; Blau and McKinley, 1979).

More recently, another definition, which we will adopt in this book, has been proposed by scholars working in engineering and technology management. This definition places a stronger emphasis on *how the elements of the system are related to each other* – in other words, on interdependencies (Baldwin and Clark, 2000; Suh, 2001; 2005). This approach, originally developed by Simon (1962), allows for the possibility that the degree of complexity may vary in systems of equal size.

To see how this definition may help in conceptualising complexity, imagine a white goods company with three product lines:[1] dishwashers, washing machines and vacuum cleaners – which are sold to customers – the purchasing departments of large department stores – in three different geographic markets: north, west and south (Figure 2.1a). The company hires three sales representatives, one for each regional market. The sales representative has a number of responsibilities, such as identifying sales leads, preparing proposals, negotiating contracts, ensuring product delivery and monitoring customer satisfaction. For simplicity, let us assume that the customers in the three regions don't overlap (each customer is only represented in one region), that the customers may potentially buy all three products, and that the manufacturer has the necessary capacity to meet customer demand (i.e., there is no need to prioritise between customers in the three regions). In this case we have what we can call a *simple organisation*: the performance of one unit (or, in this case, a sales representative) is largely unrelated to the efforts of other units (or, in this case, other sales representatives). The customer representatives each decide which customers to target within their respective regions, which products to offer them and how to negotiate terms and conditions.

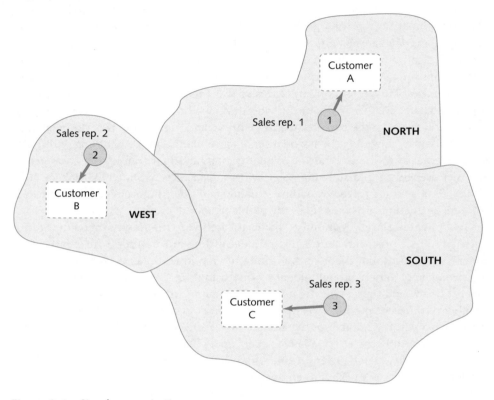

Figure 2.1a Simple organisation

However, a different situation emerges if management decides to organise sales by product rather than by geography. In other words, one representative takes responsibility for dishwashers, one for washing machines and one for vacuum cleaners. In this case, the performance of one unit (sales representative) will most likely be highly dependent upon the decisions and actions of the others (Figure 2.1b). Sometimes, the action of another sales representative may affect performance negatively. For example, if a client has a limited budget to spend on home care products, the efforts of sales representative 1, selling dishwashers, may be hampered if sales representative 2 has already secured a sale for washing machines to the same customer. However, the interdependencies may also lead to positive performance effects, for example, when an existing relationship with a client who has bought vacuum cleaners leads to a sale of washing machines and dishwashers later on. In this case, the decision to re-structure the company creates a *complex organisation*:[2] Multiple interdependencies emerge between roles/units. The main effect of the inter-dependencies is that actions and decisions in one role/unit potentially affect the performance of other units. With a product line structure, a sales representative will most likely be unable to reach their personal goals without affecting the perform-ance of the other sales representatives. They will probably need to spend a lot more time coordinating with the other two sales representatives, for example, to avoid tar-geting the same client with competing bids.

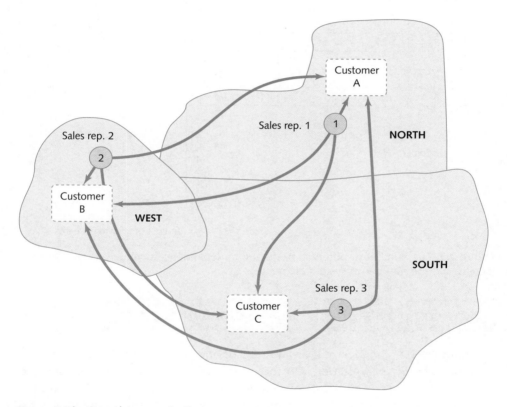

Figure 2.1b Complex organisation

According to this reasoning, a large organisation is *complicated* but not necessarily *complex*: Complexity is primarily about interactions, not about size (Suh, 2005). On the other hand, it is true that the number of potential interdependencies increases dramatically with size: a system with two elements has two potential bilateral inter-actions (A → B and B → A); a system with three elements will have six bilateral interactions (A → B, A → C, B → A, B → C, C → A, C → B), and so on. In practice, then, the challenge of managing complexity will usually be much more significant in large organisations than in small ones (see Figure 2.2).[3]

Number of system elements	Number of potential interdependencies	Increase from adding one system element
2	2	
3	6	4
4	12	6
5	20	8
6	30	10

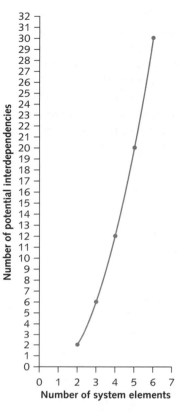

Figure 2.2 The number of potential bilateral interdependencies created as a result of increases in the number of system elements

How complexity affects organisational functioning

A certain level of complexity is always present and is necessary for sustaining the operations of any organisation. On the other hand, excessive levels of complexity produce a range of organisational consequences that may critically affect the performance of organisations. In the following, let us review some of the studies discussed in the literature related to this issue.

The most immediate consequences of complexity are *increased time and cost* of completing projects or performing business processes. Frederick Brooks (1975), in his classic work on the *Mythical Man-Month*, was perhaps the first to point out that complexity was a key cause of overruns for IT projects. When schedule slippage occurs, the typical response of a project manager is to add more manpower. Yet Brooks frequently observed that *adding manpower to a late project makes it later*. The explanation is straightforward. Project managers forget the existence of interdependencies between software engineers when estimating the required work effort – software engineers spend a lot of time communicating with each other to coordinate their work and resolve issues that relate to different components or modules of the software system. Adding more manpower leads to a further increase in coordination cost, which may sometimes offset the effect of the added capacity. (The increase in coordination cost will depend on the size of the project as well as the degree of interdependency between the different modules that the software engineers are configuring.) For example, adding two new software engineers to a project of four engineers introduces 18 new potential interfaces (4 engineers have 12 possible interdependencies; 6 engineers have 30 possible interdependencies) (cf. Figure 2.2).

Whereas Brook's work was based largely on anecdotal evidence, there are also empirical studies that examine the relationship between organisational complexity and productivity. One example is the research reported in Hihn et al. (1990), who considered the relationship between the structure and performance of software projects. Complexity was measured by indices that reflected the number of interfaces that the project team would need to handle. For example, complexity was rated as low if the software was developed within one section of the organisation, and high if it involved several divisions or external partners. As expected, productivity was lower for the projects with a more complex structure.[4] Importantly, it was also found that the effect of volatility (e.g., changes in requirements during the project) was smaller for the projects with a simple structure than for projects with complex structures. In other words, the simple project teams seemed to have a better ability to respond to change.

Carillo and Kopelman (1991) examined the relationship between organisational structure and productivity in 234 branches of a US bank. The structural variables included size, the number of hierarchical levels in each branch and the ratio of staff versus production workers. The results indicated that there was a negative relationship between size and productivity, and between the number of hierarchical levels and productivity. The smaller branches had approximately 31 per cent greater efficiency than the larger ones, and the branches with one hierarchical level were approximately 44 per cent more productive than branches with five levels.

Complexity affects the propensity to commit errors, which in turn influences both quality and the risk of accidents. A common error is simply to omit one step in a process – a worker in a production facility may forget to fasten a bolt or a nurse may drop administering a pill. Errors might also occur because people misinterpret instructions or procedures, or apply the wrong procedure. Some studies show that the defect rates in production processes are strongly related to *the number of process steps* executed (Hinckley, 2003). The same conclusion was reached by researchers looking at errors in hospitals, who found that the likelihood of an adverse event increased by 6 per cent *for each day* a patient spent in a hospital (Andrews et al., 1997). The key implication of these studies is that simplifying work processes may be the single most effective means of reducing defect rates.

Yet the most serious consequences are not related to errors to individual steps in a process, but to the more systemic risk that is created in highly interlinked systems (both technological and organisational). Today, unanticipated *interactions among components* is the most frequent source of serious accidents (Perrow, 1984). Each component of a system may be safe when viewed in isolation; however, with increasing complexity it becomes difficult both to identify risk sources and to mitigate risk when it is detected. Complex interdependencies essentially mean that a failure of one component can quickly propagate through the system in unexpected ways.

> In October 1996, Aeroperú Flight 603 crashed into the Pacific Ocean, killing 9 crew members and 61 passengers. The aircraft investigation revealed that the cause of the accident was a piece of masking tape accidentally left over the so-called static ports (air intakes) by cleaning personnel. The blocked static ports led the basic flight instruments to relay false airspeed, altitude and vertical speed data, which created complete confusion in the cockpit, as the pilots believed they were flying at a safe altitude, when in fact they were approaching sea level. The trial following the accident identified both defective design by the Boeing Company, the aircraft's manufacturer, and negligent maintenance procedures as contributing to the accident.[5]

The underlying cause of the Aeroperú accident was clearly a failure to anticipate that such a minor error – a failure to remove a masking tape during cleaning – could have such catastrophic consequences. This failure may be due both to the complexity of the airplane itself, from a purely technological standpoint, combined with the difficulty of interchanging information among sub-teams of a large development project. It is likely that the design of the static ports and the design of the flight instruments were done in two separate sub-teams of Boeing's development organisation.

Complexity also makes it difficult for leaders of organisations to define a coherent structure and clear accountabilities. The result is that sub-units in complex organisations often pursue goals that are ambiguous. This phenomenon has been the subject of several studies among public management scholars, although the current evidence does not necessarily suggest that level of goal ambiguity is higher in public than in private organisations. Chun and Rainey (2005) examined the existence of goal ambiguity in US federal agencies. They defined ambiguity as the extent to which an organisational goal or set of goals allows leeway for interpretation. But they also distinguished between different facets of ambiguity, for example, ambiguity may be related to the interpretive leeway in understanding or explaining the actual mission, in selecting specific actions to accomplish the mission, in evaluating the progress toward accomplishing the mission or in prioritising among multiple goals that the unit has been given. In their study, the level of goal ambiguity correlated with federal employees' ratings of organisational and management effectiveness. As hypothesised, goal ambiguity was negatively related to both.

In some organisations, employees do not even agree about how the boundaries in the organisation are drawn. In a study of 43 teams in a large multinational company, Mortensen (2004) found that people in only 13 of the 43 teams agreed who the members of their team were. Teams that exhibited such *boundary disagreement* reported significantly lower performance than those experiencing no boundary disagreement. Interestingly, it was found that the team members were confident when asked to name team members, and were unaware of the existence of boundary disagreement among teammates. Mortensen (2004) explains that people have differing frames of reference on which they base their evaluation of a typical team member.

Ambiguity and goal conflicts at the organisational level may negatively affect role clarity (i.e., create *role ambiguity*) at the individual level (Pandey and Wright, 2006). In a study in an insurance company, Posner and Butterfield (1978) found that role clarity was positively related to perceptions of job satisfaction, personal influence, and task-oriented leadership. An independent measure of effectiveness showed that members in high-performing offices had greater role clarity than those in low-performing offices. Interestingly, they found that *role clarity was higher at higher organisational levels*. This finding may be interpreted in several ways. At higher organisational levels, there may exist more objective, outcome-based measures that can be used to define individual managerial roles (e.g., a senior manager can be made directly accountable for unit profitability). However, it may also indicate that higher-level managers ignore the need for proper definition of jobs at lower levels of the organisation.

Researchers have studied soldiers working in situations where the mission is unclear and success a remote possibility. For example, the soldiers that were deployed as part of the US operation in Somalia in 1992 arrived there motivated and committed, but as the operation wore on, many became demoralised and disengaged due to shifts in the overall mission and vague rules of engagement, which made it difficult for the soldiers to protect civilians (Britt, 2003). As pointed out by Britt (2003), there is a common misconception that job engagement is a personality trait and that motivated people will throw themselves with equal enthusiasm into pretty much any job. Yet the research actually shows that those employees that are the most engaged in their work report the lowest levels of job satisfaction when their roles are ambiguous.

In a study conducted with 125 middle managers, the combination of high amounts of interdependency and role ambiguity (e.g., ambiguity caused by unclear or hidden interdependencies toward other units or individuals) was identified as a key source of stress. Managers confronted with such a challenge may be dependent on others for resources or support in order to perform their tasks, yet be unsure about with whom or about what they are supposed to coordinate (Wong et al., 2007). On the other hand, the study also concluded that some managers are able to handle a great number of interdependencies, as long as there is sufficient clarity with regard to goals and structure.

A lack of structure and accountability may also make it more difficult to ensure that employees comply with ethical standards. Fleming and Zyglidopoulos (2008) argue that organisational complexity in some cases has amplified the severity and pervasiveness of fraudulent practices, including the large-scale corruption that occurred in cases such as Enron, Arthur Andersen, WorldCom and Barings Bank. A 'fog of complexity' makes deception difficult to understand and control, because activities are conducted outside the boundaries of normal managerial control. Moreover, they hypothesise that complexity will make it more likely that deviances from acceptable business practices gain momentum and escalate into organisational phenomena: 'A lie told in the past by individuals can spread into the future by making any effort for honest reporting misleading at best . . .' (p. 16).

Finally, complexity has important implications for strategic decision makers. One would expect, for example, that it would become harder to forecast future results the more complex a business is. There is no study on this issue employing the same definition as we introduced above, but if we accept size as a proxy for internal complexity, we may use a study described in Meyer (2002) that was conducted in a global pharmaceutical firm. This study plotted the accuracy of revenue forecasts for various country subsidiaries of the firm as a function of their size. The measure of size was prior year sales, while the measure of forecast accuracy was the percentage deviation of actual from projected sales in the current year. The data showed that forecast accuracy declined sharply with size. Complexity thus essentially increases overall uncertainty by decreasing the probability that a given strategic decision will have the intended effect (Suh, 2001).

Rising complexity

The existence of diseconomies of scale, such as factors leading to high internal complexity of large firms, has been acknowledged by economists since the 1920s (Canbäck et al., 2006). What is more problematical, however, is that the overall level of complexity seems to be increasing, independent of firm size. Unfortunately, there are no studies that track the same indicator of complexity over a significant amount of time. The studies that have been conducted employ different definitions and methodologies. This means that we have an incomplete picture of the degree of complexity and its evolution over time. Nevertheless, when piecing together the findings from different studies, a fairly clear trend emerges.

The design of organisations has changed considerably during the last couple of decades. A number of studies have documented the introduction of cross-functional, horizontal processes and the increasing prevalence of project-based work. Whittington et al. (1999) found a significant increase in 'horizontal linkages' in a study conducted in European companies between 1992 and 1996. They also found evidence of delayering, that is, that organisations were removing management levels. Some have argued that old hierarchies have been dismantled; it is probably more accurate to say that hierarchy is being complemented by the use of flexible and dynamic organisational arrangements, such as temporary project teams and cross-functional business processes.

Organisations have become much more 'coordination intensive', a development that has been spurred by the introduction of new communication technologies (Malone, 2004). Some indirect evidence for this trend can be found by looking at the usage of communication technologies and the frequency of meetings in organisations. Information technologies, such as e-mail, have made it possible to coordinate by communicating with far more people, more quickly, at a much lower cost than before. Several studies show that the volume of corporate e-mail traffic increases by about 10 per cent per year. One study looked at the time period from 2003 to 2006, and concluded that corporate e-mail volume increased by 36 per cent during this period.[6] Most experts expect the volume of e-mail traffic to continue to increase.

Another relevant indicator of the amount of coordination is corporate meeting activity. There are no studies of corporate meeting activity that have been repeated over a longer period of time, but we can combine data from various studies conducted at different points in time. The trend from these seems very clear: both the frequency and duration of meetings have increased markedly. A conservative estimate is that managers currently spend 50 per cent of their time in meetings, on average. For senior executives the estimate is even higher – up to 70 per cent. This can be compared to a study conducted in the 1960s, which showed that managers only spent 3½ hours per week in planned meetings (somewhat more time was spent on unplanned meetings) (Romano and Nunamaker, 2001).

By and large, the effect of these changes may be positive. Delayering may reduce costs, improve accountability and decentralise decision making, and improve the speed of decision making and the quality of communication (as there are fewer levels across which one needs to share information). The increase in horizontal linkages may lead to increased integration and thereby reduce the effect of organisational 'silos'. The greater reliance on project-based work may contribute to increased speed and flexibility.

Although the overall effect may be positive, many observers have noted that these changes have also led to increasing complexity, which is placing new demands on managers and employees. There is now ample evidence that this issue is becoming a concern for business leaders. This issue was first identified in a PwC survey in 2006, which included responses from 1,400 CEOs globally (PricewaterhouseCoopers, 2006). Overall, more than three-quarters of the CEOs stated that complexity had increased during the preceding three years (that is, during the 2003–2006 period) (see Figure 2.3). When asked about which business initiatives contributed most strongly to increasing complexity, the respondents rated 'Extending operations to

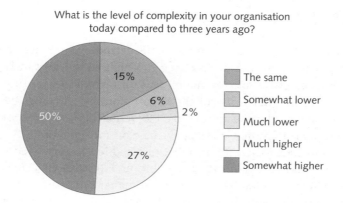

Figure 2.3 Excerpt from PwC's Global CEO study conducted in 2007
Source: Based on data reported in PricewaterhouseCoopers, 2007

new territories' as most important. Extending operations to new territories (particularly foreign countries) introduces complexity in several ways, for example, by requiring the company to modify products or add product variants, establish additional organisational units (e.g., country subsidiaries) and adapt to a new set of laws and regulations. Although the respondents considered external factors as important drivers of rising complexity, it is clear that they also believed that complexity could be reduced by improving the internal organisation. No less than 97 per cent of the respondents indicated that they were engaged in at least one improvement programme to reduce internal complexity. 'Organisational structure' was rated the second most common focus area for these improvement programmes, after 'Information technology'.

The trend has been confirmed in more recent studies conducted by IBM (2010) and the Economist Intelligence Unit (2011). In the IBM study, the participants indicated that they expected the level of complexity to continue to increase. The Economist Intelligence Unit survey included an item specifically about the role of internal, organisational factors. The results confirm that many executives view the structure of the organisation as a source of complexity (Figure 2.4).

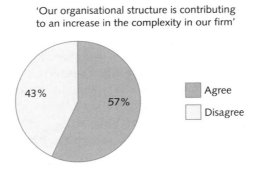

'Our organisational structure is contributing
to an increase in the complexity in our firm'

43%   57%   ■ Agree   □ Disagree

Figure 2.4 Excerpt from the Economist Intelligence Unit's report
Source: Based on data reported in Economist Intelligence Unit (2011)

The same trends are evident in studies considering other functional areas. In the IT area, a key topic for debate has been the high complexity in IT infrastructure and applications platforms. The main focus for many IT leaders during the last decade has been to simplify work for the IT function, by reducing the number of applications and standardising around large ERP (enterprise resource planning) systems. There is support that these efforts have paid off for some firms. A study of 623 large US firms concluded that ERP installations had led to improved productivity and performance, particularly for those combining ERP with CRM (customer relationship management) and SCM (supply chain management) systems (Aral et al., 2006). However, other experts have warned that the implementation of ERP systems in some cases have increased, rather than decreased complexity:

. . . companies ended up having several instances of the same ERP systems or a variety of different ERP systems altogether, further complicating their IT landscape. In the end, ERP systems became just another subset of the legacy systems they were supposed to replace.

(Rettig, 2007, p. 23)

To manage this growing complexity, IT departments have grown substantially: As a percentage of total investment, IT rose from 2.6% to 3.5% between 1970 and 1980. By 1990 IT consumed 9%, and by 1999 a whopping 22% of total investment went to IT. Growth in IT spending has fallen off, but it is nonetheless surprising to hear that today's IT departments spend 70% to 80% of their budgets just trying to keep existing systems running.

(Rettig, 2007, p. 21)

There is also a growing interest in the implications of complexity for supply chain management. Product proliferation has been identified as a key driver of complexity in the supply chain. One study estimated that 1.7 products models are being introduced for every product being discontinued (Hoole, 2006). An additional factor is outsourcing: Activities that were previously conducted within the organisation – such as manufacturing, distribution, accounting and IT – are now performed by external suppliers. In some cases work is being 'offshored' to suppliers in low-cost locations, and there is said to be 3,500 outsourcing providers in India alone. Although modern supply chain management methods have led to increased quality, speed and flexibility, some authors (e.g., Blecker and Kersten, 2006) argue that it has simultaneously led to dramatically increased complexity. In particular, scholars associated with Cranfield University in the UK have questioned the introduction of 'Lean' practices and argued that these practices sometimes increase vulnerability of the supply chain (Peck, 2005). The main focus of Lean is increasing efficiency. The tight coupling between the activities in a Lean process (such as the elimination of inventory in the system to 'buffer' any interruptions) means that operational difficulties at a single supplier can affect every other organisation in the supply network.

The 2008–2009 financial crisis was also partly attributed to rising complexity, both within individual firms and in the finance industry as a whole. In a speech, Ben Bernanke, the chairman of the US Federal Reserve Board, emphasised that the complexity of credit cards plans and mortgage products in some cases served to disguise unfair and deceptive practices, and made it difficult for even the most diligent consumers to evaluate the features of different products and make appropriate choices (Bernanke, 2009).

Many observers have commented upon the interconnected nature of the financial system, where a failure of individual components may destroy the whole. As stated by the deputy governor of the Bank of France, Jean-Pierre Landau (2009, p. 1): 'Transmissions of shocks occur through networks . . . this potentially creates numerous feedback loops and amplication effects.' New techniques for managing financial risk made it possible to spread the risk more broadly, but also meant that the network of counterparties expanded in scale and complexity, which in turn led to a loss of information, making it hard to assess the real risk profile of the underlying assets.

Herring and Carmassi (2010) linked these challenges to organisation design issues in their analysis of international financial conglomerates. They concluded that the complexity of the corporate structures of the conglomerates itself was a source of significant systemic risk, which also impeded timely regulatory intervention and disposition. They concluded that several large financial institutions have become 'too complex to fail'.

Why is complexity allowed to grow?

The findings and viewpoints reviewed so far are rather uncontroversial. There is a broad consensus among both scholars and practitioners that complexity has been increasing. Few people would disagree with the assertion that complexity has potential negative effects, and few people would deliberately seek to increase complexity. So the paradox we have to address is why complexity is still increasing in many organisations.

One possible explanation could be that the level of *internal* complexity in an organisation largely reflects the increasing level of *external* complexity. The proponents of this view often refer to Ashby (1956), who formulated the law of *requisite variety*. This law states that the variety within a system must be at least as great as the environmental variety against which it is attempting to regulate itself. As Galbraith (2000, p. 2) stated, 'A company's organisation must be as complex as its business . . . If the business is simple, the organisation can be simple.'

Without doubt, a firm's environment is an important driver of internal complexity. There are examples in practically all industries of external changes that force companies to introduce more complex internal structures. The introduction of a new regulatory framework (e.g., the Sarbanes-Oxley act, or the Basel II or Solvency II conventions) may force all banks to implement new (and potentially very complex) audit and governance processes. More differentiated customer needs may lead manufacturing companies to offer a higher number of new product models, which increases internal complexity (e.g., by the introduction of new manufacturing processes as well as the establishment of organisational roles and units responsible for each of the new products, etc.). In the telecom business, the introduction of new infrastructure standards, such as 4G networks, may force telecom firms to change their internal product development process and consider new business models.

However, the fact that organisations in the same industry are subject to the same environmental forces does not necessarily mean that they respond by adopting identical structures. As pointed out by Gresov and Drazin (1997), environmental contingencies dictate the functions, and not the structure of an organisation (cf. the distinction between functions/functional requirements and structure/design parameters discussed in Chapter 1). Today, for example, many telecom firms experience that basic telephony services are being commoditised, and that future survival depends on the ability to offer new services, such as mobile banking, social networking, games and location-based services (e.g., route planners, restaurant guides). But managers of telecom firms have many choices with regard to how this strategy should be pursued, and even more with regard to how specific initiatives should be organised. For example, there are different ways in which to access the required skills and technologies – a telecom firm may establish alliances with or acquire content providers, or attempt to build the required skills internally. Alternatively, it may essentially outsource content development, by offering its network and subscriber base to a content provider that essentially develops a service independently (Ende, 2002).

Research by organisational economists also supports the notion that managers exercise strategic choice and consequently, that the increase in complexity cannot be attributed solely to external factors. The basic proposition of the transaction cost approach was that diseconomies of scale increase with increasing size. But Williamson (1975) also pointed out that there are factors that may moderate the (predicted negative) relationship between firm size and performance. Two important moderating factors that he mentioned were appropriate organisation of activities within the firm and effective governance practices. The role of these moderating factors was confirmed in the study reported in Canbäck et al. (2006). There is also some indirect support for this hypothesis in the studies that consider the relationship between firm size and performance. Some of these studies show that smaller firms outperform larger firms (Dhawan, 2001) while others show that larger firms outperform smaller firms (Schmalensee, 1989). It is important to note that these studies simply correlate financial performance with size – they do not measure the level of complexity directly. Nevertheless, the inconclusive results suggest that some managers are able to keep the level of complexity in check even as the firm grows.

If we accept that managerial choice plays a role, it is important to explain why managers sometimes make suboptimal decisions. We also need to understand why the overall level of internal complexity seems to be increasing for firms in many industries. We do not have definitive answers to these questions, but we may encounter some likely explanations by considering the nature of decision-making processes within firms. It is also useful to consider the methods that are available to managers and the advice that managers have received from leading management gurus with regard to organisation design.

It is well established that decision makers simplify the structure of intractable problems in order to select a course of action (e.g., Schwenk, 1984). When considering alternative options for organising a firm, managers may thus fail to see the real implications of alternative models, and inadvertently select organisational models that increase rather than decrease complexity.

There are various cognitive biases that may play a role. One bias identified by Heath and Staudenmayer (2000) is 'partition focus', that is, the tendency for people to partition a task prematurely, resulting in subsequent integration problems. For example, when faced with a new project, software managers tend to immediately divide the effort into five or ten pieces, and assign each piece to a development team. Once allocated a responsibility, software engineers (as other workers) often display another limitation – which Heath and Staudenmayer call 'component focus': more effort is devoted to completing one's own piece of work than on understanding how the piece fits into the overall system. Only in later stages of the project is it discovered that there are significant interfaces between the work pieces, which require intensive communication between the different teams before they can be resolved.

Another possible explanation is a phenomenon called 'the tyranny of small decisions' (Haraldsson et al., 2008). Over time, managers in organisations make local, independent decisions, which are relatively insignificant when seen separately, but which create complexity in a cumulative manner over time. Decisions about local issues often occur 'under the radar' of senior executives. In some firms, senior executives are primarily concerned about the composition of their own leadership team and the performance of their direct reports, and may rarely question the organisation of units one or more levels below in the organisation, unless they receive reports of dysfunctional practices or problems. This means that sub-unit managers have relatively ample latitude in defining roles and responsibilities within their own units or in units that they control indirectly (e.g., by holding the role as internal customer or resource provider to those units). The actual design of large organisations is the result of hundreds of small compromises and adjustments that are made to resolve local issues.

It is also likely that the adoption of new management concepts and organisational forms has contributed to the increase in complexity. The traditional functional organisation – with different functions for sales, manufacturing, service and so on – was a frequent target of criticism during the 1980s and 1990s. It became clear that the internal functions frequently represented isolated 'silos' that in fact aggravated people's pre-existing 'component focus'. Important new organisational concepts were introduced to counter this tendency, such as the idea of end-to-end processes and cross-functional teams. However, at times, new roles and structures are simply added *on top of* the existing formal organisation. For example, in an attempt to create greater process orientation, companies have typically created roles for managers as the 'process owners' of new defined end-to-end processes. However, this creates an immediate challenge in terms of accountability, as two dimensions of managers are now responsible for process performance (the process owners and the respective functional managers).[7] A national railway company went one step further by introducing – in addition to the two dimensions of functions and processes – a *third* dimension of 'process coordinators', who were supposed to facilitate coordination between functional managers and process owners. As Heath and Staudenmayer (2000) observed, coordination problems are frequently repaired by introducing even more coordination mechanisms. The challenge of integrating the 'process dimension' into the organisation's systems of roles and accountabilities has until recently received little attention by the proponents of techniques such as Re-engineering, Lean and Six Sigma.

Developing a new agenda for managing and re-designing complex organisations

The evidence pointing to negative implications of complexity and the indications that complexity is increasing raise the question of how one can respond in a more effective manner. How can organisations be designed in a manner that minimises complexity, or prevents the build-up of complexity? The following section discusses two possible ways in which to confront this challenge. The first is related to the need for a clear definition of the concept itself. Second, we consider the organisational strategies that leaders may adopt to manage complexity.

Definitional framework

In the PwC study cited above, only 4 per cent of CEOs indicated that they had a way of measuring the internal complexity of their firms. At the most fundamental level, we cannot expect to be able to reduce complexity unless we have a method that lets us identify, document, and ideally, measure it. In Chapter 1, we introduced the difference between functional requirements and design parameters. This distinction makes it possible to conceptualise complexity by viewing it from two different angles. The first is based on axiomatic design theory (Suh, 2005) and considers the relationship between functional requirements and design parameters. The second considers the relationships among design parameters (Eppinger, 2001).

A simple example, drawn from political philosophy, may serve as an illustration. The French philosopher Montesquieu, who some call the French equivalent of Adam Smith, was the first to outline the three basic functions of government: Legislate (create laws), Enforce (implement and enforce laws), and Provide for Justice (interpret and apply law and resolve disputes). These are essentially functional requirements for the design of governments. The functions are performed by three different systems: the judicial system (the courts), the elected legislature (i.e., the parliament, or the congress in the US) and the executive branch of government (state institutions including law enforcement agencies). Montesquieu's real innovation, however, was in pointing out that effective government required *separation of powers*. The influence of any one power should not be able to exceed that of the other two, either singly or in combination. In Table 2.1 these interdependencies have been mapped in a design matrix.

Modern political systems vary in their degree of separation. For example, in parliamentary systems, the prime minister and the cabinet are drawn from the parliament, and the members of parliament often also select the leaders of the executive branch of the government. (According to Saunders (2006) a full separation of powers would imply, for example, that members of the executive should be independently selected.) Nevertheless, all democratic systems maintain some degree of separation and it is interesting to note that *coupling* (a lack of separation, i.e., interdependence) between these functional requirements is usually associated with ineffective or dysfunctional government. For example, in some African states, corruption and interference from politicians or governmental officials threaten judicial independence. Given our definition here, such governments would represent a more *complex* design. In countries governed by despotic leaders, the legislative, judiciary and executive powers are sometimes in the same hands. Although there is essentially only one design parameter here, this is also an example of a coupled design, as functional requirements cannot be satisfied independently (Suh, 2005).

Table 2.1 Design matrix illustrating the design intent for a democratic government (X signifies a strong relationship)

	Design parameters		
Functional requirements	Elected legislature	Judicial system	State institutions
Legislate	X		
Provide for Justice		X	
Enforce			X

Montesquieu also noted, however, that the three systems of government were dependent upon each other. A judge relies on the laws made by elected politicians in order to impose a sentence. The executive branch of the government also relies on the laws written by the legislators as well as the interpretation of the law made by the courts in order to carry out their mandate (see Figure 2.5). These dependencies are related, but not equivalent, to the interdependencies between functional requirements described above, as they concern what we in organisation design terminology would call *process dependencies*: one unit (or individual role in an organisation) is reliant upon decisions, information or deliverables produced in another unit (or by another individual) in order to perform its activities. From this perspective, complexity can be defined as the existence of process interdependencies or, more generally, interdependencies *between design parameters*. In this case, the interdependencies fall below the diagonal (the matrix is 'lower triangular'). A lower triangular matrix usually implies that design parameters must be set in a sequence (or be performed sequentially, if they represent steps in a work process). In a society, for example, laws must be passed before they can be used by a court to pass a sentence. In a completely

		Design parameters		
		1	2	3
#	*Design parameters*	Elected legislature	Judicial system	State institutions
1	Elected legislature			
2	Judicial system	X		
3	State institutions	X	X	

Figure 2.5 Design structure matrix (DSM) showing process interdependencies between the three branches of government in a democratic society

uncoupled design (i.e., a matrix with no interdependencies), parallel processing would be possible. Nevertheless, lower triangular matrices are still preferable to matrices with entries above the diagonal. Entries above the diagonal result in higher complexity as they may imply cyclical dependency relations, i.e., that processes require iteration back and forth before they can be completed.

The same principles may be used to analyse private corporations. The CEO of a corporation corresponds to the head of government, the shareholder meeting to parliament, and the company board to the members of cabinet (Benz and Frey, 2007). These bodies carry out separate functions, and their role and composition are regulated by law in many countries. Indeed, the principle of division of power is central in some theoretical frameworks used to analyse corporate governance issues, most notable in *agency theory* (Jensen, 1983). Agency theory is concerned with the so-called principal–agent problem, which refers to relationships where one party (the principal) delegates work to another (the agent) who performs the work. The key concern is conflict of interest between the principal and the agent. For example, a company owner will be motivated to increase shareholder value, whereas a CEO will be motivated to maximise his or her own remuneration, power or status. Agency theory specifies various mechanisms that ensure that the agent does not deviate from the preferences of the principal in the execution of the task. Proponents of agency theory have introduced specific proposals for changes in order to increase monitoring and control of management, such as splitting the role of the chairman and the CEO, increasing the number of independent directors on company boards, and separating the auditing function from the executive; for example, by requiring that members of audit committees be independent directors.

As pointed out by Jensen (1983), agency theory essentially formalises principles that have evolved from long experience and thus have proved to have survival value. A widely practised principle is to separate operations responsibility from accounting responsibility. In most companies, the person who receives cash will not be the same as the one who keeps the record of the transaction, nor will the same person be able to both authorise and receive payments.

Frey and Benz (2007) argue, however, that the principle of division of power is still applied much less strictly in private corporations than in public institutions. They propose that the independence of the auditing process could be further improved by allowing the shareholders to elect the members of the audit committee and perhaps also the auditing firm. Frey and Benz argue that key principles from public government, such as competitive elections, may be applied to strengthen corporate governance in a number of other areas as well.

Example 2.1

We can revisit the home care products company used as an example in the introductory part of this chapter to illustrate how organisational designs may be mapped by means of design matrices (Table 2.2a). When organised geographically, the functional requirements are in principle independent. Although a similar design *intent* may motivate the introduction of a product line organisation for the sales unit, the actual result may, given the assumptions described above,[8] look similar to the situation depicted in Table 2.2b, in that the achievement of one requirement may have positive or negative impact on the ability to satisfy the other functional requirements (because this impact is probable, but uncertain, it has been marked with an x, whereas the primary relationship has been marked with an X).

Table 2.2a Design matrix showing interdependencies between functional requirements and design parameters for sales department organised geographically

	Design parameters		
Functional requirements	Sales representative 1	Sales representative 2	Sales representative 3
Maximise revenues for dishwashers, washing machines and vacuum cleaners in the north region	X		
Maximise revenues for dishwashers, washing machines and vacuum cleaners in the west region		X	
Maximise revenues for dishwashers, washing machines and vacuum cleaners in the south region			X

Table 2.2b Design matrix showing interdependencies between functional requirements and design parameters for sales department organised by product line

	Design parameters		
Functional requirements	Sales representative 1	Sales representative 2	Sales representative 3
Maximise revenues for dishwashers in the north, west and south regions	X	x	x
Maximise revenues for washing machines in the north, west and south regions	x	X	x
Maximise revenues for vacuum cleaners in the north, west and south regions	x	x	X

The process interdependencies related to realising this strategy may be depicted as in Figures 2.6a and 2.6b. The first matrix represents a simple organisation and the second a complex organisation with several process interdependencies.

Design parameters

#	Design parameters	1	2	3
		Sales representative 1	Sales representative 2	Sales representative 3
1	Sales representative 1			
2	Sales representative 2			
3	Sales representative 3			

Figure 2.6a Design structure matrix showing the relationship between different design parameters in sales department organised geographically

Design parameters

#	Design parameters	1	2	3
		Sales representative 1	Sales representative 2	Sales representative 3
1	Sales representative 1		X	X
2	Sales representative 2	X		X
3	Sales representative 3	X	X	

Figure 2.6b Design structure matrix showing the relationship between different design parameters in sales department organised by product

Discussion

Two definitions of complexity have been described. The first defines complexity as interdependency (coupling) between functional requirements and design parameters. According to this definition, a complex organisation is one where two or more design parameters (e.g., sub-units) address the same functional requirement. A design matrix (Suh, 2005) was used to illustrate the existence of coupling. Coupling means that attempts at achieving a particular FR may impact the ability to achieve one or more other FRs. In organisations, coupling increases uncertainty (it becomes less clear for decision makers which levers to pull to achieve a given outcome), reduces accountability (more than one sub-unit is responsible for achieving a given outcome, or may influence the outcome indirectly) and creates goal conflicts (achievement of one sub-unit's goals may compromise the ability of another sub-unit to achieve its goals). The overall effect of high complexity is a *decreased probability that the organisation will be able to achieve all of the goals that it is pursuing* (Suh, 2005).[9]

The second definition states that complexity is due to interdependencies between design parameters; this was illustrated by means of a design structure matrix (Eppinger, 2001). According to this definition, a complex organisation is one with many cross-unit interdependencies that requires frequent coordination and information exchange. Process interdependencies create coordination costs (because two or more sub-units need to adjust to each other's plans and actions) and reduce organisational flexibility (because changes cannot be made independently in one sub-unit, without affecting the functions served by another).

We may add that it is not only the existence of an interdependency that counts, but also our degree of knowledge of the existence of the interdependency, and the relative uncertainty and predictability of the interdependency. In today's more fluid organisations, it may not always be clear with whom a manager should interface with in order to complete a task. This has given rise to what is called *hidden interdependencies* (Wong et al., 2007). A lack of knowledge of interdependencies may thus in itself be a source of complexity. (We discuss this topic further in Chapter 7.)

An important implication of this definitional framework is that it points to the possibility of creating analytical tools to support organisation design processes. The most frequently used tool, the organisation chart, only displays one dimension of the organisation – the formal reporting structure – and often conceals the inherent complexity of a design. An organisation chart shows (at best) the design parameters of a current or future organisation, but not how the design parameters interact or how they address functional requirements. It is, therefore, difficult to use organisation charts as a means for comparing and evaluating different design options that are developed as part of a re-design process. The matrices used in this chapter (e.g., Table 2.1 and Figure 2.5) are alternative tools that can be considered. They can be used to extract the key features of an organisation design and may thus allow systematic comparison and evaluation of design options.

One should perhaps distinguish between two types of measures that organisations can use to gauge the level of complexity. The first is 'direct' measures reflecting the structural designs. One could use the design matrix and design structure matrix to map an organisation (or parts of it). (The level of interdependence, as well as the total number of interdependencies, are factors that can quantified in such a mapping.) Second, one could use indicators that reflect the various consequences that complexity may have. Both objective, work process data (e.g., cycle time, cost, quality) and perceptual measures (e.g., employee surveys that include items regarding job design, goals and structure etc.) may be used for this purpose.

Organisational strategies

There are basically three generic strategies that one can adopt in the face of increasing complexity (SerdarAsan, 2009) (Figure 2.7). An important premise is that one is able to distinguish between necessary and unnecessary complexity. Although there is no objective way to identify the exact level, we can, in principle, define necessary complexity as the level of complexity needed to perform the functions of a system, and unnecessary complexity as complexity that does not provide additional value to the system (the organisation), or that can be avoided with little or no loss in the functions performed.

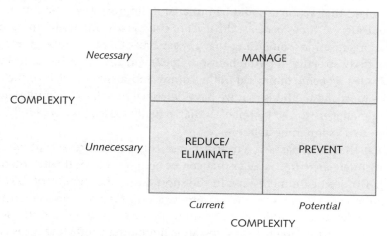

Figure 2.7 Strategies for dealing with organisational complexity
Source: SerdarAsan, 2009

Above we described how companies sometimes adapt their structure in response to external changes. Managerial choices in such cases influence both the level of *necessary* and the level of *unnecessary* complexity. If customer needs are changing, or becoming more differentiated, the response may be to increase the frequency of product upgrades or develop entirely new products. Some increase in internal complexity may be an unavoidable result of such changes. At the same time, such moves may also lead to an increase in unnecessary (i.e., avoidable) complexity. The introduction of new product offerings may result in duplication of business processes, the introduction of new product components (where standard parts could have been utilised) incompatible infrastructure (e.g., two or more IT systems), and the establishment of organisational roles and units with conflicting goals and KPIs (key performance indicators). Similarly, the adoption of a new regulatory framework may be necessary, and also lead to important benefits for individual companies, such as improvements in internal control and audit processes (Wagner and Dittmar, 2006). However, it may also result in unnecessary complexity. At times, the adoption of new governance processes leads to the establishment of multiple internal governance bodies and a multiplication of the steps that need to be performed in order to authorise a business decision. The end result may be to increase costs and slow down strategic decision making.

It is an important research question to identify what level of complexity a given type of organisation can sustain, and what level of complexity is likely to be dysfunctional and damage performance. However, even if more objective methods are developed to assess the level of complexity, in the end it is the key stakeholders in the organisation who themselves must identify complexity as an issue. So it may be appropriate to say that it is when stakeholders *perceive* organisational complexity to be too high, that actions should be initiated to improve the situation. It is possible that outsiders at times perceive the level of complexity differently from managers inside the organisation; something that appears chaotic to an outsider may in fact have an orderly structure (cf. Abrahamson, 2002). On the other hand, insiders may also be blinded by being immersed in the culture and mental models of their organisation; the tools and methods that we have described here have an important role in sensitising managers to the complexity that actually exists, and hopefully, in spurring action to do something about it.

Provided that one has arrived at a consensus about the acceptable level of complexity, there are two strategies that can be employed to deal with internal complexity that is deemed unnecessary. In the short term, one should try to reduce the level of unnecessary complexity. For example, a firm may be able to reduce organisational complexity by standardising business processes, minimising the number of individual roles performing the same job and eliminating conflicting goals and KPIs.

The key strategy to deal with *necessary* complexity is to manage it. Large firms consist of multiple operating units, utilise many different production processes, employ diverse technologies and rely on a global network of suppliers. They may also be characterised by highly layered hierarchies and intricate governance processes. If the firm's management believes that the level of complexity is necessary to sustain its operations, it should attempt to reduce the impact of the complexity on the organisation's performance. For example, to avoid confusion among employees, managers may make an effort to explain how the organisation is structured and clearly communicate how the key processes are performed and how roles and responsibilities have been allocated. The firm may also try to develop the individual skills required to work in a complex organisation, for example, improving communication and negotiation skills may allow managers to handle complex cross-functional and cross-unit collaboration in a productive manner.

Although periodic re-design may be required in order to reduce or eliminate complexity, the ideal strategy is to prevent the build-up of complexity, by selecting designs that minimise complexity in the first place, so that one avoids the need for frequent fixes or restructuring exercises. Ideally, one should not only select the design option that is optimal today – but one that also ensures that the level of complexity will be manageable in the future. The organisational model that is selected should be sufficiently robust to accommodate changes that may occur in products, markets or internal processes. Of course, this is easier said than done. There are organisations that alter their structure almost every year and change back and forth between organisational models based on product or geography, or between centralised and decentralised structures. However, one may succeed in creating more robust designs by making a conscious effort to evaluate the inherent complexity of any proposal aimed at changing the organisation and by selecting a design that minimises (unnecessary) complexity.

The sequence in which these strategies is applied is not arbitrary. Managers who are concerned by the level of complexity in their firms sometimes suggest introducing training courses and change programmes aimed at increasing collaboration, reducing inter-unit conflicts and so on. However, such initiatives do not address the root causes of the issue, and one may thus find that the level of complexity increases further as a result. It seems clear that the ideal sequence is to first establish what the necessary level of complexity is, and then initiate actions to reduce any unnecessary complexity, before strategies to manage the necessary complexity are employed.

Summary and conclusion

A number of studies documents that organisational complexity may negatively affect the productivity of individual employees, the performance of projects and processes and the overall financial performance of a firm. Rising levels of internal complexity in large organisations is partly a result of rising environmental complexity, but it also reflects managerial choices, including the implementation of inappropriate organisational designs. Research confirms that firms of similar size and in the same industry differ with regard to the level of internal complexity.

Until recently, there has been a lack of systematic methods for managing or reducing complexity. This situation is changing with the introduction of more precise definitions and of tools that can be used to map and re-structure interdependencies between functions and design parameters. In this chapter, we reviewed two slightly different conceptualisations of complexity. The first defines complexity as the existence of coupling between functional requirements, positing increased uncertainty as the key implication. The second defines complexity as the existence of interdependencies between design parameters, positing increased coordination cost as the key implication. These definitions are complementary, however, and provide the basis for building a systematic approach to assess complexity and to develop organisation design interventions that can support leaders in dealing proactively with complexity.

Design propositions

Objective   *Maximise the effectiveness of large organisations by dealing proactively with complexity*

    2.1   Periodically assess the level of, and consequences of, organisational complexity.

    2.2   Implement systems, tools and processes that can help reduce the impact of *necessary* complexity (MANAGE).

    2.3   Re-design organisational structure, processes and/or individual roles when complexity is deemed unnecessarily high (REDUCE).

    2.4   When selecting new organisational models, processes and individual roles, other things being equal, select designs that minimise complexity (PREVENT).

Objective   *Systematically evaluate the level of complexity of alternative organisational models*

    2.5   Map the correspondence between functional requirements and design parameters by means of a design matrix and identify instances of (actual or potential) coupling.

    2.6   Map the relationship between different design parameters in a design structure matrix (DSM) and identify (actual or potential) interdependencies that may increase coordination costs (e.g., that may cause iterations, delays).

Review questions

1   How does the definition of complexity proposed in this chapter differ from the definition traditionally employed in organisation theory?

2   What are the indicators that suggest that internal complexity is increasing in many organisations?

3   How does complexity affect organisational functioning?

4   What strategies should managers adopt in order to deal proactively with rising complexity?

5   Does the existence of process interdependencies imply that there is coupling between functional requirements?

6   Consider an organisation that you are familiar with (e.g., a business firm, a university, etc.). Map the correspondence between functional requirements and design parameters using a design matrix and identify potential instances of coupling. Are there alternative designs with fewer instances of coupling?

Research questions

1   How can we more precisely assess the level of 'necessary' versus 'unnecessary' complexity?

2   What is the relationship between the perceived level of risk among decision makers and the level of internal complexity in an organisation?

3   What indicators could be used to more systematically assess how the level of complexity within organisations develops over time?

4   What are the performance effects of adopting different strategies for dealing with complexity?

Notes

1   I here extend on an example borrowed from Ethiraj and Levinthal (2009).

2   One could imagine other scenarios, where the effect would have been the opposite. For example, a product line organisation might lead to a lower degree of complexity than a geographical organisation if customers operate across different geographies yet perform purchasing centrally.

3   The total number of potential interactions between n structural elements of a system is $n(n-1)$.

4   In empirical studies of the effects of organisational complexity, it is important to control for other factors that may lead to performance differences, such as the size and complexity of the task itself. In the Hihn et al. (1990) study, the productivity data were adjusted based on differences in the nature of the project task and the experience level of the project team members.

5   Source: http://en.wikipedia.org/wiki/Aeroper%C3%BA_Flight_603.

6   These estimates were derived from the following report authored by Australia's Information and Communications Technology agency: http://www.educationau.edu.au/sites/default/files/SPAM_information.pdf.

7   In a study reported in Pritchard and Armistead (1999), 'confusion or ambiguity between functions and processes' was ranked as one of the greatest difficulties in implementing process-based organisations.

8   Note that the design matrix shown only holds for the specific case described above (cf. Figure 2.1). One may think of many scenarios, such as one in which the same customer is represented across the three regions, where a product-based structure would be less complex than a geographically based structure. Thus the argument being made is not that a geographically based structure is better per se.

9   As a consequence, one would thus expect that the degree of complexity is related to the risk level as perceived by decision makers: the more complex the organisation, the higher the risk associated with the achievement of functional requirements.

Case study

The functions and structure of a hospital

Wikipedia describes a hospital as follows:

> A hospital, in the modern sense of the word, is an institution for health care providing patient treatment by specialized staff and equipment, and often, but not always providing for longer-term patient stays.
>
> (http://en.wikipedia.org/wiki/Hospital)

Clearly, treating people who are ill is the defining characteristic of a hospital. But as pointed out by Healy and McKee (2002), a hospital also performs other functions. For example, a hospital may be an important setting for teaching and research and be an important source for local employment.

According to Payne (2006, p. 759), health care organisations face enormous pressure to meet two conflicting functional requirements: 1) Provide the highest possible quality and technologically advanced care possible; and 2) Maintain tight cost control on all services rendered. For example, providing higher quality may imply spending more time with the patient, having specialists deliver services rather than generalists, providing services locally, and investing in the latest medical equipment. Maintaining cost control may imply spending less time with the patient, letting generalists deliver services, centralising service delivery and investing in less expensive equipment. The conflict between these two requirements is further complicated by the fact that the end user (i.e., the patient) has incentives to demand the highest quality care yet is normally not the payer of the services rendered.

Hospitals have traditionally been organised based on medical specialisation, with one department for each sub-discipline (see Figure 2.8). A common criticism of this organisational structure is that it creates obstacles for an efficient patient flow. Patients often need to make multiple visits for tests performed by different departments. Delays are created if specialists from different departments need to collaborate in forming a diagnosis or providing treatment, resulting in excessive waiting time for patients.

As Figure 2.8 indicates, hospitals may be viewed as dual hierarchies (Harris, 1977). Medical staff usually admit and treat patients without interference from the administration. The administrators have the responsibility for creating the support infrastructure and make resources available for the medical staff. (Note that these two internal groups also represent the two functional requirements described above: efficiency is mainly the concern of the administrators, whereas quality care is mainly the concern of the medical staff.)

Discussion questions

It may be helpful to discuss the following questions in groups, document the results on a flip chart or presentation slides, and then compare the results of the discussions in the different groups.

1 How would you formulate the main functional requirements for a general hospital?

2 What are the design parameters that address these functional requirements?

3 Discuss further examples of how functional requirements may sometimes be in conflict.

4 Consider whether there are any design options that may resolve the conflict between quality and cost control efficiency. It may be helpful to first decompose one or more of the functions; the design options may relate to the formal structure or to systems, work processes or medical procedures in the hospital.

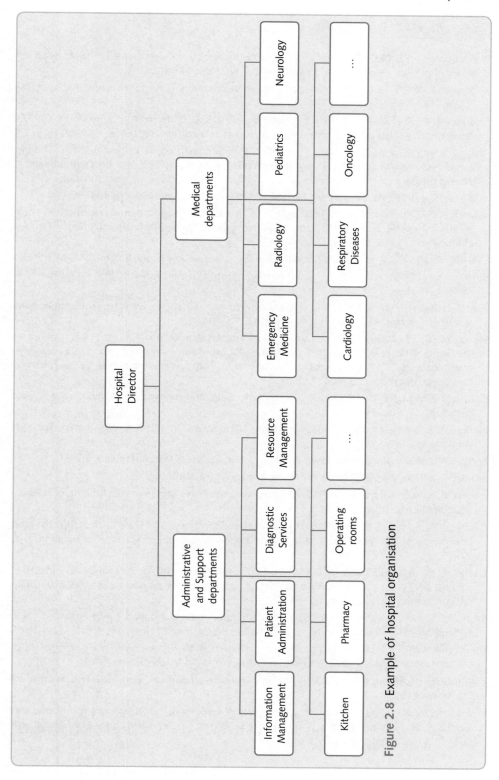

Figure 2.8 Example of hospital organisation

References

Abrahamson, E. (2002). Disorganization theory and disorganizational behavior: towards an etiology of messes. *Research in Organisational Behavior*, 24, 139–80.

Anderson, P. (1999). Complexity theory and organisational science. *Organization Science*, 10, 3, 216–32.

Andrews, L. B., Stocking, C., Krizck, T., Gottlief, L., Krizck, C., Vargish, T. and Sieger, M. (1997). An alternative strategy for studying adverse events in medical care. *Lancet*, 349, 309–13.

Aral, S., Brynjolfsson, E. and Wu, D. J. (2006). Which came first, IT or productivity? The virtuous cycle of investment and use in enterprise systems. MIT Center for Digital Business Working Paper.

Ashby, W. R. (1956). *An Introduction to Cybernetics*. London: Chapman & Hall.

Ashmos, D. P., Duchon, D. and McDaniel, R. R. Jr. (2000). Organizational responses to complexity: the effect on organizational performance. *Journal of Organizational Change Management*, 13, 6, 577–94.

Baldwin, C. and Clark, K. (2000). *Design Rules: The Power of Modularity*. Boston, MA: MIT Press.

Barney, J. (1996). *Gaining and Sustaining*. Competitive Advantage. Reading, MA: Addison-Wesley.

Benz, M. and Frey, B. S. (2007). Corporate governance: what can we learn from public governance? *Academy of Management Review*, 32, 92–104.

Bernanke, B. S. (2009). Financial innovation and consumer protection. Speech given at the Federal Reserve System's Sixth Biennial Community Affairs Research Conference, Washington, DC, 17 April. Available on-line from: http://www.federalreserve.gov/newsevents/speech/bernanke20090417a.htm.

Blau, J. R. and McKinley, W. (1979). Ideas, complexity, and innovation. *Administrative Science Quarterly*, 24, 200–19.

Blecker, T. and Kersten, W. (2006). *Complexity Management in Supply Chains*. Berlin: Schmidt Verlag.

Britt, T. W. (2003). Black hawk down at work. *Harvard Business Review*, January, 16–17.

Brooks, F. (1975). *The Mythical Man-Month*. Reading, MA: Addison-Wesley.

Burton, R. M. and Forsyth, J. D. (1986). Variety and the firm's performance: An empirical investigation. *Technovation*, 5, 9–21.

Canbäck, S., Samouel, P. and Price, D. (2006). Do diseconomies of scale impact firm size and performance? A theoretical and empirical overview. *Journal of Managerial Economics*, 4, 27–70.

Carillo, P. M. and Kopelman, R. E. (1991). Organisation structure and productivity: effects of subunit size, vertical complexity, and administrative intensity on operating efficiency. *Group & Organisation Management*, 16, 44–59.

Chun, Y. H. and Rainey, H. G. (2005). Goal ambiguity and organizational performance in U.S. Federal Agencies. *Journal of Public Administration Research and Theory*, 15, 4, 529–57.

Dhawan, R. (2001). Firm size and productivity differential: theory and evidence from a panel of US firms, *Journal of Economic Behavior and Organization*, 44, 269–93.

Economist Intelligence Unit (2011). *The complexity challenge*. London: The Economist Intelligence Unit.

Ende, Jan van den (2002). Modes of governance of new service development for mobile networks: A life cycle perspective. Working paper, Erasmus Research Institute of Management (ERIM), Rotterdam School of Management.

Eppinger, S. (2001). Innovation at the speed of information. *Harvard Business Review*, 79, 1, 149–58.

Ethiraj, S. K. and Levinthal, D. A. (2009). Hoping for A to Z while rewarding only A: complex organisations and multiple goals. *Organisation Science*, 20 (1): 4–21.

Fleming, P. and Zyglidopoulos, S. C. (2008). The escalation of deception in organizations. *Journal of Business Ethics*, 81, 4: 837–50.

Galbraith, J. (2000). *Designing the Global Corporation*. San Francisco, CA: Jossey-Bass.

Gresov, C. and Drazin, R. (1997). Equifinality: functional equivalence in organisational design. *Academy of Management Review*, 22, 403–26.

Haraldsson, H. V., Sverdrup, H. U., Belyazid, S., Holmqvist, J. and Gramstad, R. C. J. (2008). The tyranny of small steps: a reoccurring behaviour in management. *Systems Research and Behavioral Science*, 25, 1, 25–43.

Harris, J. E. (1977). The internal organization of hospitals: some economic implications. *Bell Journal of Economics*, 8, 2, 467–82.

Healy, J. and McKee, M. (2002). The evolution of hospital systems. In M. McKee and J. Healy, *Hospitals in a changing Europe*. Buckingham: Open University Press.

Heath, C. and Staudenmayer, N. (2000). Coordination neglect: how lay theories of organizing complicate coordination in organizations. *Research in Organizational Behavior*, 22, 153–91.

Herring, R. J. and Carmassi, J. (2010). The corporate structure of international financial conglomerates: complexity and its implications for safety and soundness. In Berger, A. N., Molyneux, P. and Wilson, J. (eds), *Oxford Handbook of Banking*. Oxford: Oxford University Press.

Hihn, J. M., Malhotra, S. and Malhotra, M. (1990). Volatility and organizational structure. *Journal of Parametrics*. September, 65–82.

Hinckley, C. M. (2003). Make no mistake – errors can be controlled. *Quality and Safety Health Care*, 12, 359–65.

Hoole, R. (2006). Drive complexity out of your supply chain. *Supply Chain Strategy* (Newsletter from Harvard Business School Publishing and the MIT Center for Transportation and Logistics), December–January.

IBM (2010). *Capitalizing on Complexity*. Summers, NY: IBM.

Jensen, M. C. (1983). Organization theory and methodology. *Accounting Review*, 56, 319–38.

Landau, J.-P. (2009). Complexity and the financial crisis. Introductory remarks at the Conference on 'The macroeconomy and financial systems in normal times and in times of stress', jointly organised by the Bank of France and the Deutsche Bundesbank, Gouvieux-Chantilly, 8 June. Available on-line from: http://www.bis.org/review/r090806c.pdf

Malone, T. W. (2004). *The Future of Work*. Boston, MA: Harvard Business School Press.

Meyer, M. W. (2002). *Rethinking Performance Measurement: Beyond the Balance Scorecard*. Cambridge: Cambridge University Press.

Mortensen, M. (2004). Antecedents and consequences of team boundary disagreement. *Academy of Management Best Papers Proceedings*.

Pandey, S. K. and Wright, B. E. (2006). Connecting the dots in public management: political environment, organizational goal ambiguity and public manager's role ambiguity. *Journal of Public Administration Research and Theory*, 16, 4, 511–32.

Payne, G. T. (2006). Examining configurations and firm performance in a suboptimal equifinality context. *Organization Science*, 17, 756–70.

Peck, H. (2005). The drivers of supply chain vulnerability: an integrated framework, *International Journal of Physical Distribution and Logistics Management*, 35, 4, 210–32.

Perrow, C. (1984). *Normal Accidents: Living with High-Risk Technologies*. New York: Basic Books.

Posner, B. Z. and Butterfield, D. A. (1978). Role clarity and organizational level. *Journal of Management*, 4, 2, 81–90.

PricewaterhouseCooopers (2006). 9th Annual Global CEO survey: Globalisation and Complexity; Inevitable Forces in a Changing Economy.

Pritchard, J. P. and Armistead, C. (1999). Business process management – lessons from European business. *Business Process Management Journal*, 5, 10–32.

Rettig, C. (2007). The trouble with enterprise software. *Sloan Management Review*, 49, 1, 21–7.

Romano, J. and Nunamaker, F. (2001). Meeting analysis: findings from research and practice, *Proceedings of the Thirty-Fourth Annual Hawai'i International Conference on System Sciences*, 1, 1–13, Washington, DC: IEEE Computer Society.

Saunders, C. (2006). Separation of powers and the judicial branch. *Judicial Review*, 11, 337–47.

Schmalensee, R. (1989). Intra-industry profitability differences in US manufacturing: 1953–1983. *Journal of Industrial Economies*, 37, 337–57.

Schwenk, C. R. (1984). Cognitive simplification processes in strategic decision-making. *Strategic Management Journal*, 5, 111–28.

SerdarAsan, S. (2009). A methodology based on theory of constraints' thinking process for managing complexity in the supply chain. Doctoral thesis, Technical University of Berlin, http://opus.kobv.de/tuberlin/volltexte/2009/2406/pdf/serdar_asan_seyda.pdf

Simon, H. A. (1962). The architecture of complexity. *Proceedings of the American Philosophical Society*, 106, 467–82.

Suh, N. P. (2001). *Axiomatic Design: Advances and Applications*. New York: Oxford University Press.

Suh, N. P. (2005). *Complexity: Theory and Applications*. New York: Oxford University Press.

Wagner, S. and Dittmar, L. (2006). The unexpected benefits of Sarbanes-Oxley. *Harvard Business Review*, 84, 133–40.

Whittington, R., Pettigrew, A., Peck, S., Fenton, E. and Conyon, N. (1999). Change and complementarities in the new competitive landscape: a European panel study, 1992–1996. *Organisation Science*, 10, 5, 583–600.

Williamson, O. E. (1975). *Markets and Hierarchies: Analysis and Antitrust Implications*. New York: Free Press.

Wong, S., DeSanctis, G. and Staudenmayer, N. (2007). The relationship between task interdependency and role stress: a revisit of the job demands-control model. *Journal of Management Studies*, 44, 2, 284–303.

Chapter 3

Managing the organisation design process

Overview

Background

- Leaders periodically initiate organisational re-design processes in order to improve performance
- The quality of the re-design process itself is an important predictor of the quality of the organisational model that is developed – and of its acceptance and implementation

Challenges

- Unless managed skilfully, re-design processes can easily result in suboptimal outcomes:
  - Omitting the link between functions and structure may lead to *misalignment* between the organisational model that is developed and the strategy of the organisation
  - A failure to fully consider the many interrelated elements of organisational models may lead to *incoherent* designs
  - Lack of proper involvement of key stakeholders in the re-design process may lead to a *withering of trust*, which in turn reduces voluntary compliance with the new organisational model

Key question

- How can we manage re-design processes in a manner that allows us to *align* the organisation with the strategy, create *coherent* designs, while building *trust* among key stakeholders (including employees affected by the change)?

Proposed approach

- Develop a structured methodology that leaders can use to plan, develop and implement new organisational designs

- Ensure that the methodology addresses the challenges related to creating alignment, coherence and trust

- Consider how the methodology may be further improved by means of field testing and systematic research on design processes

Introduction

The more complex an organisation is, the harder it is to re-design. Leaders who undertake to re-design their organisations frequently encounter problems that are best described as 'messes' – problems that are difficult to solve because of incomplete, contradictory and/or changing requirements (Ackoff, 1999). Leaders may also be subject to considerable pressure from stakeholder groups and individuals who frequently hold different views and who press for a solution that is favourable, given their interests and position in the organisation. How can we structure the organisation re-design process in a way that enables leaders to handle such challenges in a constructive manner?

Most experienced leaders have personal experience from developing and changing organisations. They may hold strong personal preferences with regard to the approach to follow when initiating a re-design process, based on observations of the success or failure of past attempts. Such personal knowledge is clearly valuable and will always influence how one approaches a re-design process. Yet it is also important to acknowledge the limitations of personal knowledge. Personal knowledge is *tacit* and thus difficult to verify and to disseminate. Relying on tacit knowledge alone makes it difficult to create a cumulative learning process in which organisation design principles are gradually refined and improved over time.

The development of a methodology, containing guiding principles, frameworks and tools, is one way to create *explicit knowledge* about re-design processes.[1] A methodology ensures that an effective way to solve a problem is codified and that it can be shared among a larger group of people. It helps in creating shared 'mental models' and may thus contribute to 'cognitive coordination' among participants in a design process (Werr et al., 1997). A methodology may also serve as a basis for developing a gradually more sophisticated knowledge base about re-design. A methodology may comprise a set of *design propositions*. As discussed in Chapter 1, design propositions should reflect the current state of academic research but should also be revised and improved based on 'field testing', by observing the outcome of actual re-design processes where they have been applied.

The purpose of this chapter is to develop a methodology that may provide a basis for systematic and cumulative improvement of knowledge over time. It goes beyond existing methodologies by incorporating some key elements of the axiomatic design approach described in the preceding two chapters, for example, by emphasising the link between functional requirements and design parameters. The methodology has been developed 'in the field' and refined during repeated re-design projects. Yet methodology only represents a first step. Disagreements do exist among practitioners with regard to some issues and their gaps in the formal knowledge about re-design processes. We acknowledge this by formulating several research questions that are described in the Discussion section.

Requirements to design processes

In line with the axiomatic design philosophy, one should start the development of a re-design methodology by considering the purpose and the requirements that such a methodology should fulfil. Although there will always be some situation-specific requirements to design processes, we here suggest that there are three generic requirements that practically all re-design processes must fulfil in order to be successful. These requirements are to create *alignment* with strategy, *coherence* and consistency between design elements and *trust* among stakeholders participating in and affected by the design.

At the most fundamental level, organisational models that are developed during a re-design exercise should aid the organisation in realising its strategic goals. In other words, the organisational model needs to be *aligned* with strategic goals. This in turn requires that the strategic goals are known. Moreover, the strategic goals need to be sufficiently clear to allow a design team to make choices that may prioritise one design criterion (e.g., costs) at the expense of another (e.g., customer service). Yet as observers of organisational decision making have noted (e.g., Pache and Santos, 2010; Pfeffer, 1982), leaders sometimes encounter fundamental disagreements about goals. Large organisations consist of several stakeholder groups, with different interests and interpretations of the organisation's purpose, mission and goals. Overcoming such disagreements is often the most difficult part of a design exercise.

A CEO of an engineering firm initiates a discussion in his management team about how the firm's Research & Development unit should be organised. In particular, he is considering whether to split and decentralise the unit's resources among the firm's different business areas. During the process, this proposal meets with considerable resistance, as the R&D staff believe that decentralisation would force it to become more like a support function, driven by the business-areas' short-term needs, making it difficult to maintain its current research capabilities. The CEO concludes that the unit lacks a clear purpose: Should its main purpose be to support product development, or to develop entirely new technologies?

> A governmentally funded body responsible for food certification is reviewing its organisational structure. Half way through the design exercise, it becomes clear that there exists some ambiguity with regards to its mission. Staff members mention difficulty in prioritising different projects, aimed at different users or target groups. This leads to a discussion of who the primary beneficiary is of the body's services: Is it the consumer, who will be able to enjoy safer and higher quality food? Is it the government, which funds its activities? Is it the farmer, the supplier of the food ingredients? Or is it the supermarket chains that buy the products from the farmer, and, that should be able to increase both margins and volume when products are certified?

An effective organisation design process should enable key stakeholders to identify and improve unclear or conflicting goals that preclude the development of viable designs and, once this has been achieved, ensure that new designs are aligned with the organisational strategies.

The next challenge is developing a design that is *coherent* and consistent. Many senior executives start the re-design process by changing reporting lines for top level executives, with (apparently) little appreciation for the effects that such changes may have on how cross-unit processes are carried out.

> The CEO of an insurance company decides to restructure the company. The new structure consists of three main units: Sales, Customer Service and Claims Handling. After settling on the composition of his leadership team, he 'empowers' each of the new unit managers to work on the organisational design of his/her unit. The head of the sales unit chooses to organise by geography (North, West, South). The head of Customer Service prefers to organise by customer group (consumers, businesses, etc.). The head of the claims unit prefers to organise by product (life and non-life insurance). After implementing the new structure, it becomes clear that problems in the horizontal business processes – spanning Sales to Customer Service to Claims Handling – are producing delays and increasing cost. The CEO gradually realises that the pieces don't fit – the units have not been designed to enhance the organisation's overall performance.

When organisation re-design processes are initiated, the purpose is rarely to optimise one part of the organisation in isolation but rather to improve *system* (i.e., *organisational*) performance. This can only be done by looking both at the individual units and at how they interact in carrying out the organisation's processes. Although lower-level units may be empowered to develop the specific designs for their own units, it is necessary to *coordinate* the design processes centrally in order to ensure a focus on system performance.

Third, the design process should ensure that the design is actually implemented. As members of organisations, most of us observe intentions that are not realised and plans that are only partially implemented.

Hood et al. (1985) studied the effects of 10 reorganisations of British government departments. The reorganisations consisted in both mergers and demergers of government departments. The intention of the mergers was to bring separate units under one roof to make government policy more coherent and get people to work together (The Economist, 2009). Yet Hood et al. (1985) observed that the changes had had little effect on the way people worked and on how different sub-units would collaborate with each other: 'The Ministry of Defense in its current form was stitched together from the separate military departments in the 1960's, and it's often said that even now you can see the joints' (The Economist, 2009, p. 38). Hood et al. refer to the 'Law of inertia' to explain why reorganisations fail to produce the intended effects.

A global oil services firm introduced a new product-based organisation. The new structure implied that people that had previously been part of functionally defined units would now be transferred to one of the three product units that were established. An evaluation some months later revealed that the new structure had been implemented in different ways in the various offices worldwide. At the Houston office, the regional president had re-allocated workers' offices to ensure that team members were co-located. At the Oslo office, on the other hand, many people were still in the same offices as before, four months after the new structure had been announced. As one manager remarked: 'For us . . . there really was no distinct shift between the old and the new organisation. . .people don't feel that they are part of a new team. . .'

As Russell Ackoff states (1981), no design has ever been created that humans aren't able to subvert. Yet one may ask what the conditions are that motivate managers and employees to voluntarily comply with, rather than subvert, a design that has been selected as the preferred model by their organisation's decisions makers. Both systematic research and practical experience point to three crucial factors that influence the likelihood that employees will actively support the implementation of organisational changes.[2] The first is the degree to which employees understand the rationale for initiating the change, and for the particular design that has been selected. The second is related to the ability to influence the outcome of the process by means of participation in the decision process. The third is the degree to which employees see a pay-off for them personally from implementing the organisational changes, for example, whether a new design will provide roles that create opportunities for learning, growth or career advancement. In short, managers need to create *Trust* in the re-design process and its outcomes.

The challenge of creating *alignment*, *coherence* and *trust* can be converted into requirements for the design process (see Table 3.1). The purpose of the remaining part of this chapter is to outline a methodology that is intended to maximise the chances that re-design processes in complex organisations will fulfil the requirements – that is, that the participants in the process are able to develop designs that are aligned with strategic goals, which are coherent, and which create trust and thus are likely to be implemented and complied with by organisational members.

Table 3.1 Key challenges in re-design processes and how these are addressed by the design methodology proposed

Challenge	Examples of techniques recommended
Creating *alignment*, i.e., ensuring that the chosen model is aligned with the company's mission and strategies	• Facilitation techniques to clarify mission and purpose • Use of mapping tools to identify correspondence between goals (functional requirements) and organisational variables (design parameters)
Creating *coherence*, i.e., improving the performance of the entire system, as opposed to optimising individual parts	• Central coordination of design process • Explicit consideration of the *interdependencies* between sub-units • Sequencing of activities (strategic design before operational design) • Coordinated re-configuration of *Operating model*, *Resource model* and *Governance model*
Creating *trust*, which is necessary for the chosen organisational model to be accepted and implemented by the organisational members	• Methods that allow key stakeholder groups to participate in the design process • Development and use of explicit decision criteria • Careful operationalisation of the design and systematic transition planning

Many managers working in large organisations will be able to recount instances of dysfunctional organisation design processes. Leaders may have been unwilling to consider new options and may have simply resorted to the same solutions that have been used in the past; decisions processes may at one point have disintegrated into political manoeuvring among key players, or decision makers may have selected solution alternatives that would obviously fail to address the underlying causes of a well recognised problem. In fact, such problems are so commonplace that many managers and employees probably doubt the feasibility of attempting to create alignment, coherence and trust. They have come to the conclusion that organisational re-design is primarily a political process that only a handful of key players are likely to be involved in.[3] Rather than creating a dedicated re-design project as advocated here, some managers may put more faith in the more frequent and gradual adjustments that line managers carry out to roles and processes within the various sub-units of the organisation.

Obviously, no methodology for conducting a decision process will by itself resolve such issues; a methodology will only serve its purpose if there is a pre-existing commitment to addressing organisation design issues in a systematic and transparent manner. Nevertheless, the overall assertion here is that one is unlikely to achieve a successful re-design of large and complex organisations using unsystematic methods or overly political strategies. The first question to a line manager contemplating an organisational re-design it thus what kind of process the line manager envisages. The methodology described in this chapter is primarily intended for those managers willing to articulate their decision criteria, to test their own assumptions and to involve relevant stakeholders throughout the process.

We should acknowledge that the process advocated here is relatively time-consuming and requires some project support. (In a large organisation, either internal or external project resources should be assigned to support the process through the different phases described below.) Indeed, a key assumption is that making quick decisions is not a valid goal in itself. What counts – in terms of improving corporate performance – is what one may call 'time to value', that is, *the amount of time that elapses before the intended benefits of the organisational model are realised*. A systematic re-design pro-cess requires an investment of time. Not only does it take time to perform the actual project activities (e.g., data collection and analysis); the process often requires negotiation between different stakeholder groups and frequently sets in motion psychological processes where new concepts and ideas, that may immediately seem new or foreign, gradually mature and become accepted as potential solutions.

The purpose of the methodology is not to eliminate all 'politics' in the process; which would be impossible in any case. However, the methodology is built on the assumption that there are productive and unproductive ways of handling the political aspects of an organisation design process. In accordance with theories on negotiation (Fisher and Ury, 1983), it is assumed that it is easier to create productive dialogue if one can first obtain commitment toward general principles and decision criteria, and delay the discussion regarding individual roles to a later stage in the process. It is also assumed that it is easier to discover effective design solutions – and to implement them, once selected – when different stakeholders have been involved throughout the process. It may be impossible to design an 'optimal' model, but it may be possible to create a design process in which participants jointly create new designs, evaluate decision alternatives, implement the design, and also adjust elements of the design that do not work as intended.

In the following, a set of tools used to produce 'deliverables' that document the outputs of each step of the process is described. Documenting information has a value in itself; for example, it improves the ability to effectively share information among a group of stakeholders. Written records of the design process also allow 'traceability', that is, the ability to document on what grounds a given design option was selected. This in turn facilitates learning as outcomes can be compared more directly to prior decisions and decision criteria. However, even more important is the role that these tools play in shaping the design process itself. To take a simple example, using an organisation chart as the main tool in the design process is likely to lead to a somewhat narrow focus on the formal reporting structure. A tool, on the other hand, that explicitly includes other organisational dimensions (such as process interdependencies) may to a significant degree change what information is collected, how stakeholders perceive the key design challenges, and potentially also widen the range of design alternatives that are considered.

This chapter advocates a 'fact-based' approach by describing how data about the organisation can inform design decisions. Yet it does not claim that organisation design can or should be a fully 'analytical' process. An analytical process does not in itself produce a solution. As Georges Romme (2003) has pointed out, to create a new design, it is often necessary to transcend the current definition of the problem, and this is particularly the case with 'messy problems' (Ackoff, 1999) with contradictory requirements. Messy problems require creative re-conceptualisation to be resolved. A methodology thus does not remove the need for creativity. A methodology may, however, aid managers in focusing the problem solving efforts on the right issues, in planning and managing the design process, and in testing and validating ideas that are generated.

Sequence of activities in re-design projects

The methodology proposed here is divided into three main phases: analysis, design and implementation. These phases may in turn be divided into nine more detailed steps (see Table 3.2). In the following we describe in more detail how to perform each step using examples from actual re-design projects.

Table 3.2 Phases and steps of the proposed methodology

Phase	Step
1 Analysis	1 Set the agenda
	2 Analyse the current organisation
	3 Define design criteria
2 Design	4 Develop the organisational architecture (strategic design)
	5 Select the preferred model
	6 Operational design
3 Implementation	7 Create transition plan
	8 Implement
	9 Evaluate

Step 1: Setting the agenda

Organisational re-design processes potentially entail significant costs yet have uncertain outcomes. Even a limited restructuring of a single department often takes months to implement, saps time and attention from core activities and may result in key members leaving the department, if they are disappointed with their new roles. In a larger, multi-unit organisation, the costs and risks multiply. A poorly executed re-design process may cause a deterioration of the organisation's long term financial performance. Experienced leaders are well aware of such risks. How, then, are re-design processes initiated? The risks inherent in changing the organisation implies that no re-design will be initiated without a strongly perceived need for change.[4]

For most management teams, there are many issues competing for attention, and it usually requires a strong champion to ensure that 'the organisation' enters as an item on the decision-making agenda. Key decision makers must be confronted with the issues, reminded of the need to act and become convinced that organisation re-design is an appropriate solution. The key purpose of this initial step, which is called 'Setting the agenda', is precisely to create a consensus among key stakeholders about the need for change.

A fundamental insight in organisational behaviour is that motivation to change is created when key stakeholders perceive a significant gap between the *current* and the *potential* performance of their organisation (or of an organisational sub-unit).[5] To evaluate *current performance* one may use both perceptual and objective data. There are numerous sources of data that may be consulted. Obviously one should make use of whatever standard measures the organisation uses to track the performance of its processes (e.g., time, quality and cost) and financial results (e.g., profitability of different sub-units). Other useful sources are employee surveys and customer surveys, which document how the organisation is perceived and in many cases contain findings that reflect strengths and weaknesses of the current organisational model.[6]

To evaluate what the *potential performance* level is, or should be, it is natural to start with the organisation's strategic goals and ask managers to consider the organisational implications of the goals. One may also compare the organisation to other similar organisations, or to an idealised view of what the organisation would look like, if it were optimally designed (Sachs, 1999). Of course, the gap between an organisation's current and potential performance is not static, and may widen during the design process. The gap may increase because managers perceive that the actual performance is decreasing, or because the potential performance increases (i.e., the ambition level is raised) (see Figure 3.1).

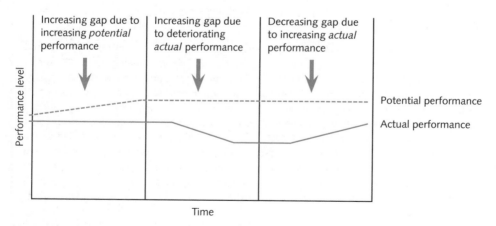

Figure 3.1 Changes in an organisation's actual and potential performance over time[7]

It can be helpful to ask managers to evaluate the organisation's relative performance level in the early phase of a design process (see Example 3.1). If leaders indicate that there is a gap between their current and their potential performance, one can then examine the factors that prevent the organisation from achieving its optimal performance level. In this manner, it is possible to confirm that stakeholders do perceive that there exists a potential for performance improvement, and that an organisational re-design would be the appropriate intervention to realise this potential.

Example 3.1 **Assessing the gap between current and potential performance**

In a survey distributed in a large telecom company, 300 senior managers were asked to evaluate the current performance of the company relative to competitors and compare it to the performance level they believed the company would need to attain in order to realise its strategic objectives. The results were visualised in a chart similar to the one shown in Figure 3.2. At the time of the survey, the company was experiencing increased competition from smaller and more nimble competitors.

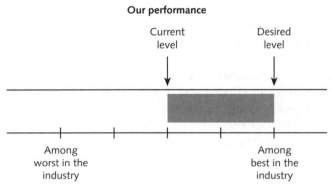

Figure 3.2 Rating of potential versus current performance

In the survey, managers were not only asked to evaluate their overall performance, but also to rate performance related to 10 different capabilities, ranging from 'Customer understanding' to 'Realising value from IT'. Nine out of 10 managers indicated that gaps existed between current and potential performance with regard to most of these capabilities. The managers were also asked to explain what prevented them from achieving their optimal performance level. They contributed more than 1,300 comments. These comments were then analysed to pinpoint the underlying causes of the capability gaps. It was concluded that a common denominator for many of the gaps was organisational complexity, which resulted in an inability to take timely decisions and/or difficulty in mobilising resources in support of strategic objectives and/or low productivity. For example, managers were concerned that an inordinate amount of time was spent on internal processes, rather than on external, market-focused work.[8]

It should be emphasised that the goal is not to develop solutions in this initial phase, nor to identify the exact cause of any problems. The goal is simply to consider whether organisation design is a contributing factor to a performance gap, and, if this assumption is confirmed, develop a shared consensus among key stakeholders about the need to act. This should allow the creation of a clear *mandate* for a re-design process. By mandate we here refer to an explicit decision to form a re-design project, a clarification of the desired outcomes and a timeline and overall plan for the project. It is also helpful if leaders at this point can agree on some key principles for how the process should be executed: Who should be involved? How will decisions be made? Do we aspire to a design process that will produce *alignment*, *coherence* and *trust*? It is important to set the tone early about the guiding principles – and ensure that one has a common understanding of what they entail. It is much more difficult to introduce such principles later in the process, if one discovers that the process begin to derail in an unexpected direction.

Most leaders will need some kind of support in the re-design process. The type and level of support required will depend on the complexity of the change that is considered. In a large organisation undertaking significant change, it is customary to form a dedicated project team with internal and/or external resources. The key responsibilities of the project team is to plan the overall re-design process, collect and analyse data about the organisation, facilitate management meetings, develop design options and support the implementation of the chosen model. In a smaller firm, or in a large firm undertaking less radical changes, it may suffice to have a part-time internal or external advisor supporting the leader. In any case, if multiple units are affected by the decisions that are made, we assume that *central coordination* of the process will be required in order to achieve a coherent design. This does not imply that designs are developed in a 'top-down' fashion, on the contrary, we shall advocate the use of a highly participatory approach. The need for coherence does mean, however, that decisions cannot be taken in isolation as different sub-units are interdependent; each plays a role in the same work processes and changes in the structure of one unit may positively or negatively affect the ability of other sub-units to perform their tasks.

Step 2: Analysing the current organisation

Occasionally, managers may question whether it is necessary to spend time and money analysing the current organisation. Once a project mandate is formed – why not proceed directly to designing the new organisation? Indeed, some 're-organisations' simply consist in a quick re-drawing of the formal reporting relationships for the senior executives of the organisation. However, the information that is most readily available, such as organisation charts, usually provide little or no relevant information about how work processes are performed, how resources are currently utilised, or about interdependencies that exist between units. In addition, it is not uncommon to find that managers have divergent views about how the current organisation actually works – something which usually leads to divergent views regarding how it *should* be designed in the future. By investing time in analysing the current organisation, one collects data that are vital in order to take appropriate decisions regarding future designs and also creates a foundation for building trust in the process, by involving managers and employees in identifying improvement areas and potential solutions. This in turn makes it possible to implement the chosen design in less time and at a lower cost. Thus one should not underestimate the value that can be derived from analysing the current organisation in an early stage of the re-design process.

We have found it useful to provide three key deliverables in this phase. The first is a high-level map of the key units and their main interfaces, which we refer to as the *Operating model* (see Figure 3.3).[9] It is intended to capture the essence of how the organisation currently works, in a user friendly format, without requiring a full blown process mapping. The map may be created in a workshop setting, with representatives from the organisation or the sub-unit being analysed, or a consultant may draw the map based on information derived from interviews with managers and employees. In either case it is often necessary with a few iterations before one arrives at a map that everybody feels adequately expresses the current design. Although the resulting map is important in itself, and will become indispensable in the subsequent design steps, equally important are the questions that are raised in constructing the map, and the ability this confers to create a shared understanding among the participants in the process.

It is helpful to follow certain conventions when drawing the map. One can mimic a 'value chain' logic by placing suppliers on the left of the diagram, the target organisation in the middle and its customers or users on the right. Similarly, one may place management teams and governing bodies (e.g., steering groups) in the upper part of the diagram and more operationally focused units in the bottom part. One should strive to identify the most important interdependencies between the units by focusing on the key outcomes that the units are responsible for providing. (One will end up with a much more complicated drawing if one instead focuses on the many cross-unit *activities* that are performed in order to achieve a certain outcome.) In most cases, this type of map makes it possible to summarise the workings of an entire organisation on one page; however, it is of course possible to produce similar maps for different sub-units if additional detail is needed.

The second deliverable is a list of *functional requirements* for the organisation. As described in Chapter 1, this term has been borrowed from systems designs terminology, and basically entails defining the required outputs. One starts with the overall question: What are the desired results (or outcomes) that this organisation is accountable for delivering? One then breaks down this top-level requirement into sub-requirements. The format for this deliverable is shown in Tables 3.3a and 3.3b. (It is advisable to use verbs in the description of functional requirements, and nouns for the design parameters.) As in other fields, such as engineering and IT, requirements express 'what' the system should produce, or what outcomes it should be able to provide, and should ideally be *solution neutral*, i.e., the requirements should not presuppose the choice of a given organisational structure or otherwise limit the choice of certain solutions. The challenge of describing *how* requirements are to be fulfilled will be handled in the subsequent phase of the re-design process, in which organisational units, processes and roles will be designed that *perform* the functions that have been defined in the current planning step.

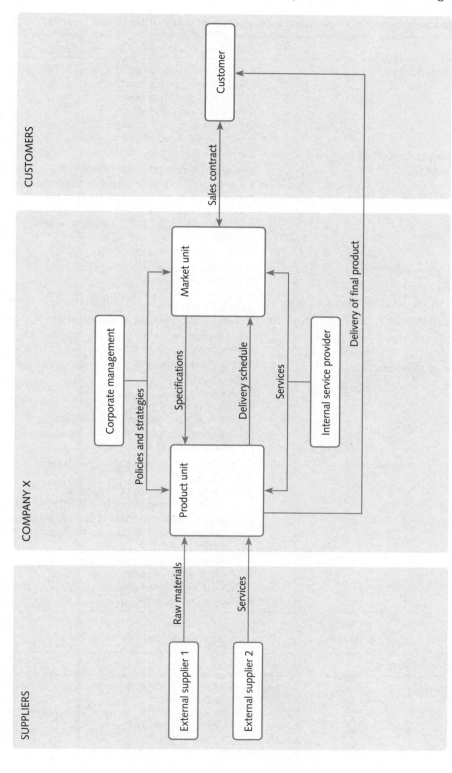

Figure 3.3 Generic template for documenting an organisation's Operating Model

Table 3.3a Examples of high-level functional requirements (from actual client projects)

Organisation	Functional requirements
Software firm (SoftCo)	1 Sell software products and services 2 Provide customer support 3 Manage software products 4 Build software products 5 Develop next generation product concepts 6 Support sales and marketing process
Governmentally funded body responsible for food certification	1 Perform farm audits 2 Manage food certification programmes 3 Contribute to increased recognition of and market access for food products that have been certified 4 Develop new certification programmes and services 5 Plan and administer processes
Geophysical company	1 Market and sell services 2 Develop multi-client library 3 Perform seismic data acquisition services 4 Provide data processing services 5 Perform data interpretation services 6 Manage projects 7 Provide geoscience support
IT function in global engineering firm	1 Manage IT Operations (Service Management) 2 Develop applications 3 Maintain applications 4 Provide project support 5 Provide information management services 6 Manage relations with internal customers 7 Manage global IT resources
HR function in oil services firm	1 Develop individual capability (training and development) 2 Motivate and manage performance (performance management) 3 Shape the workforce (staffing and succession) 4 Build workgroups & culture (survey feedback processes) 5 Perform personnel administration processes 6 Manage employee data 7 Support expatriation process 8 Analyse and report HR data

Table 3.3b Example of decomposition of a functional requirement

Functional requirement	Sub-requirements
3 Manage products	3.1 Capture customer requirements 3.2 Define product road map 3.3 Follow up implementation of customer requirements 3.4 Perform technical marketing of products 3.5 Monitor customer satisfaction

It is helpful to not only identify a list of requirements, but to consider how they interrelate. (This may be done more formally by means of a design matrix as described in the previous chapter.) In some complex organisations, a mapping of the functional requirements will reveal the existence of conflicting requirements, that is, requirements that can only be satisfied by undermining other requirements. The root cause is often compromises that have been built into the current organisation due to a lack of clear strategies or priorities, or because of disagreements between different stakeholders. To resolve such issues, it may be necessary to take a step back and reconsider the very mission and purpose of the organisation (or of a sub-unit that has been made accountable for fulfilling conflicting requirements). Stephen Haeckel (1999) suggested a useful exercise, in which the organisation's key stake-holders are asked to identify the organisation's *reason for being*. The reason for being expresses the organisation's purpose, or what it exists to do, as opposed to what it must do to exist (specific examples are provided in Chapter 5). By reducing any ambiguity that may exist about purpose in this manner, one is more likely to suc-ceed in developing a set of clear requirements for the organisation.

While developing the operational model and the functional requirements, one should also ask managers to assess strengths and weaknesses of the current organ-isational design, particularly in light of any new strategic goals or changes in the business environment. Pre-existing sources of data, such as employee and customer surveys, may also be scrutinised for information that shed light on current organisa-tional functioning. The final deliverable in this step, then, is a list that summarises these findings and their implications for the new design.

Some additions and variations of the above process may be warranted, depending on the scope and purpose of the re-design project. In 'operational level design' at the sub-unit level, it may be necessary to consider business processes and interdependen-cies in more detail than the high-level map described above (Figure 3.3) suggests. It may also be necessary to collect information about individual roles and responsibili-ties as well as the hierarchical structure within the sub-unit. (For 'strategic', corporate level re-design projects, it will usually suffice to cover the senior management roles at this stage.) Finally, many re-design projects will involve the re-allocation of resources, for example, if cost reduction has been defined as one of the objectives for undertaking the re-design. In such cases, it will be necessary to collect information about current resource utilisation. At times, the company's existing databases or ERP systems do not contain sufficiently detailed data (or do not contain data in the appro-priate format) and it may therefore be necessary to collect this information directly from managers, for example, in the form of a survey where managers estimate how resources are utilised across different projects, products and business processes.[10]

Step 3: Defining design criteria

Many managers who contemplate the introduction of a new organisational model proceed directly to the solution stage, by outlining different alternative organisational models. If we return to the requirements for the design process (Table 3.1 above), it is clear that this approach is problematical for both political and psychological rea-sons. Presenting only the outputs of a thought process – such as a new organisational model – often generates resistance that complicates the implementation of the model. Stakeholders need to understand the rationale behind the choice of the solution and, ideally, be provided the chance to influence how that rationale is construed.

A key assumption is thus that we should make the decision criteria – which we call *design criteria* – explicit; moreover, that we should enlist extensive participation in defining the design criteria to ensure that they reflect the concerns and interests of the key stakeholders. For this reason the third step that we suggest is to identify a set of design criteria that expresses the desired characteristics of the future organisational model. Examples would be 'Our future organisational model should help us become more customer-focused', or 'The new organisation should help us reduce costs' (see Tables 3.4a and 3.4b for further examples). Some design criteria will likely follow as direct implications of the corporate strategy – for example, an organisation that has established a growth strategy will need an organisation that is capable of delivering growth. Other design criteria can be derived from interviews with line managers, and may relate to, among other things, issues that they consider to be important in realising strategic objectives or factors that impede or facilitate organisational effectiveness more generally.

Table 3.4a Examples of design criteria

Organisation	Design criteria
Software firm (SoftCo)	1 Promote integration/interoperability between our products, and with other products used by target customers 2 Allow us to capture the requirements of customers in our target markets 3 Help us build effective teams, with members who are able to work closely together 4 Create clarity with regard to accountability (of roles/units) 5 Allow the development of next generation solutions 6 Be scaleable to support growth
Governmentally funded body responsible for food certification	1 Ensure balanced resource utilisation across our different food certification programmes 2 Increase the orientation toward our key stakeholders/users 3 Realise synergies between our different areas of work 4 Ensure developmental opportunities for our staff 5 Lessen the administrative burden for the director
Geophysical company	1 Promote business development (e.g., commercialisation, mergers and acquisitions) 2 Create clarity with regard to accountability 3 Ensure that customers perceive us as one integrated geophysical company 4 Prevent conflicts between product areas regarding resource utilisation
IT function in global engineering firm	1 Contribute to a more flexible cost base 2 Increase 'manageability' of IT 3 Increase business focus of IT 4 Support operation as a single enterprise 5 Facilitate cost effective delivery of IT services
HR function in oil services firm	1 Ensure that the Group HR function can effectively support the implementation of key strategic HR initiatives 2 Ensure that units in different business areas receive a consistent service level from HR 3 Establish Group HR as a strategic partner to line managers

It is important to distinguish between *design criteria* defined in this manner and *functional requirements*[11] (cf. Step 2 above). The main purpose of developing design criteria is to aid decision makers in selecting among alternatives; this means that they are temporary, that is, mainly relevant in the design process itself (in Step 3 and in the evaluation phase, Step 9). Different organisational models will to a greater or lesser extent satisfy the design criteria. Functional requirements, on the other hand, are intended to describe the 'functionality' of the organisation, or, put differently, the *required capability* of the organisation. All of the organisational models that are developed in the design phase should satisfy the functional requirements, otherwise they will not constitute viable decision alternatives.

The main purpose of design criteria is to allow systematic evaluation of different alternative organisational models. However, as the above description should have made clear, the role of design criteria extends far beyond that of serving as a tool for *decision making*; they not only help select between a set of alternatives, once developed, but also aid in the development of the alternatives and in the subsequent implementation of the preferred alternative. On the one hand, design criteria set boundaries on the solution and – if correctly formulated – ensure that the outcome of the design process will be aligned with strategic goals and current needs of the organisation. On the other hand, because design criteria are explicit, as opposed to tacit or implicit, they make it possible to include a large set of stakeholders in a dialogue aimed both at refining the criteria and in building support for the organisational changes that they may lead to. In fact, managers may *test* the validity of the criteria – and the stakeholders' commitment to them – by posing the question: 'If we are able to design an organisation that satisfies the design criteria – which you have all contributed to formulating – would this organisation help us address our current challenges and achieve our goals?' If the response is affirmative, one is ready to proceed in the process; in the reverse case, one needs to repeat this step one more time. Thus, the formulation of design criteria allows managers to combine an analytical approach to decision making with extensive participation.

Some managers may have doubts about the realism of the approach advocated here. One concern is that it is simply too difficult to identify precise and relevant design criteria. Thinking in terms of criteria requires a relatively analytical mindset, and some people will have difficulty articulating criteria, although they may be perfectly able to distinguish between the relative attractiveness of various options, once presented as more concrete solution models. A facilitator in the design process may employ a couple of helpful techniques to address this challenge. One is to avoid asking the participants about the design criteria directly, but rather infer the criteria based on how participants describe strengths and weaknesses of the current organisation. Similarly, one may also allow the current step (Step 3) to overlap somewhat with the subsequent step (Step 4), by 'zig-zagging' between the development of the criteria and the development of organisational models (cf. Suh, 2001). The facilitator may ask different participants to first describe an ideal organisational model and then ask them to consider what benefits this model would confer.[12]

A related question is how detailed the criteria need to be. (The examples provided in Table 3.4a indicate that the level of detail will differ from one organisation to the next.) Sometimes design criteria are stated at such a high level of abstraction that it is virtually impossible to disagree or challenge the proposed criteria. The key principle here is that the criteria should be specific enough to allow decision makers to differentiate among the alternative models that are being proposed.[13] For example, in one of the examples provided in Table 3.4a, the client was comparing three relatively simple models for organising the IT function in a global engineering firm. In order to differentiate between the models it was necessary to decompose the criteria to more detailed criteria as shown in Table 3.4b.

Table 3.4b Example of decomposition of design criteria

5 Facilitate cost effective delivery of IT services	5.1 Achieve more effective resource utilisation and management
	5.2 Contribute to lower application maintenance costs
	5.3 Facilitate lower infrastructure costs
	5.4 Allow re-use of systems, processes and procedures across units

Perhaps the most important concern is that 'political' considerations will outweigh any design criteria developed through a participatory process. In one company, the manager who led the re-design process expressed doubts that the CEO would in fact make use of the design criteria, derived from extensive interviews with the key managers in the organisation (as well as with the CEO himself). It may be counter-productive to initiate a participatory process if there is no real intention to make use of the input provided by the participants. It may in some cases be worthwhile discussing this issue openly with the executive initiating the re-design process and explore whether it is possible to change the conditions under which the re-design is being conducted.[14] The leader may fear losing control, in that the final outcome may be different from what he or she had in mind when the re-design was initiated, and thus 'reserves the right' to short circuit the participatory process by imposing his or her own preferred model. In such cases, one should attempt to create a higher level of trust in the process; for example, by revisiting the original intent and discussing the rationale behind the chosen design approach. If the leader's own criteria differ from those of the organisation's other stakeholders, it may be worth investigating the cause of the discrepancy. It may be a 'political issue'; the leader may possess information related to the choice of the organisational model that he/she does not want to share with the followers. But the discrepancy may also be due simply to different interpretations of the organisation's strategic challenges and their organisational implications. If so, it will obviously be helpful if these interpretations can become the subject of open inquiry among the participants in the design process.

Step 4: Develop the organisational architecture (strategic design)

The purpose of this step is to develop, describe and evaluate alternative organisational models. A set of functional requirements were defined in Step 2. The first question in Step 4 is what the design parameters are – that is, the organisational units, processes and roles – that are required to ensure that the functional requirements are fulfilled. (This process essentially *allocates accountabilities* to different organisational units.) As suggested in Ackoff (1999), it may be helpful to distinguish between those requirements that are related to providing *inputs* (i.e., internal services), to manufacturing or delivering outputs (i.e., *products or services* to end customers) and to *marketing* and *selling* products or services. This leads to an initial grouping of the organisation into three types of units – input units, output or product units, and market units (this concept will be discussed in more detail in Chapter 4). Table 3.5 shows, in generic form, how high level functional requirements can be mapped to design parameters.

Table 3.5 Generic form of table mapping functional requirements to design parameter

	Design parameters		
Functional requirements	Input units	Output (Product) units	Market units
Provide internal services	X		
Market and sell services		X	
Manufacture products/Deliver services			X

Once the accountability for different functions (functional requirements) has been defined, the main task is to consider the required *linkages* between different sub-units, roles or processes. For example, two interdependent sub-units may be linked hierarchically, by establishing a reporting relationship to the same manager, or they may report to different managers yet coordinate informally, or be linked in terms of an internal value chain where one unit is defined as the internal supplier and the other as the internal customer. Different ways of analysing the linkages and interdependencies between sub-units will be discussed more fully in Chapter 7.

Alternative organisational models that are developed in this phase will likely differ in terms of a number of factors. One of the alternatives may imply a shift in the resource model, in that a unit that is currently a cost centre would be transformed to a profit centre. Another alternative may imply a need to build informal networks across units in order to support information sharing and collaboration. A third alternative may hinge on the establishment of new decision forums (for example, a product innovation board with representatives from different business units). None of these changes will appear on the usual organisation chart that only displays individual positions or units and their reporting lines.

In Chapter 1, we discussed five 'layers' of design parameters (Table 1.3). All of these may need to be considered in an organisation re-design process. At a minimum, we would suggest that *each alternative model* that is developed in this step should be described in terms of its Operating model, Resource model and Governance model.

- A chart illustrating the key units and their main interfaces (cf. Figure 3.2 above) and a table mapping the organisational units against the functional requirements, can be used to document the proposed *Operating model*.

- A chart showing the nature of resource flows and a description of each unit's financial accountability (whether the unit is defined as a revenue centre, profit centre, cost centre, etc.) can be used to describe the proposed *Resource model*.

- A chart showing the formal reporting relationships and a description of decision processes and governance bodies may be developed to express *the Governance model*.

A more complete description of the alternative models would include a definition of customer–supplier roles of the main internal units and a consideration of the informal mechanisms that are necessary for a model to function as intended; for example, whether a model presupposes that different units find informal ways to coordinate their efforts or share knowledge.

A final element that may be relevant is *costs*. At this stage one rarely has the information required to perform a detailed analysis of the cost impact of the alternatives being considered. Nevertheless, one may consider some of the key *cost drivers* associated with the different models that are developed. As an illustration, different organisational models may differ sharply in terms of *the number of roles per level* and *the number of locations*. Although one has yet to draw a complete organisation chart covering all levels, one may still consider the top 4–5 levels of the organisation and count the number of management positions per level for each of the alternatives that are proposed. Similarly, one may create a simple table with the key work units and their proposed location in the different alternatives.

The approach that we advocate is clearly broader than the stereotypical process of redrawing reporting lines on the organisation chart. At the same time, it should be noted that the required documentation is not necessarily very extensive. The key purpose is to capture the essence and provide stakeholders with sufficient information to evaluate the main alternatives against each other; only the selected model will be specified in detailed (in Step 6 described below).

Step 5: Selection

The purpose of this step is to select the preferred model. The first task is to compare the proposed models against the design criteria. Although the formal leader of the organisation normally has the final say, other stakeholders – either the management team or a larger group of participants – may be involved in evaluating the alternative models or in forming a recommendation to the leader.

When attempting to compare the proposed models against each other, one may discover that the design criteria have not been formulated in a specific enough manner to allow meaningful comparison. If a design criterion is 'increase customer focus', how is this used to differentiate between alternative models? Is a more decentralised model good or bad for customer focus? The solution is obviously to decompose the criterion further, for example, customer focus may relate to the ability to understand customer requirements, to develop new products, to serve customers in certain regions and segments and so on.[15]

The same holds for the solution alternatives that one is comparing against each other. It is obviously important that not only the key features but also that *the implications* of each alternative are well understood. It can be helpful to perform a 'dry run' to spell out the differences. One may develop specific examples of hypothetical decision processes, or ask managers themselves to consider how they would behave in each of the proposed models:

> 'In our first alternative, IT has been defined as an internal service provider and the line organisation as the internal customer. In this model, who has the authority to take decisions regarding changes to the IT infrastructure?'

> 'In one of the alternatives we have developed, Sales is organised regionally. If you were the head of Sales, how would you ensure that we coordinate across the regional sales units to serve larger, global accounts?'

Once one is confident that the criteria are sufficiently precise, and the alternatives well understood, one can start evaluating the alternatives against each other. Most practitioners do not use complicated scoring systems to compare alternatives, other than asking executives to rank design criteria and evaluating the models against the criteria (e.g., using a simple three-point scale, see Example 3.2). More advanced methods would certainly add sophistication, but the concern is that they would not make up for the loss of transparency and simplicity; more complicated scoring systems require more of an 'expert' approach and are less convenient in a group setting.[16] The key priority in this step should rather be to avoid some well-documented and frequent decision errors, such as taking decisions based on insufficient data, a narrowing of focus (the tendency to focus on a small sub-set of alternative choices) and the tendency to view more favourably the decision alternative about which one has the most information (Bazerman, 1994). If one follows the steps proposed here, one should minimise the chances of making such errors.

At this point, some of the participants in the process may have growing concerns about the risks of introducing changes to the organisation, while others may express disappointment if none of the proposed new models appears to be 'optimal'. One may include the current organisational model as one of the alternatives that is considered (as it is always an option not to change anything) and evaluate the current model using the same criteria. Experience suggests that few management teams, when asked to make such a direct comparison, express that they prefer their current model to the alternatives developed during the re-design process.

In describing the development of design criteria above, we noted that participants may sometimes wonder whether political concerns will override the input that they provide to their leaders during the process. However, in the decision phase, the reverse situation is also likely to arise. Leaders may harbour concerns about the objectivity of the input that they have received from their followers. Re-designs inevitably change the power structure in organisations. Leaders may thus suspect that the preferences that are voiced during the re-design process reflect the personal interests of various stakeholders rather than their professional judgement of the relative merits of different options.

There appear to be three possible ways in which to mitigate this particular concern. First, by emphasising design criteria rather than solutions in the early stage of the process, as we have recommended, it should become easier to separate the substantive issues from personal interests. Second, by including a larger group of managers in the design process, one ensures that the design criteria also reflect the views of people (including middle managers) outside the current leadership team (although it is clear that allegiances to senior executives in some cases may colour their assessments).[17][18] Third, we do not believe that the final decision should be a democratic one, even if a larger group of people are involved in developing and evaluating alternative models. It is the prerogative of the leader to select the organisational model, and vesting the decision authority in the leader is particularly important in situations where one or more of the design alternatives imply a considerable change of status, authority or economic rewards for one or more of the key stakeholders in the organisation.

Example 3.2 Developing a new organisational model for SoftCo

The following example may serve to illustrate how one proceeds from having developed design criteria to the selection of a preferred model. The case is drawn from a software company (referred to as 'SoftCo') that provides advanced modelling tools that are used by large oil companies to estimate the size of oil reservoirs and optimise oil production. The managing director initiated a re-design of the firm following the formulation of a new strategy. His initial concern was the lack of customer orientation and unclear prioritisation of product development resources. A slightly simplified version of the firm's current operating model[19] is shown in Figure 3.4. The figure illustrates the key interdependencies between the two main functions, Product development and Sales (the latter comprised of several regional offices that also deliver services and support). In addition, there was a small marketing team at the company's headquarters. The allocation of responsibilities is listed in Figure 3.5.

An important function in software firms is *Product management*, which includes technical marketing tasks such as the identification of customer requirements as well as planning activities such as the definition of product 'road maps' (i.e., plans for future software releases) (Cusumano and Selby, 1995). In SoftCo, this role had been allocated to the Product development unit, rather than to Marketing, Sales or a dedicated Product management unit. The central Marketing unit focused primarily on providing support for the local marketing and sales activities performed by the regional offices, although it was also formally responsible also for feeding back data about customer requirements. As can be seen from Figures 3.4 and 3.5, the Product development organisation would both define and build the software products. In

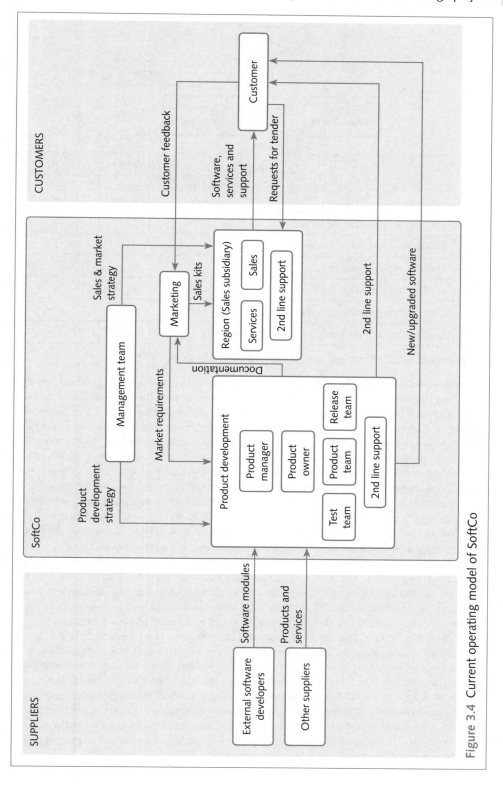

Figure 3.4 Current operating model of SoftCo

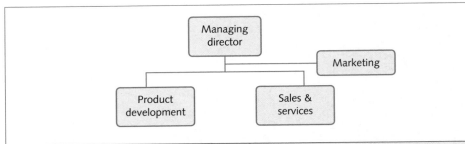

#	Function:	Accountable unit:		
		Sales & services	Product development	Marketing
1	Sell software products and services	X		
2	Provide customer support	X		(x)
3	Manage software products		X	
4	Build software products		X	
5	Develop next generation product concepts		(x)	
6	Support sales and marketing process			X

Figure 3.5 SoftCo's current organisational model (FRs vs DPs)

fact, this dual role would be performed by the same person within the product development organisation, namely the *product manager*, who was responsible for software development and technical marketing (e.g., producing product documentation aimed at 'technical buyers'). However, rather than being an impetus for more customer-focused technical work, the experience with this model was that marketing activities, such as identification of customer needs and the development of technical marketing materials, were consistently deprioritised, due to a lack of resources in the product development organisation. There was also dissatisfaction due to a lack transparency and accountability, particularly with regard to the allocation of product development resources. Requests for changes to existing software and for new features would come from many sales offices and regions, as well as from the Marketing unit. Managers felt that the current model made it difficult to prioritise different requests, representing needs of different market segments; at times the product development organisation would seemingly favour the requests from the most vocal sales office rather than features aimed at the strategically most important customer segment. Finally, there was a concern related to a lack of effective collaboration both within and across management and product development teams. One contributing factor was the highly dispersed nature of the teams, which frequently included staff members based in different physical locations.

During the process, two alternative organisational models were developed (see Figure 3.6). Both would create an explicit internal customer role and limit the accountability of Product development to that of building software products. The two alternatives differed mainly in terms of which unit would hold this responsibility. The first alternative depicts a relatively common model for software firms, where a product management (or product marketing management) function identifies the customer requirements for the products and is held accountable for the product's commercial performance. In the second alternative, this responsibility is allocated to the sales function (or more precisely, to a sub-unit reporting to a senior vice president overseeing Sales and marketing).

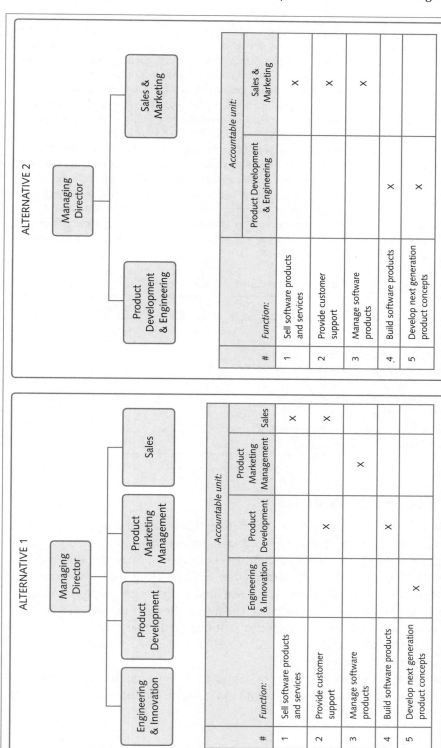

Figure 3.6 Alternative organisational models developed during the re-design process at SoftCo

All members of the management team participated in evaluating the models against each other (see Table 3.6). The consensus was that both of the alternatives would strengthen the firm's customer orientation. Overall, establishing Product management as a separate function (Alternative 1) was viewed as the best option by the majority of the team. There were concerns that organising Product management within Sales (Alternative 2) would create a short-term focus, with the risk of product management resources being utilised as support personnel for sales managers in busy times (it was mentioned that it would be analogous to the problems, described above, resulting from having placed Product management within Product development). It was also mentioned that subjugating Product management within Sales would lead to less clarity about roles and responsibilities. At the same time, the team agreed that Alternative 1 involved some risk of creating tension between the teams belonging to the respective units, and that it would be critical to establish effective work processes across product development, product management and sales. Another prerequisite that was mentioned was allocating sufficient capacity to enable a new Product management unit to fulfil its mandate. It was decided to look more closely at these issues in the transition planning phase (see Example 3.2 (cont.) below).

Table 3.6 Evaluation of alternatives against design criteria

| | Evaluation | | |
Design criteria	Current model	Alternative 1	Alternative 2
Increase customer orientation by improving identification and prioritisation of customer requirements	☹	☺	😐
Help us build effective management and product development teams	😐	😐	☺
Create clarity with regard to accountability (of roles/units)	☹	☺	😐

Step 6: Operational design

So far in the process, we have been considering organisational models at a relatively high level of abstraction: The purpose of Step 4, for example, was to describe alternative organisational models at a sufficient level of detail to allow decision makers to evaluate the models against each other. Once one has selected the preferred model, however, it is necessary to *operationalise* the model. The main purpose is to reduce the implementation time by clarifying the implications of the selected model as much as possible and create a blueprint that can guide the transition to the new model. This involves detailing the high-level *Operating model*, *Resource model* and *Governance model* developed in Step 4.

To complete the *Operating model*, one may start by detailing the design of the sub-units of the organisation. One may define the mandate for different sub-units of the new organisation by describing their key purpose, the outcomes that the units are accountable for and the key performance indicators that will be used to measure their performance. (More specific techniques for supporting operational level design shall be discussed in Chapter 5.) One may then consider how the new model will impact working processes; in particular, those that cross unit boundaries. It is rarely necessary to do a full-blown process mapping to implement a new organisational model, but one should identify those working processes that are directly affected by the organisational change in order to clarify interfaces and specify how different units are to collaborate (e.g., at what step in a process handovers should occur or how two interdependent units are to coordinate their work).

Another important question is *sizing* – how many people are needed in each unit? One can estimate the required size of units based on assumptions about the volume of business and the productivity of teams and individuals. For routine, transactional jobs, it is possible to use formal methods for calculating required capacity described in the operation management literature (see e.g., Slack et al., 2004). For example, the required number of staff in a customer support centre can be calculated based on the expected number of calls and the duration of each call. For more complex jobs such as the ones described in Example 3.2, it is difficult to use formal methods, as there may not be a fixed set of inputs or outputs variables. Nevertheless, in most organisations it may be possible, over time, to develop guidelines to support capacity estimation (e.g., 'we need one test engineer for every five developers').

To operationalise the *Governance model* one defines the hierarchical structure of the organisation, that is, the number of layers, the type and number of roles at each level and the formal reporting relationships (see Chapter 6 for a detailed discussion). The governance model should also specify the leadership teams and decision forums in the new organisation, i.e., their mandate, participants, meeting frequency and so on.

Similarly, the *Resource model* may be operationalised by defining more precisely the financial resource flows in the company. The resource flows will depend on the financial accountability of each unit (i.e., whether a unit is defined as a profit, cost or revenue centre) and the transfer pricing principles chosen by the company for transactions between internal units. Some services are likely to be charged on a cost basis, whereas others may be charged out based on a market rate.

In this step one also defines *individual roles and responsibilities*. At a minimum, the requirements of key leadership roles are defined, but depending on the scope of the change and the implementation approach, it may also be necessary to define roles for all levels of the new organisation. Experience suggests that relatively short and simple role descriptions will suffice. The definition of individual roles can be seen as a further decomposition of requirements and design parameters. One may thus rely on already existing pieces of documentation from the preceding steps in the process in defining individual roles.

Example 3.2 (*continued*) Operationalising the selected organisational model in SoftCo

Returning to the case described above, let us consider how SoftCo approached the key activities in the operational design phase. An internal working group was formed and charged with the task of defining key roles, clarifying interfaces and estimating resource needs.

A major advantage of the new model was the ability to create distinct internal customer and supplier roles, allowing greater clarity with regard to accountability. The Product management unit would represent the 'Voice of the customer' – defining 'what to build' – capturing market requirements and defining new product features (as well as supporting product roll-outs). Product development would be the internal supplier, developing software in response to the requirements set by Product management (determining 'how to build it'). Both of these units would be led by a vice president (VP), who would be part of the management team. The VP for Product management would lead a team of product managers, managing the product from a market perspective, whereas the VP for Product development would lead a team of *technical* product managers, taking ownership of technical product requirements and supporting development projects.

A key question was how to structure the units at the next level. As pointed out by Galbraith (2002), if each sub-unit is designed according to its own logic, managers are forced to work across a high number of interfaces, creating significant barriers to lateral processes. For this reason, a 'mirror image' structure was chosen in SoftCo, where both Product management and Product development were structured based on (client) work flows, which corresponded broadly to different software packages or modules (or different sets of functionality within the software). For example, some users will use SoftCo's software tools to support seismic exploration, whereas others would use it for reservoir modelling or simulation. With the mirror image structure, each product manager within Product management would have one primary partner within Product development (see Figure 3.7). In addition, other roles were defined, such as the Chief architect, with responsibility for integration across products.

It was estimated that each of these roles would require a full time position. The financial cost of the new structure was then calculated, taking into account that some capacity would be freed up in the current Product development and Marketing functions (by transferring tasks to Product management). Even though the establishment of the new function would involve a significant additional cost (through the establishment of new product manager positions), this cost was considered in relation to the company's growth projections. Investing in a stronger product management function was seen as critical in order to achieve further growth. (The ability to identify and prioritise customer requirements had been defined as the most important design criterion earlier in the process.) In addition to the increase in capacity, the new model also provided scalability – the size of the organisation may be scaled up or down without changing the basic logic. For example, if the work load is less than anticipated for a certain module, it is possible to combine the responsibility for two workflows into one role. If the work load increases, it is possible to add staff members supporting each product manager. It is also possible to add new product manager roles (although it may then be necessary to introduce another vertical layer, in the form of a senior product manager role, in order to maintain a reasonable span of control).

The internal working group also considered how the new organisational model would affect key working processes and interfaces. One example would be the process of updating the product road map based on proposals for new or improved functionality. One clarification that was made was that the product managers should receive the proposals and take them through the different stages of evaluation. It was also decided that the VP of Product management should present the full project proposal to the Product board (in the current model, this was done by the Product development VP). The changes from the current model are highlighted in Figure 3.8.

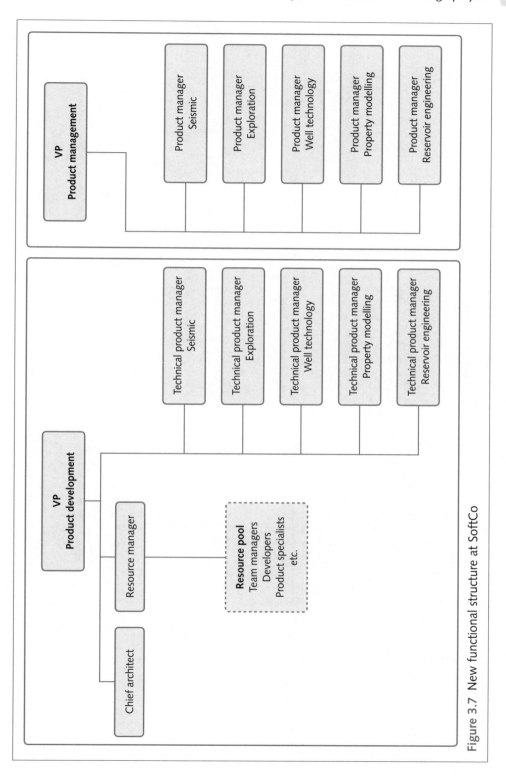

Figure 3.7 New functional structure at SoftCo

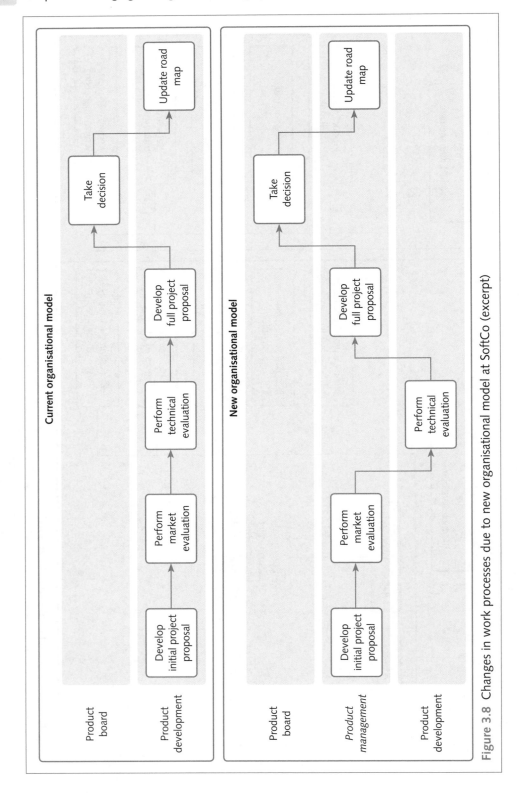

Figure 3.8 Changes in work processes due to new organisational model at SoftCo (excerpt)

Step 7: Transition planning and Step 8: Implementation

The purpose of the transition planning step is to select the overall transition approach and to create a plan that minimises implementation costs and 'time to value', that is, the time that elapses before the intended benefits of the new model are realised. Typical implementation activities that need to be prepared include the distribution of information to employees (and possibly customers and other stakeholders), changes in infrastructure (physical facilities, IT tools, etc.), and the recruitment of people to new roles.

There are five – somewhat interrelated – questions that one may consider before selecting the transition approach:

1 *What is the scope of the proposed change?* It goes without saying that the transition approach, and the effort required to implement the new design, will depend on the scope. A new design may affect a single unit or role, a few sub-units or an entire organisation. The implications of the change may range from a relatively limited impact on the formal reporting structure to a complete re-definition of processes, roles and infrastructure.

2 *What is the likely reaction among key stakeholders to the proposed re-design?* Obviously, a radical re-design that significantly alters status or power relationships will need a different approach than one which meets the expectations of the key stakeholders.

3 *Are there dependencies between the elements of the plan?* For example, dependencies are created by resources constraints. One typical example is when employees who will staff a new unit in the organisation cannot be relieved of their current responsibilities before new roles and processes are established somewhere else in the organisation. The extent of such dependencies will have an impact on the timing and sequencing of different activities.

4 *To what extent is a centralised approach to implementation required?* The degree of centralisation of an organisation will have an impact on how new organisational models are implementated. In tightly integrated companies, organisational changes are usually directed from the centre. In more loosely coupled organisations, new designs may constitute recommended (or even optional) blueprints, where the responsibility for implementation (and perhaps also for operational design) is delegated to sub-units.

5 *What approach do we want to take in allocating people to new roles?* In some re-design processes, units are kept largely intact and the change only affects the leaders of units. Other re-design processes, however, may affect the roles of a larger group of managers and employees. If this is the case, one must consider how to manage the internal staffing process.

From a change management perspective, it is usually desirable to implement a new organisation design gradually, in separate phases. For example, many of the large companies that introduced Shared Services organisations during the 1990s did not establish a global shared services unit covering all functions from the start, but instead focused on an initial set of core functions (e.g., accounting and payroll), or a limited geographical area, and then gradually increased the functional and geographical scope. Many companies have found that it is most effective to test out new organisational designs in a single unit before they are adopted on a company-wide basis. A gradual approach obviously limits the risk of interference with core operational processes of the firm and provides managers with the opportunity to adjust and refine the design solution before it is rolled out on a larger scale.

However, larger re-design exercises may necessitate the redistribution of tasks and the transfer of personnel involved in key operational activities in the business. In these cases, one must develop fairly detailed implementation plans and consider the dependencies between different implementation activities. For example, consider a bank that establishes a customer support centre in order to centralise telephone and e-mail support to customers. The customer centre is to be staffed by employees recruited from branch offices. However, these employees currently perform tasks in the branch office that need to be handed over to other employees before the staff members can be released and transferred to the central customer centre. And the ability of other employees to take on these tasks may in turn depend on receiving additional support from the customer centre. When interdependencies of this type exist, one must implement several elements of the new organisational model in a synchronised fashion.

Employee communication is sometimes viewed as the key element of the implementation phase. However, in the approach described here, communication is not an activity that is added at the end of an executive planning process in order to 'sell' the proposed change. Communication is rather an on-going activity, and if the preceding steps have been completed, the key requirements for achieving stakeholder acceptance should already be in place. First, it should be possible to communicate a clear rationale for the change, based on strategic consideration and analysis of organisational functioning (Steps 1 and 2). Second, it should be possible to present a clear plan for how the process will unfold and the implications for the individual employee, based on the operationalisation of the organisational model and the transition plan (Steps 6 and 7). The chances of gaining acceptance for the proposed changes will have been increased by including representatives from different units in the process (e.g., in developing design criteria and in identifying areas of improvement in Steps 2 and 3) and by allowing the members of sub-units to fine-tune elements of the design during the implementation process.

There are generally two approaches one can take in planning an internal staffing process in those cases where a larger group of people must be allocated to new roles. The traditional approach is that leaders appoint their subordinates in a 'cascading' process, i.e., leaders of top-level units are appointed first, and they in turn appoint their direct reports and so on. The main advantage of this approach is speed; an entire organisation with several hundred or even thousands of employees can be staffed in the course of a few weeks. However, this approach is sometimes implemented in a manner that compromises trust. People may not be consulted about alternative roles. Managers under time pressure will often select people that they already know rather than taking the time to carefully define job requirements and consider alternative candidates. The alternative is to create an internal recruitment process where all new positions are announced (e.g., on the company intranet) and where employees are encouraged to apply for one or more positions. This approach has been used by some firms during large transformations such as mergers. Until recently, the main drawback of this approach was the protracted time (and cost) resulting from having to describe all new positions, distribute information, process applications and optimise the allocation of people based on their preferences and the company needs. However, software tools are beginning to appear that allow such internal staffing processes to proceed quickly, even when thousands of employees need to be re-allocated to new roles.[20]

Step 9: Evaluation

No matter how much care one takes in planning an organisation re-design process, there will always be elements of the design that don't work as well as intended. Yet few organisations carry out *systematic, planned evaluations* of organisation re-design processes. This means that elements of the design that do not work as intended are not detected and corrected by management, although they may cause great frustration among lower-level employees. This may cement an attitude that the new design is cast in stone, and that one should refrain from attempts at improving it. Much has been said and written about the ability of managers and employees to undermine new designs by resisting to fully implement the designs. Equally common, however, may be the tendency to implement proposed designs exactly as proposed by management, without informing management of the need for adaptations.

Given the costs and risks involved, one may ask why organisations do not carry out evaluations as a routine aspect of organisational re-design processes. We can only speculate that it may be due to a combination of lack of executive time and attention, and perhaps also individual defensive mechanisms (Argyris, 1990). Leaders who have succeeded in introducing a particular solution may not enjoy being confronted with indications that the solution is less effective than promised. Unfortunately, such an attitude will in itself decrease the chances that the design will be successful in the first place; since nearly all design solutions are dependent upon an openness to adapt to the particularities of the organisation and a willingness to improve the design over time.

In addition to correcting elements of the design that do not work as intended, performing evaluations also contribute to *organisational learning*. In evaluating a re-design project, one may both ask to what extent the design is achieving its intended benefits (here it is logical to refer to the design criteria that were defined), and to what extent the re-design *process* was deemed effective. Experience suggests that asking stakeholders to provide their input in such reviews not only uncovers areas for improvement, but frequently also helps to identify important accomplishments that deserve recognition. Most managers and employees notice not only the inevitable errors and shortcomings of the processes, but also how creating new designs bring out creative ideas, forge new ways of collaboration and help in implementing long overdue changes to their organisation.

Although few organisations explicitly include evaluation as a step in the organisation re-design process, an encouraging trend is the inclusion of items related to organisation design in annual employee surveys. The items being used may not correspond exactly to the design criteria of re-design projects, but nevertheless provide important feedback on issues such as the clarity of goals and accountabilities, customer focus and process performance; some firms also tap more directly the degree of satisfaction with new organisational models.

Summary and discussion

This chapter has outlined a 9-step methodology for re-designing complex organisations (see Table 3.7 for a summary). The overall goal of the approach is to minimise the 'time to value' of new designs. To achieve this, it contains a design process aimed at maximising *alignment, coherence* and *trust*. The methodology also incorporates some key element of the axiomatic design approach, in particular, an explicit consideration of functional requirements in relation to design parameters (i.e., organisational units, processes or roles). The most important techniques and interventions are formulated as a set of *Design propositions* see below.

The approach presented here builds and extends on existing methodologies and has been successfully applied on a number of client engagements. Nevertheless, the development of this approach has also raised a number of questions that deserve both academic research and pragmatic experimentation in order to develop even more effective methodologies in the future. Five research questions will be described here.

The first question relates to the development of solution models. Romme (2003) has suggested that one should begin generating solutions models very early in the design process. He argues that one risks locking the thinking of people by focusing too much on the current system. Some consultants also prefer to develop a couple of 'straw man' solutions early on in the process to galvanise interest and drive the discussions forward. In this chapter we have advocated a different approach, however, as should be evident by the methodology summarised in Table 3.7. The key assumption is that it is critical to have a good understanding of the current organisation before one attempts to re-design it. Another concern is that by introducing solution models too early, one may lead participants to fixate on one particular, seemingly attractive model, before data have been collected about the real challenges that the organisation faces. As there are divided opinions on this issue, however, it is suggested that it become a topic for further systematic investigation.

Table 3.7 Proposed steps in the organisation design process

Step	Main purpose	Typical deliverables /outcomes
1 Set the agenda	Establish consensus regarding the need for change and the approach to follow	• Decision to re-design organisation (or review) • Project mandate and plan
2 Analyse the current organisation	Create a shared understanding of current organisational functioning	*At a minimum:* • High-level map of units and interfaces (Operating model) • Functional requirements *For operational-level design projects:* • Detailed map of processes and interdependencies
3 Define design criteria	Articulate the criteria by which a new design should be selected	• A set of design criteria, agreed among key stakeholders
4 Develop the organisational architecture (strategic design)	Develop designs that satisfy the functional requirements defined in phase 2	• Two or more alternative designs (visualised as *Operating model* and, if relevant, *Resource and Governance model*) as well as traditional organisational charts indicating reporting lines • Estimate of the costs associated with the alternative designs
5 Select model	Select the preferred design based on evaluation of alternative solutions against design criteria	• Evaluation of alternative models • Selected model
6 Operational design	Develop a complete description of the selected model	• Detailed descriptions of the Operating model, Resource model and Governance model • Description of key individual roles and responsibilities
7 Create transition plan	Create a plan for transitioning to new structure	• Transition plan (may cover creation of new roles/units, recruitment to new positions; communication with employees, changes in IT systems and infrastructure, etc.)
8 Implement	Implement changes according to the transition plan	• Depending on the selected design
9 Evaluate	Evaluate to what extent the new design fulfils its purpose and make any necessary adjustments	• Evaluation of the effectiveness of the model (given the criteria that were used to select it) • Corrective actions

There is also a difference – both philosophical and practical – between those advocating 'idealised planning' and those representing an approach to planning and design more characterised by iterative, small steps (termed 'muddling through' by the political scientist Charles Lindblom (1959)). Russell Ackoff (1999) has been a strong advocate for creating an *idealised model* in the initial phase of the design

process. The purpose is to help managers and employees resolve organisational problems by creating a shared model of how the organisation would look if they could
design it anew, without any constraints. On the other hand, there are occasions
when management teams are not able or motivated to engage in 'visionary' thinking
and where the only chance to gain traction is to initiate the re-design exercise as an
incremental adjustment of the current organisation. Either approach could be useful
in certain situations, however, and it would be useful for practitioners to know more
about which approach to select under what circumstances.

As most other design methodologies, the approach described in this chapter makes
a distinction between 'strategic' and 'operational' design. *Strategic design* is concerned
with the so-called 'umbrella structure' (Nadler and Tushman, 1997), the overall design
of an organisation, whereas *operational design* refers to the more detailed design of
sub-units, roles and processes. Is this distinction really valid? To what extent can you
make 'macro'-level decisions without 'micro'-level knowledge? In some cases, it is relatively straightforward to re-design the overall structure of an organisation, provided
that the various sub-units are supposed to stay intact. For example, the CEO of a firm
may decide to swap some managerial roles or make changes in the reporting structure
of the top executives with no intention of altering the actual work processes at lower
levels. However, there are also situations in which changes at the strategic level of a
firm should not be considered without fairly detailed knowledge about the workings
of the sub-units that constitute the organisation. This is the case when the strategic
design level changes may affect the interfaces between the sub-units, or when work
processes at an operational level warrant a different strategic design in order to be
effective. The main research proposition would be that the success rate of re-design
efforts is higher when key decision makers are well informed about the functioning
of their organisation. There could also be cases where it would be appropriate to select
the overall design of a firm based on 'bottom-up' analysis of roles and interdependencies, as opposed to a 'top-down' analysis of requirements. If so, it may erase the
traditional distinction made between 'strategic' and 'operational' design.

A related question is at what point one should staff managerial positions during
the design process. Many executives prefer to quickly select managers to staff the
key positions once a decision has been made regarding the overall, strategic design.
The managers that have been selected are then made responsible for developing
the detailed, operational design for their units. Many executives believe sub-unit
managers should be accountable for designing their units. Some leaders may also
be concerned about uncertainty breeding among the managers in the organisation
during the design process, which could lead some to resign amidst doubts about
their future role in the new organisation. On the other hand, by nominating leaders for specific positions too early, one risks closing off design options that would
have been possible if the positions were not yet filled. By delegating the operational
design work to sub-unit leaders one also risks overemphasising the unit-specific
needs at the expense of the coherence of the overall model. An alternative is involving key managers in the process in temporary working groups, yet delaying the
formal nomination of leaders to a later stage in the process when the design of the
complete model has been determined. In this approach one thus waits until the
implementation phase to add managerial names to the organisation chart.

This chapter has highlighted stakeholder involvement as a necessary means to build trust and secure voluntary compliance. This is also a prerequisite for ensuring that the design is based on valid information about current organisational functioning, which in turn influences the extent to which design solutions will be well aligned and coherent. We have assumed that there will be a central design team collecting and analysing information, developing design ideas and co-ordinating the transition process. (In a large organisation, the central design team will typically include both internal and external resources.) However, there are consultants who go further and advocate a fully participatory process, where much of the design task is delegated to managers and employees themselves. One example is the large group methods used by Gil Steil, an American consultant (Steil and Gibbons-Carr, 2005). The key element in this approach is to gather all key stakeholders (up to several hundred) for facilitated workshops. These workshops essentially deal with all of the steps outlined in this chapter, and in the same sequence, but compressed into 3–5 days of intensive problem solving. The key assumption is that the real experts are the people that are already employed by the organisation and that a new organisation can be designed faster if all its members (or a group with representatives from all of the main units) are gathered together in the same room. An important question for future research is thus to clarify to what extent large group methods may constitute an alternative to traditional approaches for managing the design process.

Design propositions

Objective   *Create an effective organisation re-design process (i.e., a process that minimises 'time to value')*

3.1   Develop design options that are *aligned* with organisational goals and strategies by:

a   identifying and resolving unclear or conflicting goals at an early stage of the design process

b   ensuring that key stakeholders have a common understanding of the organisation's *'Reason for being'*

c   explicitly linking *design parameters* (i.e., organisational units, processes and roles) with *functional requirements*

3.2   Ensure that design options that are developed are *coherent* by:

a   establishing a central design team to coordinate data gathering, analysis, model development and implementation

b   ensuring that key stakeholders have common view of current organisational functioning, before they consider alternative future designs

c   mapping and evaluating the organisation's units and their interdependencies (current and future Operating model)

3.3   Ensure that the process creates or maintains *trust* and that the selected design is voluntarily complied to by:

    a   sequencing the design process to allow the development of design criteria (i.e., *principles*) to occur before the development of alternative organisational models (i.e., *solutions*)

    b   involving key stakeholders in analysing the current organisation, defining design criteria, developing organisational models and evaluating options

    c   actively communicating to employees the rationale and the benefits to the organisation and the individual employee from adopting the chosen model

    d   preparing a systematic and well structured transition process to implement the chosen model

    e   using a transparent staffing process where individuals' preferences are taken into account when filling positions

Review questions

1   What are generic requirements to organisation design processes?

2   What are the nine steps of organisation design processes proposed in this chapter?

3   How do executives or other change agents 'set the agenda', i.e., persuade other stakeholders that a re-design is required?

4   What are the advantages of collecting data about current organisational functioning in an early phase of a re-design process?

5   Why should one define explicit design criteria?

6   What is the difference between design criteria and functional requirements?

7   This chapter advocates the use of a systematic, 'facts-based' methodology. What are the benefits of such a methodology, and what are the potential concerns some managers may have about it?

8   The chapter argues that involvement of stakeholders is necessary to build trust. Does this imply that the design decisions are to be taken collectively (e.g. by the management team or a larger group of managers)?

9   What are the key questions that one should consider in selecting the transition approach?

Research questions

1 At what point in the design process should one start to develop models of the future organisation?

2 In what situations is the 'idealised design' approach advocated by Russell Ackoff most effective? In what situations would it be counter-productive?

3 To what extent can you take effective 'strategic design' decisions without the knowledge of 'operational' issues (such as work process interdependencies)?

4 At what point in the design process should you staff managerial positions?

5 Do large group methods constitute a viable alternative to traditional approaches to redesigning complex organisations?

Case study

PowerCo

PowerCo is a regional energy group comprising three main business areas. It produces energy by means of hydro-electric power stations, coal- and gas-fired power plants, as well as wind farms and solar power plants. It distributes energy by operating an electricity transmission and distribution infrastructure. Finally, it sells energy to end customers through its retail unit.

The CEO of PowerCo wants to initiate a review of the organisational structure of the company. In particular, he is concerned with the organisation of the energy generation business. Currently, this division is largely structured around its physical assets (Figure 3.9). In addition to producing energy using existing assets, it also has a unit (Business development) responsible for identifying, developing and commercialising new energy producing facilities.

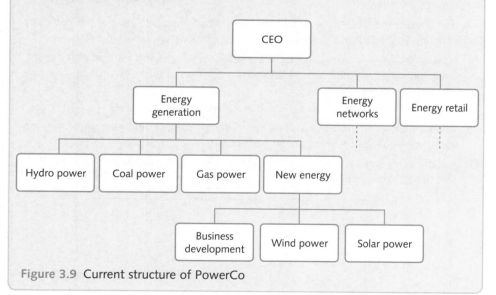

Figure 3.9 Current structure of PowerCo

The government is planning to introduce a new tax regime to reduce carbon emissions. In response to this, PowerCo recently developed a new strategy to increase its production of energy from renewable sources (including wind and solar). So far, however, the CEO has been disappointed by a lack of success in the wind and solar power businesses. These businesses are lagging competitors in terms of revenues and profit, and still contribute less than 1 per cent of the energy that PowerCo produces overall.

The CEO believes that there are both cultural and structural causes contributing to this performance gap. The energy generation business is dominated by managers with a background from managing traditional energy plants. In terms of its hierarchical position, the wind and solar power businesses are at level 4, one level below the other units in the division. He feels that the wind and solar businesses lack internal visibility in the company and that it may be hard for the leaders of these units to initiate and get approval for new projects as they must compete with larger and more profitable projects related to hydro, coal and gas power.

On the other hand, the Executive Vice President (EVP) of the energy generation division has indicated that he sees no need to change, or even review, the current structure. He believes that the wind and solar power units would be even less successful as stand-alone units as they rely on the skills and knowledge of other managers in his division related to business development, commercialisation and operational management. He has remarked that if PowerCo wants to increase its emphasis on renewable energy, it can simply do so by changing the criteria (set by the CEO and approved by the board) used to evaluate investment proposals. He is of the opinion that these businesses are still small and thus cannot be compared with the other larger and more profitable business units in his division. Finally, he points out that the solar and wind businesses are led by relatively young and inexperienced managers who are not ready to be promoted into the executive team or even to his divisional leadership team.

Discussion questions

1 Based on the information above, how would you summarise the functional requirements for PowerCo?

2 If you were the CEO, how would you present your plan to review the company structure to the EVP of the Energy Generation division?

3 How would you design a process that would seek input from a group of people, while avoiding potential biases that could result from a desire to protect their current position in the system?

4 What are some of the design options that PowerCo could consider?

5 What would be the main phases of the re-design process, and how much time do you think would be be necessary on each phase?

6 Are there any key assumptions in the CEO's or the EVP's reasoning that it is important to test? How could these assumptions be confirmed or disconfirmed?

Notes

1 Although there is little work on organisation re-design processes per se, management scholars have looked at planning more generally and found that the quality of strategic planning processes is important and may even predict corporate performance (Hart and Banbury, 1994; Dean and Sharfman, 1996). Research on strategic change has similarly demonstrated that the overall approach that leaders select, as well as the timing and sequencing of specific interventions, are important in securing a successful outcome in change processes (Huy, 2001).

2 The first two factors here are based on research on procedural justice or 'fair process' (Kim and Mauborgne, 1996). The third is derived from research on change processes by organisational psychologists (Farr, 1990).

3 The fact that new organisational models are sometimes imposed in an attempt to gain political control is well recognised in the academic literature (e.g., Morgan, 1986, p. 162; Pfeffer, 1982).

4 In fact, there is some evidence that suggests that managers frequently wait too long to make required changes (Miller and Friesen, 1980; Tushman and Romanelli, 1985).

5 The individual-level psychological mechanisms creating motivation to change are explained in 'self-discrepancy' theory developed by Higgins (1987).

6 A lot of information, down to the sub-unit level, can often be obtained from employee and customer surveys by first considering the statistical results, and then conducting a qualitative analysis of the comments made by respondents to pinpoint more specifically the causes of problems that are suggested by the statistical analysis.

7 The general format for this chart has been borrowed from Sachs (1999).

8 Of course, a performance gap as defined here may be caused by a number of different factors and these findings may not necessarily generalise to other organisations.

9 Other authors have used similar graphical tools to illustrate the workings of organisations (e.g., Ackoff, 1999; Haeckel, 1999; Rummler and Brache, 1990).

10 The organisation chart (which usually only shows the permanent positions and reporting structure) is a poor guide to estimating how resources are utilised, as large organisations increasingly rely on projects, networks and cross-functional teams.

11 Design criteria in organisation design can be compared to constraints in engineering and architectural design. For an interesting discussion of the role of constraints, see Vandenbosch and Gallagher (2004).

12 This technique is called the 'Functions follows form principle' and is discussed in more detail in Goldenberg and Mazursky (2002).

13 In some cases it may be helpful to rank the criteria. For example, if one has identified 10 criteria based on interviews with managers, one may in a brief follow-up survey ask the same managers to rank these criteria by importance.

14 Argyris (1990) describes specific interventions that can be used to deal with individual defensive routines in cases similar to the one described here.

15 Note that this does not necessarily imply that one needs a higher number of design criteria; one can leave out design criteria that do not differentiate between the solution models and select a limited number of highly specific criteria that do.

16 Nevertheless, there may be occasions where more advanced scoring and evaluation systems are warranted, and there is a large literature on multi-criterion decision making that may be helpful for those seeking guidance on the right approach (for an overview, see Triantaphyllou, 2000).

17 In circumstances where the participants have strong personal interests that may influence their views, one may reduce bias by asking participants to evaluate (e.g., rate or rank) design criteria in an anonymous survey, rather than using group discussions (see Anderson and Brown, 2010, for a review of research on this issue).

18 The current top managers will often have most to lose from a radical re-design. In a historical analysis of organisational changes in three major industrial concerns, Gammelsaeter (1991) found that new organisational models had generally been introduced by middle managers, who had more easily found support for the changes with the CEO than with other top managers.

19 The example focuses mainly on the issues related to Product development; other issues that were considered in the re-design process (e.g., the organisation of customer support) have been left out for clarity.

20 An example is a software tool called Organization Weaver, developed by the firm BrightArch (www. brightarch.com).

References

Ackoff, R. (1981). *Creating the Corporate Future.* New York: John Wiley & Sons.

Ackoff, R. (1999). *Re-Creating the Corporation: A Design of Organizations for the 21st Century.* New York: Oxford University Press.

Anderson, C. and Brown, C. E. (2010). The functions and dysfunctions of hierarchy. *Research in Organizational Behaviour*, 30, 55–89.

Argyris, C. (1990). *Overcoming Organizational Defenses: Facilitating Organizational Learning.* Needham, MA: Allyn & Bacon.

Bazerman, M. (1994). *Judgment in Managerial Decision Making.* New York: John Wiley & Sons.

Cusumano, M. A. and Selby, R. W. (1995). *Microsoft Secrets: How the World's Most Powerful Software Company Creates Technology, Shapes Markets, and Manages People.* New York: Free Press.

Dean J. W., Sharfman, M. P. (1996). Does decision process matter? A study of strategic decision-making effectiveness. *Academy of Management Journal*, 39, 2, 368–96.

The Economist (2009). 'Reshaping government: permanent revolution', 13 June, 38.

Farr, J. L. (1990). Facilitating individual role innovation. In West, M. A. and Farr, J. L. (eds), *Innovation and Creativity at Work: Psychological and Organizational Strategies*, 207–30. Chichester: Wiley.

Fisher, R. and Ury, W. (1983). *Getting to Yes: Negotiating Agreement Without Giving In.* New York: Penguin Books.

Galbraith, J. (2002). *Designing Organizations: An Executive Guide to Strategy, Structure, and Process.* San Francisco, CA: Jossey-Bass.

Gammelsaeter, H. (1991). *Organisasjonsendringgjennomgenerasjoneravledere* [Organisational changes through generations of leaders, in Norwegian, not translated]. Molde: Møreforskning.

Goldenberg, J. and Mazursky, D. (2002). *Creativity in Product Innovation.* Cambridge: Cambridge University Press.

Haeckel, Stephan H. (1999). *Adaptive Enterprise: Creating and Leading Sense-and-Respond Organizations.* Boston, MA: Harvard Business School Press.

Hart S. and Banbury, C. (1994). How strategy-making process can make a difference. *Strategic Management Journal*, 15, 4, 251–69.

Higgins, E. T. (1987). Self-discrepancy: A theory relating self and affect. *Psychological Review*, 94, 3, 319–40.

Hood, C., Huby M. and Dunsire, A. (1985). Scale economies and iron laws: Mergers and demergers in Whitehall 1971–1984, *Public Administration*, 63, 1, 61–78.

Huy, N. (2001). Time, Temporal capability, and planned change. *Academy of Management Review*, 4, 26, 601–23.

Kim, W. and Mauborgne, R. (1996). Procedural justice and managers' in-role and extra-role behavior: The case of the multinational. *Management Science*, 42, 4, 499–515.

Lindblom, C. E. (1959). The science of 'muddling through'. *Public Administration Review*, 19, 2, 79–88.

Miller, D. and Friesen, P. H. (1980). Momentum and revolution in organizational adaptation. *Academy of Management Journal*, 23, 4, 591–614.

Morgan, G. (1986). *Images of Organization*. Thousand Oaks, CA: Sage Publications.

Nadler, D. and Tushman, M. (1997). *Competing by Design: The Power of Organizational Architecture*. New York: Oxford University Press.

Pache, A. C. and Santos, F. M. (2010). When worlds collide: the internal dynamics of organizational responses to conflicting institutional demands. *Academy of Management Review*, 35, 3, 455–576.

Pfeffer, J. (1982). *Managing with Power: Politics and Influence in Organizations*. Boston, MA: Harvard Business School Press.

Romme, A. G. L. (2003). Making a difference: organization as design. *Organization Science*, 14, 5, 558–73.

Rummler, G. A. and Brache, A. P. (1990). *Improving Performance: How to Manage the White Space on the Organization Chart*. San Francisco, CA: Jossey-Bass.

Sachs, W. (1999). *Adaptation revisited*. In Proceedings of the Russell Ackoff conference, Villanova University, 4–6 March.

Slack, N., Chambers, S. and Johnston, R. (2004). *Operations Management* (4th edn). London: Pitman.

Steil, G. and Gibbons-Carr, M. (2005). Large group scenario planning: scenario planning with the whole system in the room. *Journal of Applied Behavioral Science March*, 41, 1, 15–29.

Suh, N. P. (2001). *Axiomatic Design: Advances and Applications*. New York: Oxford University Press.

Triantaphyllou, E. (2000). *Multi-Criteria Decision Making Methods: A Comparative Study*. Norwell, MA: Kluwer Academic Publishers.

Tushman, M. L. and Romanelli, E. (1985). Organizational evolution: A metamorphosis model of convergence and reorientation. In Cummings, L. L. and Staw, B. M. (eds), *Research in Organizational Behavior*, 7, 117–22. Greenwich, CT: JAI Press.

Vandenbosch, B. and Gallagher, K. (2004). The role of constraints. In Boland, R. J. and Collopy, F. (eds), *Managing as Designing*, 198–207. Stanford, CA: Stanford University Press.

Werr, A. Stjernberg, T. and Docherty, P. (1997). The functions of methods of change in management consulting. *Journal of Organisational Change Management*, 10, 4, 288–307.

Chapter 4

Designing multidimensional organisations

Overview

Background

- Many large organisations today are structured along multiple dimensions, representing markets, products and internal services
- Compared to a unidimensional structure, a multidimensional structure allows greater decentralisation, eliminates duplication or multiplication of similar subunits, better reflects the organisation's work processes and creates a more balanced leadership team

Challenges

- The organisation design literature has overlooked the differences between alternative ways in which to combine different dimensions of large organisations
- Managers and consultants also tend to refer to any multidimensional structure as a 'matrix'
- There are several ways in which to design multidimensional organisations, which differ in terms of their complexity and flexibility

Key questions

- How can the multidimensional organisation best be conceptualised?
- How can we analyse and evaluate the complexity and flexibility of alternative multidimensional designs?

Proposed approach

- Employ axiomatic design principles to distinguish between three multidimensional organisational models: the traditional matrix structure; the front-back model; and the modular organisation.

- Examine the internal and external contingencies that would favour one multidimensional model over another

Introduction

Identifying the right criterion by which to structure organisations has always been a core issue in organisation design. Traditionally, single product firms were structured in terms of the means that they used to produce outputs (Mintzberg, 1979). The means include knowledge, skills or processes that are used to produce a product or service. The resulting design is often referred to as **functional** structure, and the resulting units as *business functions* (not to be confused with the term *functional requirement* used elsewhere in this book). Purchasing, Finance and Marketing are typical examples of business functions. Similarly, hospital departments such as Cardiology, Pediatrics and Radiology are defined based on the knowledge and skills of doctors – each department corresponds to a medical sub-discipline that doctors specialise in after completing their basic medical training. But we may also include under this rubric organisations that are structured by process; as we will discuss in more detail in Chapter 5, a manufacturing plant may be decomposed by the process or activity performed by each worker, such as casting, welding and machining.

In companies with multiple products or services, the organisation is sometimes structured in terms of the *ends* rather than the means, namely, by the different products or services that it delivers. In a **product-based** organisation, the key units are responsible for a specific type of product or service, or alternatively, a product line or brand. A consumer goods company may have three product divisions: Skin care (e.g., lotions), Home care (e.g., detergents) and Oral care (e.g., toothpaste). An electronics firm may have product divisions responsible for printers, servers and personal computers. In a pure product-based structure, functionally defined units (e.g., Research and development or Production) will be organised *within* each product division.

A more recent approach is to structure the organisation based on **markets**. Units in such an organisation can either be defined by the market segments that customers are categorised into or by the geographical regions in which customers are located. A bank may be decomposed into three main units: one for individual customers; one for small businesses; and one for large businesses. A large, global company may comprise multiple national subsidiaries; a governmental institution such as the office managing education may be sub-divided into different regions and school districts.

To this list we may add the possibility of defining an organisation based on its **projects**. An offshore engineering firm may be subdivided into a few large projects, each focused on delivering a specific solution to a client (e.g., the engineering design for a particular oil platform or some of its sub-systems or components). In some cases, projects may even become more or less permanent units within organisations (Sanchez and Heene, 2004). A project team organised to launch a new product may become a department with responsibility for the new product once it has been launched.

Until recently, a fairly common assumption was that it was necessary to select one main criterion, in other words, that organisational structure needed to be unidimensional. Strategy experts (e.g., Porter, 1996) have maintained that developing a successful strategy requires the ability to focus, by prioritising the activities that contribute most strongly to competitive advantage. From this perspective, it seems natural that the relative importance attributed to each criterion (function, product/service and market) should be reflected in the organisation design and that the most important criterion should be employed when defining the highest level of the organisational structure. Simple contingency models have often been used to select the main criterion and align the organisation with the chosen strategy. If product innovation was deemed most important, companies would organise by brand or technology platform. If customer orientation was deemed paramount, a structure based on geography or customer segments would be adopted. If operational excellence was a concern, one might attempt to introduce a process-based structure (at least in parts of the organisation).

However, over time, as organisations grew in size and complexity, it gradually became clear that selecting one criterion for structuring an entire organisation might lead to compromises that result in suboptimal performance. There were also indications that companies with a unidimensional structure were rarely able to maintain the structure over time; some even oscillated between different (unidimensional) structural configurations. US chip maker Cisco is a case in point. From 1997 to 2001, it was organised as three semi-autonomous business lines, one for each main customer type: large companies, small/medium-sized companies and internet service providers. Each business line developed and marketed its own products, and had its own sales staff. In 2001, the company chose to introduce a product-based structure, and the three business lines were divided into 11 technology groups. The rationale was to consolidate engineering resources to ensure that technological solutions would be reused across customer segments. Two US academics, Gulati and Puranam (2009), examined the implementation of the new organisation more closely. Whereas the new formal structure appeared to suggest that the company operated as a 'product-centric' company, they found instead that informal networks from the previous customer-oriented organisation prevailed. For example, marketing people would continue to approach their old colleagues from engineering to solve problems or to seek advice on how to respond to customer inquiries. It is likely that the informal networks were used to compensate for the fact that new formal structure had distanced the engineers from the customers. Cisco later seemed to acknowledge that the new structure was inadequate in terms of customer responsiveness, and introduced cross-unit processes in 2004, aimed at achieving integration across technologies, and also introduced a set of 'business councils' that essentially replicated the older grouping by customer type (at higher management levels).

In conclusion, it is difficult to find one criterion that is appropriate across units that hold different roles and carry out fundamentally different kinds of activities. Of course, as in the Cisco case, people may informally compensate for this weakness, but it is arguably better to find a formal design that acknowledges the actual functions that an organisation seeks to fulfil. Consequently, many large organisations today are *multidimensional*. Units within the organisation that are responsible for the development and manufacturing of products are typically organised by brand or technology platform. Units responsible for sales and customer support are organised by geography (e.g., country) or market segment (e.g., large, medium-sized and small customers). Finally, internal service providers such as HR, IT and Accounting are typically organised by knowledge and skills.[1] Initially, organisations simply combined such units by utilising different grouping criteria at different levels of the hierarchy, creating a hybrid organisational model. For example, at the lowest level of the organisation, units would be grouped by skills and knowledge or process, then at the next level they would be combined into larger units grouped by product, which in turned would be grouped by geography. With a multidimensional structure, however, it is not necessary to select one dominant criterion at the expense of another, as it is possible to create a design where units representing different dimensions are represented *at the same hierarchical level*. This development is illustrated in Figure 4.1a–c.

It is natural to compare multidimensional organisations to the *multidivisional* organisation described in Chapter 1. In a pure version of the multidivisional model, business units are supposed to be largely independent economic units, with managers that directly control the resources required to perform its processes. Few firms are organised in this manner today. The majority of large firms have increased resource sharing and coordination between divisions (Hoskisson et al., 1993; Whittington et al., 1999). For example, firms have consolidated administrative functions into shared services units and introduced account management processes in order to coordinate sales and marketing. However, the multidimensional models as defined here go a step further by formally decoupling two or more core dimensions (such as products and regions) that are usually organised within the same division or business unit in a multidivisional company.

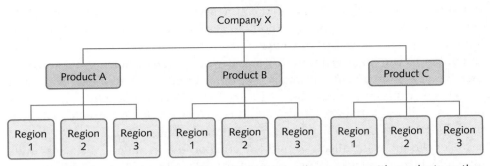

Figure 4.1a Hybrid organisation with multiple levels of grouping, with products as the main grouping criterion

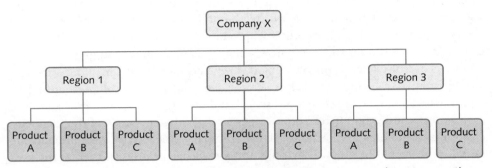

Figure 4.1b Hybrid organisation with multiple levels of grouping, with regions as the main grouping criterion

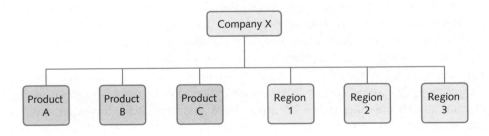

Figure 4.1c Multidimensional organisation

A multidimensional structure should confer a number of advantages:

- It should make it possible to combine the main advantages of three different organisational models: the customer orientation of a market-based structure; the technology focus of a product-based structure; as well as the economies of scale and competence building derived from a functional structure (if internal units such as IT, HR and Finance & Accounting are grouped by skills and knowledge).

- It also tends to be flatter. As Figures 4.1a–c show, two management levels may be collapsed into one in a multidimensional organisation.[2] Indeed, large firms have often introduced this design as part of an effort to 'disaggregate' their organisation by removing management layers, dividing up large units into smaller units and decentralising decision-making authority.

- A multidimensional organisation avoids the duplication or multiplication of similar sub-units that is required to create a coherent unidimensional structure when sub-units have been defined according to different grouping criteria at different levels. (Note that in the hybrid model shown in Figure 4.1a, for example, there are three sub-units responsible for Region 1, whereas only one is required in the multidimensional structure shown in Figure 4.1c.)

- A multidimensional structure will often reflect the main business processes of the organisation to a greater extent than a unidimensional organisation, which in turn will contribute to a more balanced composition of the leadership team. As indicated in Figure 4.1c, the leadership team may consist of the heads of each of the main units, representing internal service providers, products units and market units. In a hybrid structure (such as that shown in Figure 4.1a or 4.1b), the composition of the leadership team is always skewed toward one dimension.

Despite these advantages, one important challenge related to this model is *how to link* the different dimensions – representing internal functions, products and markets. Most experts would agree that the success of the model is largely dependent upon how well one is able to coordinate across the units responsible for customers, products and internal functions. However, there has been a tendency to overlook fundamental differences between alternative linking mechanisms. A leading organisation design expert, Jay Galbraith, explained that 'some form of matrix is usually employed to tie the front and the back together' (2000: p. 243). It has been common in the organisation design literature to present the matrix (i.e., a dual authority structure) as the mid point on a continuum from product to functionally based structures (or alternatively, as the mid point between functional and geographical structures) (see Figure 4.2). Managers and consultants also tend to refer to any multidimensional structure as a 'matrix'.

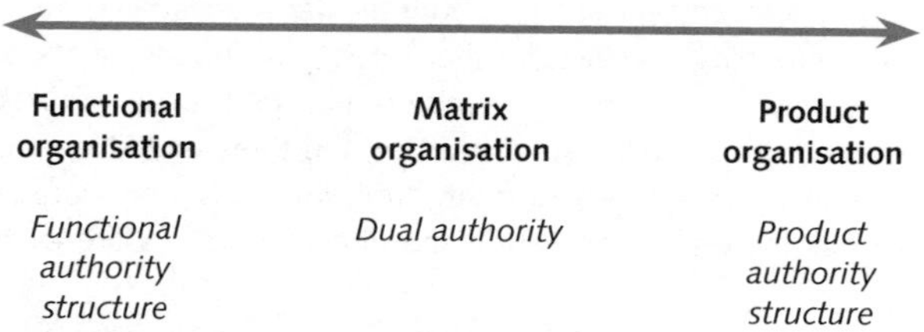

Functional organisation	**Matrix organisation**	**Product organisation**
Functional authority structure	*Dual authority*	*Product authority structure*

Figure 4.2 Range of alternative organisation design options according to Galbraith (1971; 2000)

However, a closer examination reveals that the matrix structure is only one of several alternative ways in which to create a multidimensional structure. In the remainder of this chapter we review three different approaches. In addition to the matrix structure, we examine the *front-back model* and the *modular organisation*. Utilising design matrices we show how functions are allocated across internal units and discuss the resulting flexibility and complexity of each model.

Example 4.1 Scandinavian telecom

To illustrate alternative ways of designing a multidimensional structure we use an example case from a company that we refer to as ScanTel. The example case is the result of interviews and surveys conducted in a large Scandinavian telecommunications firm in 2007 and was later revised and updated with representatives from the firm. ScanTel's mission is to offer a broad set of services (related to both fixed and mobile telephony, content and infrastructure, etc.) and serve multiple stakeholders (customers, shareholders, employees, etc.) in two main market segments: consumer (individual/residential) and business. Having evolved from a state-owned monopoly, the firm manages considerable assets (telecom network infrastructure and IT systems).

At the highest level, the functional requirement for this firm can thus be stated as follows:

FR_1 = Create value for stakeholders by offering telecommunication services

This functional requirement can be decomposed into a set of more specific, lower-level functional requirements, as follows:

FR_{11} = Provide cost-effective IT systems and applications that meet the needs of internal clients
FR_{12} = Develop and manage an efficient network infrastructure
FR_{13} = Maximise profits for Fixed telephony services
FR_{14} = Maximise profits for Mobile telephony services
FR_{15} = Maximise revenue in the Business segment
FR_{16} = Maximise revenue in the Consumer segment
FR_{17} = Perform enabling and control processes

In the following, we will review slightly different variations of this decomposition. There are often multiple lower-level functional requirements that can be chosen that all satisfy the highest level FR. It may be necessary to adjust both the decomposition of functions and design parameters (i.e., unit grouping and/or allocation of responsibilities across units) in order to improve a design. However, an important premise is that the top-level function (FR_1) remains constant. This is the case in the following discussion; the three multidimensional designs that we describe are alternative ways of realising this firm's main mission (expressed as FR_1).

The key design parameters for delivering the above functions are as follows (also see Figure 4.3):

DP_{11} = Information systems (IS) unit
DP_{12} = Operations unit
DP_{13} = Fixed business unit
DP_{14} = Mobile business unit
DP_{15} = Business market unit
DP_{16} = Consumer market unit
DP_{17} = Corporate staff unit

According to our definition above, this design is multidimensional as it places units that have been decomposed based on three different grouping criteria at the same hierarchical level (cf. Figure 4.3). There are two products units, defined based on the network infrastructure being utilised to deliver services, either fixed or mobile. There are also two market units, defined by the main customer segment that they target: business and consumer (i.e., individual/ residential) customers. In addition, there are two important internal units responsible for IT systems and the network infrastructure as well as a central staff unit responsible for HR, Finance and Procurement.

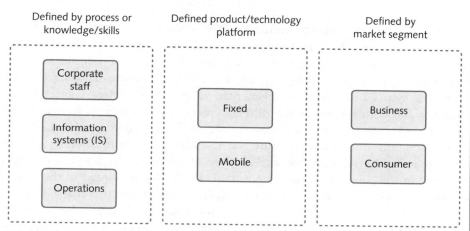

Figure 4.3 Grouping criteria used to define the key units in ScanTel

The key prerequisite for a multidimensional model is that one is able to decompose the organisation into a set of relatively independent sub-units. This in turn requires that some key assumptions, regarding market segments and product interdependencies, actually hold true. As an example, there are five key assumptions behind the model adopted by ScanTel:

1 Business and residential customers have distinct needs and therefore require different product and service packages, pricing plans, etc.
2 Customers in both segments may buy either fixed or mobile telecommunication products (or a combination).
3 There are limited interdependencies between fixed and mobile technologies, making it feasible to separate these into two units.
4 There are scale effects and other advantages from consolidating product-related processes in the back end units, as opposed to spreading them in the front units.
5 Similarly, IT and operations processes may be consolidated into internal service provider units that serve all product or market units.

Current market trends may challenge these assumptions and make it necessary to revisit the chosen structure. For example, telecom services are increasingly 'bundled' (e.g., so-called triple play offerings with a package of fixed telephone services, broadband and a mobile subscription), which sometimes require tighter integration between different product units. Moreover, the separation between consumer and business is not always relevant, as many firms buy telephone services on behalf of their employees, and essentially offer telephone or broadband subscription as an employee benefit. However, even if these trends continue they do not necessarily imply that telecom companies should revert to a unidimensional structure, but the trends will likely lead to a different decomposition of ScanTel's activities compared to the one shown here.

The matrix

The matrix structure emerged during the 1960s and had become quite common-place in large organisations by the early 1970s.[3] During this period, leaders of many divisionalised firms had become concerned about the duplication of functions (e.g., engineering, production and marketing) and the lack of coordination across divisions. The matrix structure was implemented to open up the lateral communication channels and better integrate the different parts of the company. In other firms, the main driver was increasing internationalisation. New country subsidiaries were established, and the matrix structure was introduced to ensure that key employees were focused on developing local business while being integrated in the global structure of the company (Chi and Nystrom, 1998). Key personnel in the country subsidiary would thus report both to a country manager and to a manager in one of the company's product divisions. The classic example is ABB (prior to changes introduced in 1998). A manager in, say, Spain, would report to the country manager in Spain, responsible for sales and customer support. On the second axis the manager would report to a manager in a global business area, which would be organised based on product group or technology (e.g. power transmission, industrial and building systems, financial services, etc.). The matrix form fell out of favour and was abandoned by ABB as well as by other well-known proponents such as Shell and BP several years ago. However, the model is not yet extinct; some companies have recently started to adopt matrix structures again, at least in parts of their organisation. For example, companies with plants in different countries increasingly see the plants as part of a global supply chain, rather than as country-specific resources. In such companies, a plant manager responsible for, e.g., production planning may report both to a local site director and to a supply chain manager in a global supply chain organisation. The purpose is to synchronise the global operations and to ensure that common standards apply across different sites. Another variant is the project matrix. Instead of a permanent reporting relationship to two bosses, one here refers to organisations where the 'stable' part (e.g., the functional departments) are combined with a 'changeable' part (e.g., projects) by means of matrix reporting lines. Employees report to project managers on a day-to-day basis but also belong to functional departments (representing different technical discipline).

There are many ways in which to implement a matrix. To illuminate some of the options that may exist, let us consider how a matrix could be implemented in a company such as ScanTel. In reality, ScanTel has several thousand employees, but for the sake of simplicity, we consider the effect of changing the formal structure for 21 people (Figure 4.4). For the moment we also ignore staff and internal service provider units and focus only on how to link the product-market axis. As Figure 4.4 shows, the 21 people include the EVP for each main unit, 2 managers working on sales and marketing who are already attached to one of the market units, as well as 12 employees who have yet to be allocated to a unit.

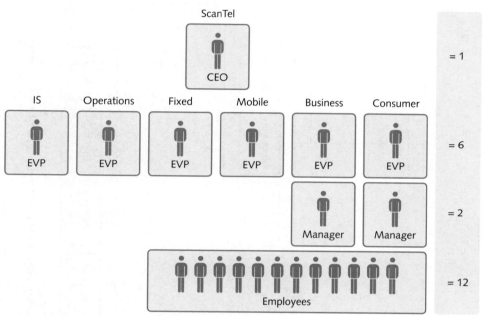

Figure 4.4 People in ScanTel that will be organised by means of a matrix in the subsequent examples (Figures 4.5–4.7)

How can we use a matrix model to organise this group of 21 people? The first question is at what level a matrix reporting structure should be implemented. The most straightforward solution is to establish dual reporting lines where the 12 employees report both to a manager in a market unit and to one of the product unit directors. Assuming that the volume of work is more or less equal across the product categories, the group of 12 can be subdivided into four groups (see Figure 4.5). The main advantage of this solution is that it avoids the introduction of any additional managerial positions, it simply sub-divides the employees into groups and links them up with the units on both dimensions by adding reporting relationships. In practice, it would mean that both the heads of the product units and the heads of the market units would influence the goals that are set, support and provide resources to the activities performed by employees, and evaluate the performance of the employees.

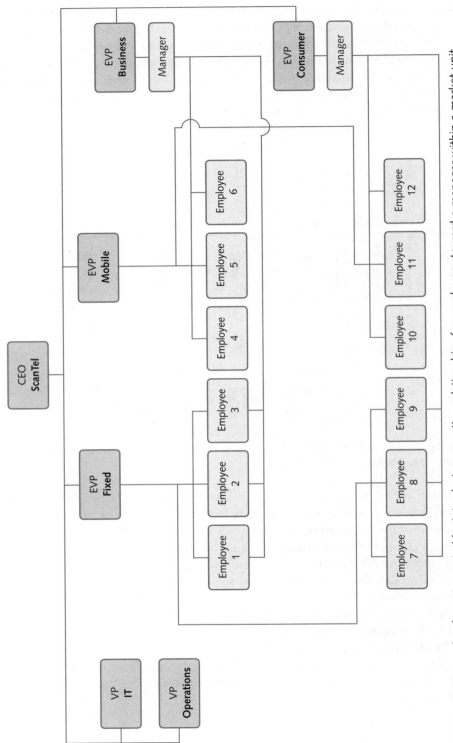

Figure 4.5 Example of matrix created by introducing reporting relationships for employees toward a manager within a market unit manager and the head of a product unit

When two organisational dimensions that are linked in such a manner have an unequal number of hierarchical layers (in this example, the product units have two layers, while the market units have three), it leads to an *unbalanced* matrix: The employees will on the product dimension report to an executive that is one level above the manager in the market unit (see Figure 4.4). Such asymmetrical power relationships present employees and managers with considerable challenges. Not only are employees supposed to manage the different and potentially conflicting expectations from the two axes of the organisation, they must do this while bearing in mind the unequal hierarchical status of their managers. The manager in the market unit may experience that he/she is being 'overruled' by the EVP in the product unit, or that he or she has no real managerial authority and will need to involve the EVP in the market unit in order to make a decision. Despite these problems, asymmetrical power relationships are relatively common in large and complex organisations (Edmondson et al., 2003).

A balanced matrix can be created in two ways. It is possible to introduce the matrix one level up, by creating additional managerial positions, and establish dual reporting lines for these positions (Figure 4.6). The managers will then report to bosses that are at the same hierarchical level (the managers' superiors will all report to the CEO). In this alternative, the employees report only to one boss as the matrix only encompasses the managers.

However, creating a balanced matrix in this manner comes at a high cost. The total number of managers would need to increase from two to four. Other things being equal, Mintzberg (1979) estimated that a matrix structure (implemented across an entire company) would require twice as many managers as a purely functional structure. Although Mintzberg's estimate seems to be correct with regard to our example here, it may in fact be too conservative. He mainly cited the increasing cost caused by the added time used for supervision, as bosses in a matrix are supposed to jointly hire, agree on goals for the employee and evaluate performance. He did not include the need to create additional positions to ensure that the structure obtains a reasonable degree of coherence and consistency. In ScanTel there are only two units along each dimension; the cost of creating a balanced matrix will increase with the number of units.

A third option is to first create an equal hierarchical structure on both dimensions of the organisation before introducing the matrix. We started from the assumption that there was one manager attached to each market unit. But new middle management positions could be created, reporting to the EVPs of the product units (Figure 4.7). If the employees instead would report to these middle managers, we would avoid the asymmetrical relationships described above. However, the assumption would obviously be that the work load of the organisation actually justifies building up a more equal structure on both dimensions of the matrix (or alternatively, that it is possible to transfer resources from one dimension to another to balance out the matrix).

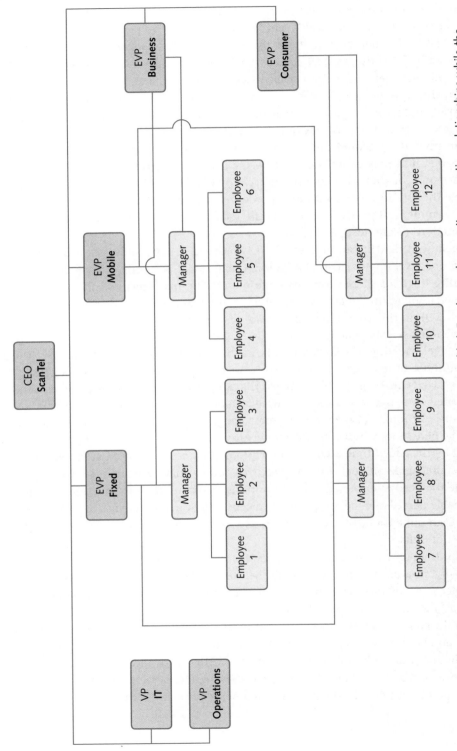

Figure 4.6 Example of matrix where additional manager positions are added. Employees have unitary reporting relationships while the managers report both to the head of a market unit and the head of a product unit

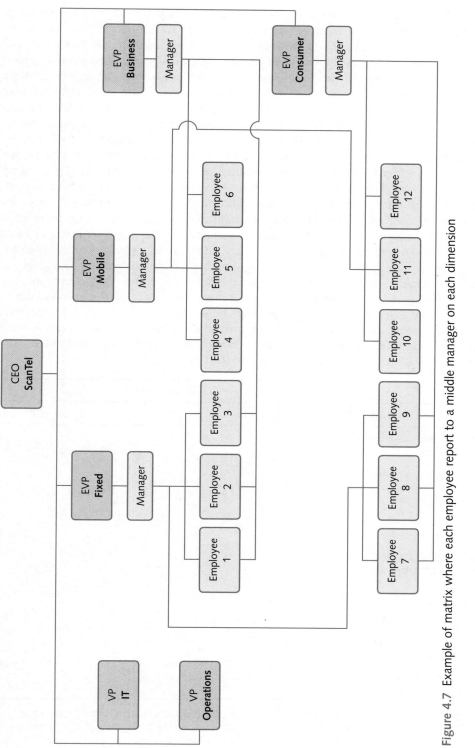

Figure 4.7 Example of matrix where each employee report to a middle manager on each dimension

Regardless of which option that is selected, a matrix will by its very nature create significant interdependencies between the units that are connected by means of the reporting structure. In a matrix, the ability of a manager or employee to attain his or her goals will to a great extent be dependent upon decisions taken in units representing two organisational dimensions (e.g., market and product units). In some cases the goals pursued by these units may be positively correlated, but they may also be negatively correlated, in which case a decision to optimise performance in one unit will undermine the ability of another unit to optimise its performance (Ethiraj and Levinthal, 2009). For example, on the market dimension, the employee may report to a superior who focuses primarily on product revenue, whereas his superior in the product unit may be measured on profit. The employee is then likely to receive conflicting directions from the two superiors. In a firm such as ScanTel, the superior on the product dimension may encourage the employee to focus on selling complex telephony solutions with high margins. The superior on the market dimension may prefer that the employee sell simpler, but higher-volume services that contribute to higher revenues. Similarly, if the product unit is responsible for developing new products, the superior on the product dimension may recognise the sales manager's efforts at promoting new and innovative technologies in the market, whereas the superior in the market unit in some cases may resist the introduction of new technologies (particularly if they only address niches in the market or represent unproved solutions that don't contribute strongly to maintaining or increasing revenues). These interdependencies represent *coupling* between functional requirements; in Figure 4.8 they are indicated with 'x's in the shaded area.

					Design parameters		
Functional requirements	*IS*	*Operations*	*Fixed*	*Mobile*	*Business*	*Consumer*	*Corporate staff*
1.1 Provide cost-effective IT systems (…)	**X**						x
1.2 Develop and manage an efficient network infrastructure	x	**X**					x
1.3 Maximise profits for Fixed telephony services	x	x	**X**		x	x	x
1.4 Maximise profits for Mobile telephony services	x	x		**X**	x	x	x
1.5 Maximise revenue in the Business segment	x	x	x	x	**X**		x
1.6 Maximise revenue in the Consumer segment	x	x	x	x		**X**	x
1.7 Perform enabling and control processes							**X**

Figure 4.8 Assumed design matrix if ScanTel adopts a matrix structure. X signifies a strong relationship between a DP and a FR, and x a moderately strong relationship. The shaded area corresponds to instances of coupling that are due to the matrix reporting structure

We should add that coupling may also be due to operational interdependencies that are unrelated to the choice of reporting structure as such. In telecommunications companies, the units responsible for IT and telephone network infrastructure have some influence on the achievement of almost all functional requirements. For example, the introduction of a new pricing scheme, developed by a market unit, may necessitate a significant re-coding effort on behalf of IT, as pricing mechanisms are sometimes 'hard wired' in the billing system (which is tightly coupled to the basic telephony network systems). Similarly, the introduction of a new product, such as television on cellphone handsets, may require network capacity increases, which may depend on additional infrastructure investments. Such interdependencies are a serious hindrance for achieving speed and flexibility in many telecoms companies. (In Figure 4.8, the 'x's' in the first two columns of the matrix indicate that the achievement of all functions is dependent upon actions and decisions in the IT and Operations units.)

As with the other two multidimensional forms that we shall discuss, the matrix was intended to allow the combination of two grouping criteria (e.g., product and market) and, in theory, achieve customer focus and economies of scale at the same time. The main change from a purely functional organisation is that it opens up the lateral channels of communication, and therefore leads to an increase in both the amount and frequency of information being exchanged between functions. Moreover, the matrix significantly alters governance processes by introducing dual reporting relationships. The two managers that intersect in a matrix structure hold joint responsibility for supervising employees, who are supposed to balance the goals of the different dimensions of the matrix. For the individual employee, the main advantage is perhaps that the matrix introduces more variety and contributes to a broadening of one's informal network as one is exposed to a larger number of individuals belonging to different units.

A key issue with matrix structures has been how employees deal with dual authority relationships. However, the primary challenge may not be having two bosses per se, but the fact that the two bosses share jurisdiction over the same work process (e.g., the sales process in ScanTel), yet are held accountable for different and potentially conflicting goals. When employees are at lower levels are unable to resolve conflicts between different goals, they are escalated to higher-levels of management. One key finding from organisations with matrix structures is indeed that higher-level managers become overloaded because lower-level managers are unable to resolve conflicts and therefore refer conflicts to the executives. In other words, an unintended consequence of a matrix structure is actually to make the organisation more centralised and to remove accountability from lower-level managers (Whitford, 2006). More recent organisational models have been developed to try to address this issue.

The front-back model

The front-back model is similar to a matrix in that it consists of decentralised units structured along different dimensions (i.e, decomposed using different criteria). However, whereas the term 'matrix organisation' may refer to any combination of dimensions (e.g., geography vs. product, project vs. functional, etc.), the 'front end' in the front-back model normally consists of market units, whereas the 'back end' comprises the product units, responsible for developing or manufacturing products. Another important difference from the matrix is that the front-back model may be implemented without dual reporting relationships. In some cases, the front and back are linked together by an internal customer–supplier interface: The market units identify customer needs, receive orders and request products and services from the units in the 'back end'. The internal customer–supplier relations may be largely informal, but the roles may also be formalised in the form of an internal market where units literally buy and sell from each other.

The market units of the front end are usually structured around customer segments at the top level, and then around customers (e.g., by having key account teams for the most important customers) (Galbraith, 2000). The key rationale is to be able to sell all the organisation's products or services (cross-selling), to provide a common interface toward the client, or to assemble solutions consisting of products and services from several back end units. Conversely, the back end units should be able to interface with any front end unit to deliver a product. The front-back model is an attempt to derive the advantages of economies of scope[4] and specialisation, or what Nadler and Tushman (1997) call leverage and focus. Leverage is gained because resources, such as product development and production, are consolidated in a product unit, and thus more easily derive advantages from scale. For example, a product unit in a home appliances company responsible for refrigerators may be able to re-use engineering designs and share production resources, even though the product is sold in many variants, or even as separate brands, by different market units. Simultaneously, focus is gained as market units are able to concentrate on a set of customers or market segments. Market units, and the various teams within them, should be able to stay in close touch with customers and have the authority to take decisions related to sales and marketing in their respective segments.

A front end structure is sometimes implemented at lower levels of the organisation, even if the overall structure of the company is organised based on geography or product. An example is a large bank that is geographically organised, with subsidiaries in many European countries. However, several of the subsidiaries have organised their corporate banking activities with a front-back structure as shown in Figure 4.9. As is common in this business, a 'relationship banker' holds the responsibility for continuous communication with customers, while product specialists develop and deliver the services that the customers require. There is also a Banking Operations unit, which performs 'back office' processing, and a corporate risk unit, which is responsible for risk assessment.

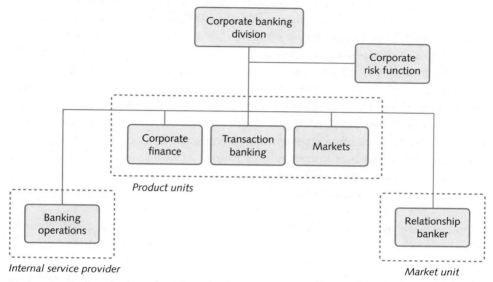

Figure 4.9 Corporate banking division of the national subsidiary of a European bank

A notable aspect of the front-back organisation is that it makes it possible to define roles and responsibilities in a manner that reduces overlaps across units. Or, in axiomatic design terms, it makes it possible – in principle, at least – to create a decoupled design (Suh, 2001) where each organisational unit performs one main function. The separation of functions is essential because it allows the definition of independent goals and KPIs. For example, unlike in the matrix organisation, sales- and revenue-related goals may be assigned only to front end units, as product units can be measured on other goals such as productivity, cost, quality or project execution. The result is a lower degree of coupling, i.e., actions initiated by units to fulfil their particular goals (i.e., satisfy the functional requirements) will to a lesser extent hamper the ability to reach other goals (i.e., other functional requirements).[5] In the case of ScanTel, we may formalise the functional requirements as follows:[6]

FR_{11} = Provide cost-effective IT systems and applications that meet the needs of internal clients

FR_{12} = Develop and manage an efficient network infrastructure

FR_{13} = Develop and launch new Fixed telephony services

FR_{14} = Develop and launch new Mobile telephony services

FR_{15} = Maximise revenue in the Business segment

FR_{16} = Maximise revenue in the Consumer segment

FR_{17} = Perform enabling and control processes

Figure 4.10 shows the formal reporting lines for employees and Table 4.1 shows the allocation of functions in ScanTel if it were to be organised according to the front-back model.

Even though the front-back model does not require the dual authority structure of the matrix, this does not imply that companies automatically avoid overlapping responsibilities or conflicting goals by implementing the model – the design intent is not always realised. For example, at the time of our interviews in ScanTel we noted that both front end and back end units had some responsibility for product development, something which managers cited as a source of friction. The more responsibilities overlap, the stronger the need for joint coordination between the front end and the back end units. And a strong need for joint coordination between the front and the back often leads to the creation of some mechanism for coordination, either an informal meeting forum or project, or a more formal integrator role. Some organisations that have attempted to implement the front-back model have created an additional, 'coordinating' layer between the front end and the back end units. In such cases, the organisation is gravitating toward a matrix form.

As discussed in Galbraith (2000), a key question regarding the front-back model relates to the balance of power. It is possible to define both the front end and the back end units as profit centres. However, it is more common to see that one axis is the dominant one, holding the profit/loss responsibility. The other axis is then usually a cost centre. Galbraith (2000) mentioned that the front end is the sole profit centre in some car manufacturers. Although systematic data are lacking, it seems to be the other way around in many other companies. For example, in a large consumer goods company, the official chart was drawn as a front-back structure, while the products units in reality dominated decision making, and directed the activities of the market units. The impression is thus that the front-back structure in many cases represents a 'push' model. This means that in the product development process, for example, the market units may provide suggestions based on customer feedback regarding possible new products, but the product units usually have the final say in deciding which technologies to employ or which products to develop.

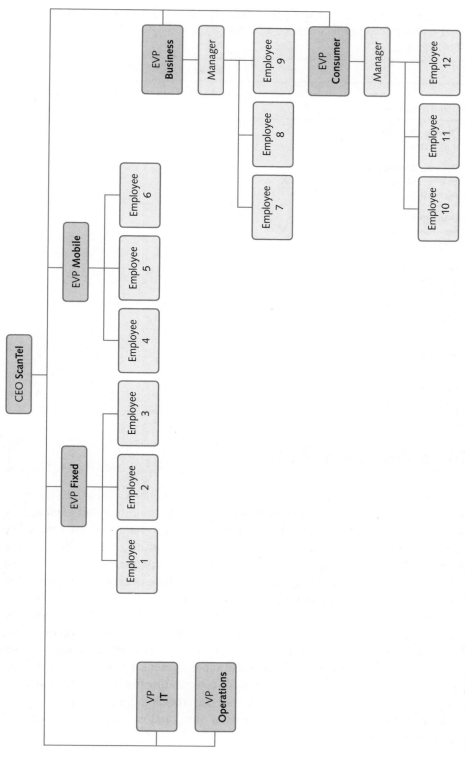

Figure 4.10 Reporting lines for the 21 people shown in Figure 4.4 if a front-back model is implemented in ScanTel

Table 4.1 Assumed design matrix if ScanTel adopts a front-back organisation. X signifies a strong relationship between a DP and a FR, and x a moderately strong relationship

Functional requirements	Design parameters						
	IS	Operations	Fixed	Mobile	Business	Consumer	Corporate staff
1.1 Provide cost-effective IT systems (. . .)	X						x
1.2 Develop and manage an efficient network infrastructure	x	X					x
1.3 Develop and launch new Fixed telephony services	x	x	X				x
1.4 Develop and launch new Mobile telephony services	x	x		X			x
1.5 Maximise revenue in the Business segment	x	x			X		x
1.6 Maximise revenue in the Consumer segment	x	x				X	x
1.7 Perform enabling and control processes							X

The modular organisation

A third alternative to structuring multidimensional organisations – the modular organisation – was first articulated by Goggin (1974) and later modified and extended by Russell Ackoff (1994; 1999).[7] The starting point is the distinction between three key functional requirements (Table 4.2). Ackoff reasoned that all organisations require certain inputs, such as people, supplies and capital. Consequently, there is a need for 'input units' that source these inputs and provide them as services to other internal units. Second, all organisations produce some outputs, whether they are products or services. 'Output units' are defined that perform this function, and will typically be grouped by product category, technology platform or brand in larger organisations. Third, 'market units' sell the outputs that are produced to external customers. Markets units may be grouped geographically or by customer segment. Finally, there may be, in larger organisations, a need for a small unit of coordinating executives. Key functions for the executives are to develop strategy and set the guidelines for the operations of the subordinate units, invest in the development of units, and monitor performance and conduct audit of units.

Table 4.2 Generic functional requirements and design parameters proposed by Russell Ackoff (1994; 1999)

Generic functional requirements	Design parameters			
	Input units	Output units	Market units	Executive office
Provide products or services that are principally consumed or used internally	X			x
Provide products or services that are principally consumed or used externally		X		x
Market and sell the products or services provided by the Output units			X	x
Perform executive functions				X

Ackoff concluded that there is no need for a matrix to link the different dimensions in a modular organisation. Instead, he proposed that there should be supplier–customer relations between roles belonging to different units. In other words, if an output unit relies on an input unit for certain services, the head of the output unit becomes the client, rather than the boss, of the employees of the input unit. Similarly, output units are the suppliers to the market units, which are supposed to represent the 'voice of the customer' within the company, both by evaluating products and services from the customer's point of view and by articulating customer needs that may be met by developing new offerings.

The modular structure is similar in some respects to the front-back model described by Galbraith. Like the front-back model, it confers both focus and leverage. Units can be highly specialised (in terms of function, product or market) yet obtain economies of scale and scope from sharing resources. Input and market units should be able to serve any output (product) unit (although they may not necessarily serve all at any time). Market units should sell all the company's products or services and thus provide a common interface for clients toward the organisation.

However, there are also a number of differences. In describing the front-back organisation above, we noted that the balance of power may differ from company to company. In some, the front end has the most authority, whereas in others, it is the back end (the product units) that essentially directs the activities of the sales and marketing people in the front end units. In the modular organisation, however, the market units always hold the internal client role, and the product units the supplier role, and not vice versa. This is a key element in creating a 'pull' system (as in the Lean philosophy) where work processes in upstream (product) units are only initiated based on specific requests from downstream (market) units.

Unlike units in a front-back model, the output (product) units within a modular organisation have no fixed assets, and only consist of a few managers (and potentially a small supporting staff). Units not only share production and market resources; they also share *human resources*. Employees are formally organised in a resource pool in one of the input units and hired out on request to output or market units (see Figure 4.11). The model implies the introduction of a dual hierarchy (Malone, 2004), which, despite the name, does not imply a matrix structure. *People managers* lead skills groups within the resource pool. However, once allocated to a project in a business unit, employees work for a *project manager*. The project manager is essentially the *internal client* of the people manager in the resource pool; there is no formal reporting relationship between them. Unlike traditional HR functions, the resource pool in a modular organisations becomes a strategic business unit. It is accountable for providing resources that business units require and for developing the skills that the company will need in the future (see Worren, 2008 for a detailed description).

Units in a modular organisation have even greater autonomy than units in the typical implementation of the front-back model. Although the executive office retains the right to override decisions of individual units, there should in practice be little need for intervention, provided that clear 'rules of engagement' have been established with regard to such issues as profit accumulation, capital investment and protection of intellectual property (see Ackoff, 1999 for further discussion). Apart from resolving issues that are escalated, the role of the executive office is primarily to design and adjust the overall organisation, that is, define the units are necessary and how they should interact. A firm may also convert an input unit to a product unit, if it turns out that there is a considerable external market for the services that it delivers.

The main difference between the modular and the matrix model is the elimination of dual functions and reporting relationships. Like the front-back model, it allows specialised units with independent performance measures. It shares with the front-back model the concept of standard interfaces between units, allowing any output (product) unit to transact with any market unit. A modular organisation may consist of a great number of individual units, with a great number of possible constellations with regard to collaboration (e.g., product unit A transacting with market unit 1 and 2, product unit B transacting with market unit 1 and 3, and so on).

The modular organisations thus confers true *reconfigurability*. Because output (product) units and market units are small and have no fixed assets, such units can easily be added, merged or disbanded quickly and at a low cost. A firm may choose to disband a unit because there is no longer any demand for the services or products that it produces, or because it is not competitive with external suppliers. Units may be created to serve new markets or because the company believes that it should 'insource' a service that has previously been purchased from an external provider.

As pointed out in Ackoff (1994; 1999), combining the modular organisation with an internal market economy contributes to even greater flexibility. All units will then be profit centres and receive income from the sale of their products and services, and pay for services rendered to them. Ackoff also proposed that units should be free both the purchase whatever they need or sell whatever they produce or provide, either internally or externally.[8] As a consequence, each unit becomes more independent (i.e., it removes *coupling* as defined in axiomatic design theory).

Even if units are not allowed to trade externally, it is possible to use market-based principles to allocate capacity internally. For example, Malone (2004) has described how internal markets may be used to allocate manufacturing capacity in a large firm with several plants. The traditional approach is based on a centralised process where a coordinating unit or executive allocates capacity based on sales forecasts from market units. In a modular organisation, the process could instead be completely decentralised – market units would be allowed to buy futures contracts for products available at specific times in the future. If the demand turns out to be less than anticipated, a market unit may sell future contracts to another market unit. In this manner capacity allocation becomes a self-regulating process that does not require management intervention (although higher-level managers obviously need to set up and monitor the process). Interestingly, internal markets should also contribute to greatly decreased complexity, in that the resource allocation process becomes much more transparent. Instead of tracking multiple forecasts and production schedules for a large number of sub-units, an electronic market system would provide information, accessible for all employees, about prices for all products in all future time periods.

If we assume that we may combine the modular organisation with an internal market, the functional requirements for ScanTel may be stated as shown in the table below.

Generic function	Specific functional requirements for ScanTel
Provide products or services that are principally consumed or used externally	FR_{13} = Maximise profits for Fixed telephony services FR_{14} = Maximise profits for Mobile telephony services
Market and sell the products or services provided by the Output units	FR_{15} = Maximise profits in the Business segment FR_{16} = Maximise profits in the Consumer segment
Provide products or services that are principally consumed or used internally	FR_{11} = Maximise profits for information systems services FR_{12} = Maximise profits for network services FR_{17} = Perform enabling and control processes FR_{18} = Maximise competence utilisation

Figure 4.11 shows the formal reporting lines of employees in ScanTel and Table 4.3 the mapping between functional requirements and design parameters (organisational units). Note that we have added a functional requirement related to the maximisation of competence (FR_{18}), which has been allocated to a new organisation unit (the People unit, i.e., a resource pool).

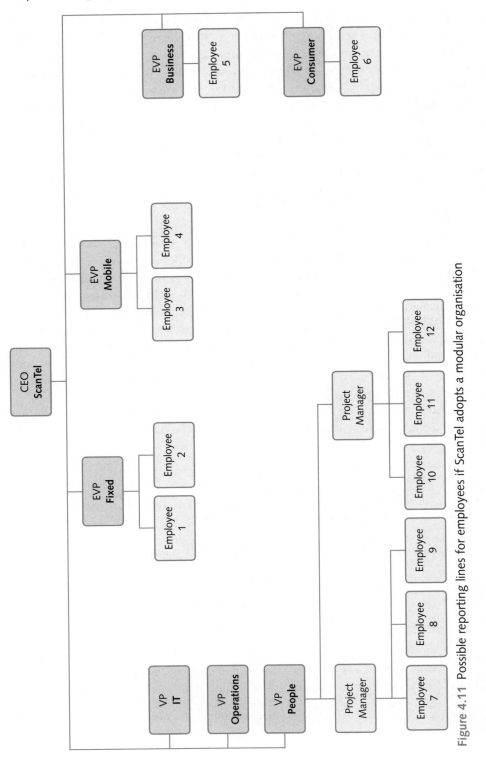

Figure 4.11 Possible reporting lines for employees if ScanTel adopts a modular organisation

Table 4.3 Assumed design matrix if ScanTel adopts a modular organisation. X signifies a strong relationship between a DP and a FR, and an x a moderately strong relationship

Functional requirements	Design parameters							
	IS	Operations	Fixed	Mobile	Business	Consumer	Corporate staff	People unit
1.1 Maximise profits for information systems services	X						x	x
1.2 Maximise profits for network services		X					x	x
1.3 Maximise profits for Fixed telephony services			X				x	x
1.4 Maximise profits for Mobile telephony services				X			x	x
1.5 Maximise profits in the Business segment					X		x	x
1.6 Maximise profits in the Consumer segment						X	x	x
1.7 Perform enabling and control processes							X	x
1.8 Maximise competence utilisation							x	X

Discussion

When the modular organisation first was conceptualised, it represented a theoretical possibility. Yet it anticipated fundamental changes that have been taking place during the last couple of decades. In many organisations today, the internal value chain is becoming increasingly virtualised in that units are free to source their input from any source, internal or external. An extreme example would be companies in commodity-based industries, such as electrical energy. The sales department of an energy company is not dependent on the capacity of the company's own power stations in order to serve a customer – once a contract is established with a customer, the energy is simply sourced from the energy commodity market. There are similar examples in other sectors. Smaller telecom companies are often 'virtual' companies that lease network capacity from larger telecom companies. Engineering companies similarly make use of external contractors in times of high demand for their services.

Reducing dependencies toward internal suppliers in this manner decreases the probability that a unit's performance will be affected by, for example, a lack of capacity in another internal unit.

Despite the advantages reviewed so far, there are a number of issues related to the modular organisation that should be examined more carefully. Perhaps the most important issue is clarifying to what extent the different functions of the respective dimensions (input, output and market) really are separable. If market units are separated from output (product) units, is it enough that market units identify customer needs and market trends, and transfer this information to output (product) units in the form of product specifications? Or is it necessary for members of output (product) units to interact directly with customers to understand their preferences, or customise solutions to their particular needs? This is the situation in corporate banking. Although the relationship manager (representing the market dimension) may sell and initiate the sale of a financial service, the actual service is often performed by product specialists who work for the client (although they sometimes may interact with client personnel at a lower level than those that the relationship manager interacts with). Vice versa, when sales people estimate the costs for a complicated engineering project, is it enough for them to rely on information supplied by an output (product) unit (e.g., historical data showing the costs of similar projects completed in the past), or do sales people need a deep understanding of the technical processes to be able to estimate the cost correctly? Or put differently, is it really possible to design a 'standard interface' in modular terms between an output (product) unit and a market unit, or does the interface have to be more permeable (Kogut and Bowman, 1995)?

Several options exist when it is not possible to fully separate output (product) units and market units (or the 'front end' and the 'back end' in the terminology of the front-back model). A company may simply integrate market units within output (product) units, essentially reducing a three-dimensional organisation to two dimensions. Sales and marketing resources will then be organised in the same unit as those responsible for developing and delivering products and services, but the company will find it more difficult to maintain a common interface toward clients across products and to sell solutions that include combinations of products or services from different output (product) units. Another option is to maintain three dimensions but place more responsibility in the market units. Homburg et al. (2000) observed that key account managers are increasingly responsible for costs in serving accounts as well as the revenues generated (on the other hand, this responsibility is not always accompanied by real authority over internal resources that influence the costs).

However, before altering – some would say diluting – the logic of the model in this manner, one may consider whether there are mechanisms that could compensate for the separation of functions that the model entails. Continuing the example of a sales process in an engineering firm, at least three possible options exist. The first is to document and standardise processes. Many engineering firms have developed standard execution methodologies consisting of repeatable processes, procedures and tools (often called work packages). These may not only specify how to execute a project, but also contain estimates of time and cost associated with different activities. Over time, these estimates can be updated to reflect the actual time and cost of implementing projects. In this manner, there may be less need for sales people to be deeply involved in the technical process, as long as they can access and correctly interpret the historical data. Another approach is to establish a cross-functional sales team that involves employees in both a market unit and an output (product) unit. This is a natural approach, particularly in the absence of reliable, historical cost data, for example, when the project involves new technologies or other uncertainties. Finally, it is possible to rotate personnel between output (product) and market units. This approach ensures that those selling products have sufficient technical insight, as well as informal networks, to draw on when there is a need for closer collaboration with engineers during a sales process.

A second issue concerns the concept of an internal market. As described above, combining the modular structure with an internal market should contribute to greatly increased flexibility. However, the main challenge is determining the boundaries of the market. Many critics of the internal market model have been concerned that it may lead to internal fragmentation. As Peter Senge noted, 'free markets don't always promote a common good, especially when the common good goes beyond the simple transactions on which the market's actors are focused' (1993, p. 91). Fostering collective action among a group of semi-autonomous units is often a challenge. It seems clear that a clear definition – and acceptance – of the executive office's role and authority is required in order to avoid fragmentation in a modular organisation. An important consideration is whether a decision, policy or process is 'modular' (i.e., aimed at enhancing unit performance) or 'architectural' (aimed at enhancing the performance of the overall system). As an example, in implementing a common IT system across different business units, costs may be reduced for the organisation because of pooling of resources (i.e., use of the same software, procedures, training courses, etc.), even though costs may increase for some individual units that previously used simpler, local IT systems. More importantly, however, a common IT system may also contribute to increased internal information sharing or allow more efficient transactions across interfaces – and thus influence the ability to forge collaboration across functions, units and geographies. If so, we are clearly talking about *architectural level* processes – which the corporate centre of a modular organisation needs to have the authority to select and implement.

Summary and conclusion

Many large organisations today are structured along multiple dimensions, representing markets, products and internal functions. Until now, one has overlooked the differences between alternative ways in which to link units representing the different dimensions of such organisations. In this chapter we have seen that there are in fact three alternative ways in which to create multidimensional designs: the traditional *matrix* structure, the *front-back* model and the *modular* organisation. Although these models may look superficially similar, they represent significantly different principles with regard to reporting relationships, coordinating processes, and allocation of resources. By acknowledging the differences between these models, we provide new design options for managers seeking to reduce complexity and improve the flexibility of large organisations.

The matrix organisation is the oldest model and appears to be the most costly, complex and inflexible of the three alternatives. Its complexity stems both from the dual authority relationships and from the existence of overlapping goals. The front-back and modular organisation provide viable alternatives for leaders that consider different options for structuring large organisations. There may be a few exceptions, where it is hard to avoid a matrix structure. In most organisations there is a need to align corporate functions at different levels, and one common method to achieve this is to establish a dual reporting structure for managers of staff functions (i.e., those responsible for accounting and finance, HR, etc.) where they simultaneously report to both the line manager of the business unit in which they work, as well as to the head of the respective corporate function. However, unlike the traditional matrix, there exists in such cases only a 'dotted-line' relationship on the second dimension; the primary reporting relationship is toward the line manager of the business unit.

The highest level of flexibility will be attained by adopting the modular organisation design. The modular organisation is explicitly based on a 'pull' philosophy, similar to the Lean philosophy (Womack and Jones, 1996). 'Pull' essentially means that no upstream unit should produce a good or service until the (internal) customer downstream requests it. In the modular organisation, this principle is extended even to human resources. Instead of having an 'inventory' of human capital in each department, waiting to be utilised, the modular organisation organises resources in a common pool and provide these resources 'on demand' to product and market units.

However, it is also clear that the modular organisation may not be the appropriate choice for all firms. Exploiting the potential flexibility of a modular organisation requires a relatively high degree of process maturity, with well defined interfaces. It also requires clear internal transfer pricing principles, an IT infrastructure that supports efficient transactions between sub-units, as well as accounting processes that allow individual sub-units to monitor their economic performance. The concept of resource pools is chiefly relevant for project-based firms of a certain size, or with workers who are geographically mobile. (A large project-based firm may establish one resource pool per location; a smaller project based firm with several offices may require employees to travel between projects for various internal clients.) For firms that carry out more stable or continuous processes, the front-back model should be the preferred choice. The front-back model relies on the well established line organisation where people are organised within one specific unit. It is possible that these two models represent different evolutionary stages in the development of large firms. Firms seeking to combine a product and a market focus may start by adopting the front-back model and later evolve to a modular design as the organisation attains a higher level of process maturity.

Table 4.4 Comparison between matrix, front-back and modular organisational structures

	Matrix	Front-back	Modular
Number of dimensions	• Two or more	• Two or more	• Two or more
Reporting structure	• Dual (or in some cases triple) reporting structure	• Is sometimes a matrix, but allows unitary reporting combined with customer–supplier relations between roles/units	• Unitary reporting combined with customer–supplier relations between roles/units
Key performance indicators	• Profit and loss may be on both dimensions, and may overlap	• Profit and loss may be on both dimensions • The structure allows independent KPIs	• Profit and loss may be on both dimensions • The structure allows independent KPIs
Organisation of resources (i.e., where people belong)	• Within each unit	• Within each unit	• In separate resource pool (neither in product nor market unit)
Organisation of 'front end'	• No particular requirement	• Always defined according to market segments	• Always defined according to market segments
Key advantage	• Increases lateral coordination	• Clarifies sub-unit roles • Reduces complexity	• Maximises flexibility
Key limitation	• High complexity due to overlapping functions and goals • Creating a balanced matrix results in higher cost (more management resources)	• Low degree of resource flexibility • One dimension (product or market) will usually dominate • Intent of model often undermined during implementation • Easily leads to asymmetries in the composition of leadership teams	• Requires a high degree of process maturity • Requires minimum size in each location, or high geographical mobility among staff • May increase risk of fragmentation

Design propositions

Objective   *Design an organisational model that maximises the effectiveness of multibusiness organisations (organisations delivering multiple products or services, or addressing multiple markets)*

4.1   Create a multidimensional model that:

    a Is built up of a set of relatively independent sub-units, each performing one distinct function

    b Contains units representing the main dimensions (e.g., internal services, products, and markets) at the same hierarchical level

    c Principally use customer–supplier relations to link units (as opposed to dual reporting lines)

Objective   *Identify the appropriate multidimensional model to fit internal and external contingencies*

4.2   Design the organisation according the the front-back model if:

    a The business environment is relatively stable and the firm relies on continuous processes to produce standard products

    b The level of process maturity is low to moderate

    c There is a limited need for internal mobility of resources

4.3   Design the organisation according to modular principles if:

    a The business environment is dynamic and/or the firm is highly project based

    b The firm would benefit from high internal resource flexibility and mobility

    c It is possible to establish the appropriate internal interfaces, systems and processes to support effective sub-unit transactions

Objective   *Reduce implementation barriers and fully exploit the value of a multidimensional model*

4.4   Ensure that the design intent is realised during implementation by avoiding overlapping or conflicting functions

4.5   Ensure that there is an enabling infrastructure to support effective sub-unit interaction and transactions (if the model includes an internal market)

4.6   Avoid fragmentation by clearly establishing the authority of the executive office to take decisions related to the architecture of the system

Review questions

1   What are the main advantages of a multidimensional structure compared to a unidimensional structure?

2   How does a multidimensional structure allow a firm to realise economies of scope?

3   What are the key differences between the matrix, front-back and modular organisation?

4   Why do matrix reporting relationships create coupling between functional requirements?

5   What are the main preconditions that must be in place in order to implement the modular organisation as defined by Russell Ackoff?

6   Can a multidimensional structure be implemented even in a small organisation?

7   Compared to a traditional organisation, do you think the modular organisation will lead to more internal competition between managers, or to more cooperative behaviour?

8   What do you think are the advantages and disadvantages for employees of being organised within a resource pool?

Research questions

1   To what extent is it possible to design a 'standard interface' in modular terms between output (product) units and market units?

2   How can modular organisations be designed to exploit the advantages of flexibility while at the same time foster the 'collective action' required to maintain coherence?

3   How can market-based resource allocation processes best be implemented in large organisations?

4   What is the evidence with regard to the effects of resource pooling?

5   How can we operationalise the concept of the modular organisation and track the degree of adoption of this model?

6   What are the performance effects of adopting multidimensional models?

7   Is the need to reorganise reduced in a multidimensional organisation (i.e., do such organisations maintain their structure over a longer period of time compared to unidimensional organisations)?

Notes

1 We define a multidimensional organisation as one consisting of a formal reporting structure where two or more dimensions are represented at the same hierarchical level (see Figure 4.1c). A 'dimension' here refers to a set of organisational sub-units having been decomposed based on a certain criterion (e.g., products, customers segments, functions, etc.). A functional organisation with *informal* coordinating mechanisms such as lateral networks does not constitute a multidimensional organisation as described here.

2 Managers in a multidimensional organisation often have a larger span of control than managers in a traditional, functional structure. On the other hand, it is possible, where there is a large number of sub-units within a dimension, to introduce an additional layer of managers co-ordinating a set of sub-units. This does not change the logic of the model described here.

3 The term 'matrix' will here be used in its original meaning, to refer to an organisation where employees have a permanent reporting relationship to more than one manager.

4 *Economies of scope* exist when the firm can realise cost savings or revenue enhancements by sharing or combining resources across multiple units (and thereby achieve 'synergies') (see Barney, 1996).

5 However, as described in Chapter 2, the removal of coupling in terms of functional requirements does not imply that one simultaneously removes *process interdependencies* between the units. In this example, the market units are clearly dependent upon the product units to deliver products.

6 To achieve an decoupled design, it is necessary to adjust the lower-level functional requirements somewhat (compare the above list of the functional requirements with those for the matrix organisation shown in Figure 4.8). The design parameters (organisational units) are the same.

7 Ackoff (1994; 1999) called this model 'the multidimensional organisation'. To avoid confusion with the two other models described in this chapter, we have chosen the term 'modular organisation' instead as it appears to conform with the criteria for defining modular systems (see Sanchez, 1995). It is also sometimes called a 'business stream organisation', where *business stream* refers to the output or product units described here.

8 The main exception is the case where the sale to a competitor of, say, a particular technology, would negatively affect the company's competitive position.

Case study

European School of Management

European School of Management is a business school with around 3,000 full-time students and 300 academic staff members. The school's mission is to develop future managers and leaders as well as to create new knowledge through its research activities. It offers both undergraduate, master level and executive education programmes. The school's main source of funding is derived from tuitions fees paid by students, but it also receives financial support from the government and from the EU for some of its research programmes.

As many other business schools, it is structured along functional lines (see Figure 4.12), in the sense that the research and teaching staff belong to an academic department depending on the area in which they specialise. (The departments are further divided into research groups/teams.) Each department is responsible for the courses in its subject area. For example, staff members in the Department of Accounting and Auditing develop and teach courses in Accounting at all levels.

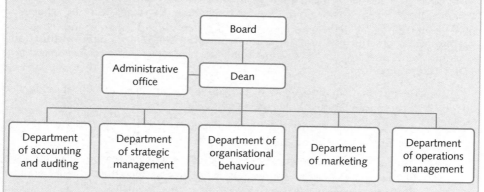

Figure 4.12 Organisation chart for European School of Management

The school recently recruited a new Dean from a US business school with a mandate to further improve the school's standing. The new Dean arranges a series of meeting with representatives from the academic departments (as well as student representatives) in order to learn more about the school's strengths and improvement areas. Several concerns about the school's organisation surface in these meetings. At the end of the meeting round, the Dean sits down and summarises the main viewpoints that have been communicated to him as follows:

1 There seems to be a lack of coordination between departments, particularly with regard to executive courses. Different departments have in the past developed partly overlapping courses and have even marketed these courses separately to prospective participants (individuals and organisations).

2 Some faculty members are concerned that the current structure does not encourage collaboration across disciplinary boundaries, particularly with regard to teaching. Each department is responsible for a set of courses and normally appoints its own

members to teach courses. In some cases, new courses could have been developed based on content from several academic disciplines, and/or utilised more highly qualified staff from another department. (The situation is somewhat different for research activities as there are a number of informal research teams crossing the department lines.)

3 The student representatives argued that the school is slow in adopting new courses and in implementing new teaching methods. Once a course is established, it tends to run for a long time, and courses on new and topical issues, such as business ethics or environmental management, have typically been adopted several years after they have become standard elements of the programmes offered at other business schools.

4 Finally, faculty members voiced strong criticism of the school's support services offered by the Administrative Office, such as facility management, IT services and secretarial support. The perception is that people performing these services lack customer orientation and fail to provide effective support to academic staff.

The Dean considers all of these issues as important improvement areas. He discusses them with his management group (the department heads) as well with the school's board, and concludes that there is a need for a systematic evaluation of the school's formal structure.

Discussion questions

1 Given the information above, how would you define the main functional requirements for European School of Management?

2 How would you tentatively describe the main design criteria that the Dean may propose based on the input he received from the meetings?

3 Could you design this business school as a multidimensional structure? If so, how? (Indicate how you would allocate responsibility between the different units along the two or more dimensions that you define.)

References

Ackoff, R. (1994). *The Democratic Corporation*. New York: Oxford University Press.

Ackoff, R. (1999). *Re-Creating the Corporation: A Design of Organizations for the 21st century*. New York: Oxford University Press.

Barney, J. (1996). *Gaining and Sustaining Competitive Advantage*. Reading, MA: Addison-Wesley.

Chi, T. and Nystrom, P. C. (1998). An economic analysis of matrix structure, using multinational corporations as an illustration. *Managerial and Decision Economics*, 19, 141–56.

Edmondson, A. C., Roberto, M. A. and Watkins, M. D. (2003). A dynamic model of top management team effectiveness: managing unstructured task streams. *Leadership Quarterly*, 14, 3, 297–325.

Ethiraj, S. K. and Levinthal, D. A. (2009). Hoping for A to Z while rewarding only A: Complex organizations and multiple goals. *Organization Science*, 20, 1, 4–21.

Galbraith, J. (1971). Matrix organization designs: how to combine functional and project forms, *Business Horizons*, February, 29–40.

Galbraith, J. (2000). *Designing the Global Corporation*. San Francisco, CA: Jossey-Bass.

Goggin, W. C. (1974). How the multidimensional structure works at Dow Corning. *Harvard Business Review*, 55, 1, 54–65.

Gulati, R. and Puranam, P. (2009). Renewal through reorganization: the value of inconsistencies between formal and informal organization. *Organization Science*, 20, 2, 422–40.

Homburg, C., Workman, J. P. and Jensen, O. (2000). Fundamental changes in marketing organization: the Movement toward a customer-focused organizational structure. *Journal of the Academy of Marketing Science*, 28, 4, 459–78.

Hoskisson, R. E., Hill, C. W. L. and Kim, H. (1993). The multidivisional structure: organizational fossil or source of value? *Journal of Management*, 19, 269–98.

Kogut, B. and Bowman, E. H. (1995). Modularity and permeability as principles of design. In Kogut, B. and Bowman, E. H. *Redesigning the firm*. New York: Oxford University Press.

Malone, T. W. (2004). *The Future of Work*. Boston, MA: Harvard Business School Press.

Mintzberg, H. (1979). *The Structuring of Organizations: A Synthesis of the Research*. Englewood Cliffs, NJ: Prentice-Hall.

Nadler, D. and Tushman, M. (1997). *Competing by Design: The Power of Organizational Architecture*. New York: Oxford University Press.

Porter, M. E. (1996). What is strategy? *Harvard Business Review*, November–December, 61–78.

Sanchez, R. (1995). Strategic flexibility in product competition. *Strategic Management Journal*, 16, 135–59.

Sanchez, R. and Heene, A. (2004). *The New Strategic Management: Organization, Competition and Competence*. New York: John Wiley & Sons.

Senge, P. M. (1993). Internal markets and learning organizations: some thoughts on uniting the two perspectives. In Halal, W. E. et al., *Internal Markets: Bringing the Power of Free Enterprise Inside Your Organization*. New York: John Wiley & Sons.

Suh, N. P. (2001). *Axiomatic Design: Advances and Applications*. New York: Oxford University Press.

Whitford, A. B. (2006). Agendas, information and conflict in matrix forms. Working paper, University of Georgia, Department of Public Administration and Policy.

Whittington, R., Pettigrew, A., Peck, S., Fenton, E. and Conyon, M. (1999). Change and complementarities in the new competitive landscape: a European Panel Study, 1992–1996. *Organisation Science*, 10, 5, 583–600.

Womack, J. P. and Jones, D. T. (1996). *Lean Thinking: Banish Waste and Create Wealth in Your Corporation*. New York: Simon & Schuster.

Worren, N. (2008). Managing the company's resource pool. *People & Strategy*, 31, 1, 42–9.

Chapter 5

Designing sub-units

Overview

Background

- Before a high-level architecture can be implemented, it needs to be operationalised by (re)designing the lower-level units that comprise the organisation
- Sub-units are (re)designed by iterative development of functional requirements and design parameters

Challenges

- Many sub-units in large organisations have ambiguous mandates or missions, making it hard to identify functional requirements
- If leaders of sub-units define the design independently, there is a risk that it may not be consistent with, or complementary to, the design of other sub-units of the organisation
- It is often difficult to obtain valid information about the work process interdependencies that should inform decisions about grouping of roles and activities
- There may also be several, competing design criteria that make it difficult to select the optimal grouping of roles or activities

Key question

- How can a sub-unit be designed in a manner that maximises the chance that its particular functional requirements will be realised, while at the same time ensuring alignment with the purpose of other sub-units and the overall organisation?

Proposed approach

- Develop a clear mission or mandate for the unit that can be the basis for identifying lower-level functional requirements

- Involve stakeholders representing higher level units and other units at the same level in establishing the mission or mandate

- Employ an analytical, 'bottom-up' approach in analysing actual work flow interdependencies to identify optimal grouping of roles

- Consider the relationship between work processes and formal structure in order to select between partitioning (dividing a unit into smaller sub-units) and integration (increasing the level of interaction between, or formally merging, two or more units)

Introduction

In the previous chapter, we considered the design of the overall *architecture* of the organisation. The overall architecture usually contains a specification of the main business areas, business units or functions (depending on the size of the organisation). In this chapter, we examine how the overall architecture is operationalised by designing (or re-designing) the sub-units comprising the organisation. If we use the multidimensional models discussed in Chapter 4 as the starting point, there will essentially be four types of sub-units that will need to be defined:

- Sales (or market) units – responsible for marketing and selling products or services

- Product (or output) units – responsible for the development and manufacturing/ delivery of products or services

- Internal service providers (or input units) – responsible for providing support, operating infrastructure or performing administrative services for product and market units

- Executive office and staff units – responsible for strategy development, policy formulation, and compliance

Each of these units may in turn be divided into smaller sub-units (departments, teams, etc.). In other words, the design process can be viewed as successively more detailed specification of the sub-systems of the organisation.

This chapter will address the twin aspects of the design methodology introduced in Chapter 1: The definition of functional requirements, derived from the sub-unit's *mission* or *mandate*, and the specification of design parameters that will ensure that the functional requirements can be achieved. Although we mentioned five types of design parameters in Chapter 1, we here focus on the sub-unit's *operating model*, that is, the main processes and work groups/teams. (In Chapter 7, the focus will be broadened to include other design parameters.)

Defining the sub-unit mission and functional requirements

In designing sub-units, a key challenge is to ensure that the sub-unit's purpose con-tributes to the achievement of the organisation's purpose *and* that the organisation enables the sub-unit to achieve things that it would otherwise not be able to achieve. (If that is not the case, the the sub-unit in question will perform better and be more valuable outside than inside the organisation.) As stated in Ackoff, 'An enterprise conceptualized as a social system should serve the purposes of both its parts and the system of which it is a part' (1994, p. 31).

However, as we have discussed in the previous chapters, the organisation's pur-pose may not always be clear. The strategies and missions developed by higher-level managers are sometimes incomplete and may contain considerable ambiguity, or even outright goal conflicts between different sub-units. Sub-unit managers who par-ticipate in the design of their unit will often need to develop and test alternative interpretations of missions or mandates, and interact with multiple constituents that must agree and accept the mission or mandate before it can be implemented.

In the following, we will consider the design of Subsea Tech, a business unit within a large engineering group that delivers oil platforms and subsea installations to the offshore oil industry. Subsea Tech is one of several business units within a *business area* (division) in this firm. The business units are legally independent com-panies, but the business area owns the majority stake of each unit. Subsea Tech designs and manufactures three main products: Pumps, compressors and actuators (actuators are devices for moving or controlling a mechanism such as a valve). The main clients are other business units in the same firm, which integrate these compo-nents into larger subsea solutions (Subsea Tech is thus currently defined as an *input unit*). The formal structure of Subsea Tech is shown in Figure 5.1. Fabrication is by far the largest sub-unit within Subsea Tech, and the one we shall focus primarily on in this chapter.

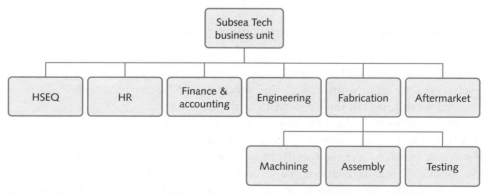

Figure 5.1 Formal structure of the Subsea Tech business unit described in the text

In the terminology introduced in previous chapters, a *mission* or *mandate* expresses the top-level functional requirement of the sub-unit (these are simply alternative terms that all refer to descriptions of a unit's purpose). Once one has agreed on the mission/top-level functional requirement, one can decompose it into more detailed functional requirements. How can we formulate an effective mission for Subsea Tech? Mission statements are sometimes criticised for being public relations attempts at improving the corporate image that bear little relation to how the organisation actually works. (For some empirical support for this view, see Wright, 2002.) How can we formulate a mission that actually creates clarity about Subsea Tech's purpose and provides guidance in the subsequent phase when roles, processes and formal structures are to be carved out? According to Haeckel (1999), an effective mission should express the organisation's *Reason for being* (why it exists), be unambiguous with regards to the *primary constituency*, and specify *the outcomes* that the unit must provide that constituency. Let us consider some alternative ways of formulating Subsea Tech's mission statement:

1 Subsea Tech exists to earn profits by delivering high quality subsea system components.

2 Subsea Techs exists to design and manufacture high quality subsea system components to internal customers while earning profits for our owners.

3 Subsea Tech exists to maximise subsea system performance for the group's end customers by delivering cost effective and highly reliable subsea system components.

4 Subsea Tech exists to provide employees with an attractive work environment and career opportunities by developing advanced components profitably for the oil industry.

What we see is that relatively minor differences in wording implies a rather different organisational purpose. In Table 5.1 each statement has been analysed by means of the framework proposed by Haeckel (1999). The primary constituent is the owner (the business area) in the first statement, the internal customers in the second statement, the end client in the third statement and the employees in the fourth. The first three statements mention 'subsea system components', while the last statement includes the term 'advanced components'. In other words, the last statement would suggest that the business unit has a more general purpose (developing *components*), while first three statements suggest that the business unit should specialise in delivering components for *subsea system installations* (which it may consider the most promising market, and one that demands the specialised expertise that Subsea Tech possesses). Also note that only the second statement specifies that the purpose of the business unit is to 'design and manufacture'. The other statements suggest that the overall purpose is to 'deliver' or 'develop' rather than design and manufacture. The second statement may thus be preferred if one would want to open up for the possibility of outsourcing the fabrication process at some point in the future. Last but not least, only the second statement indicates that Subsea Tech should limit itself to internal customers, the other three statements mention end (external) customers.

In other words, a fundamental question that would need to be clarified is whether Subsea Tech should remain an input unit, or be allowed to market and sell its products directly to external customers.

Table 5.1 Example of an analysis of alternative mission statements for Subsea Tech (based on framework proposed in Haeckel, 1999)

Action	Primary constituency	Qualifiers	Outcome
1 EARN profits	owner	Deliver high quality system components	Profits
2 DESIGN and MANUFACTURE high quality subsea components	Internal customers	Profits	Quality components
3 MAXIMISE subsea system performance	End customers	Cost-effective and reliable components	High-performing subsea systems
4 PROVIDE attractive work environment and career opportunities	Employees	Advanced components for the oil industry Profitability	Work environment and career opportunities

Which of these alternative interpretations is the most appropriate one? The owner (the business area), the external customers, the internal customers (other business units in the group), the employees and the managers of Subsea Tech may all have different interests and preferences. It will be difficult to minimise complexity and identify an effective design, unless one can get the stakeholders to agree on the fundamental purpose of the unit. The business unit leader may proactively engage the relevant constituents in interpreting and clarifying the mission. Participation by managers within the business unit should help the leader identify what Subsea Tech's unique contribution to the organisation may be. A dialogue with executives at business area and group level is required in order to ensure that the mission that is adopted is aligned with higher-level missions and strategies. Communication with other business units (including the current customers) will ensure that the unit selects a mission that is consistent and complementary to those of other sub-units within the group.[1]

In this particular case, let us assume that it is the second statement that is accepted and adopted. To '(. . .) design and manufacture high quality subsea system components for internal customers' thus becomes the top-level functional requirement. This functional requirement can be further broken down, as illustrated in Figure 5.2, into more detailed functional requirements for the core work processes performed in Subsea Tech.

Functional requirements

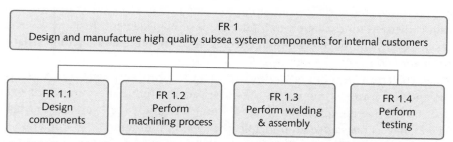

Figure 5.2 Functional requirements (FRs) for Subsea Tech identified based on the overall sub-unit mission (only FRs related to core processes are shown)

The next question is how *design parameters* should be defined to ensure that these functional requirements can be realised. If the mission statement is clear in terms of the constituents served and the desired outcomes, it should simplify the process of defining the required operating model. In this case, it is clear that *quality* is an important criterion and that specific processes or roles may be required to achieve this. The mission statement also may be interpreted as excluding some design options. It establishes that Subsea Tech will both design and manufacture components (outsourcing is thus not an option). It also specifies that it serves internal customers; if this was not the case, a business development or sales unit would probably be needed to market and sell the products externally. Despite these constraints, there is still more than one operating model that may enable Subsea Tech to realise its mission as stated here. In the next section we discuss the different options, and how one may select the most optimal one.

Defining the sub-unit operating model (design parameters)

To specify the operating model, one must consider the formal structure in relation to the work process interdependencies. We have already described the core design principle of grouping roles and sub-units to minimise interdependencies across units. This principle (formulated by Thompson, 1967) is probably not far from the lay theories that many managers hold, even if they have never been exposed to organisational theory or the organisation design literature. Most managers would agree that it is important to group related tasks or roles together. By grouping related tasks or roles together, one facilitates coordination within the unit. Application of this principle will also lead to the establishment of sub-units that are accountable for the performance of a 'whole' task (e.g., the development of a finished module or component). In dynamic and decentralised organisations, such units may to a great extent operate purposefully and autonomously, that is, be capable of setting goals, managing their own resources and solving problems that arise in the course the work, without the need for escalation to higher levels of management. In some cases, sub-units are even 'complete economic entities' that are measured on their financial performance (Zenger and Hesterly, 1997).

Nevertheless, when one examines the relationship between processes (work flow) and the formal structure in organisations carefully, one often finds examples of ineffective grouping (for a recent empirical study, see Sherman and Keller, 2011). Managers may agree, in principle, that the minimization of coordination cost should be a priority, but in practice, many grouping decisions are made on the basis of largely intuitive reasoning or custom. Von Hippel (1990) interviewed managers in aircraft manufacturers and engineering firms, and found that managers rarely analysed the work tasks and how they related to each other before making decomposition and grouping decisions:

> We have always designed aircraft bodies by dividing them into a series of cylindrical sections and assigning each section to a different task group. No one now at the company has thought about why we do this or whether it currently makes sense from any point of view. It is just the way we do it.

(p. 410)

Von Hippel concluded that in some firms, certain ways of organising are so traditional as to appear fixed, even though decomposition and grouping clearly represent variables that can be affected by management decisions. At the same time, it is important to acknowledge that it may be difficult to find an optimal grouping, even if managers are determined to apply systematic methods in finding the best organisational design for a unit. It is not always obvious what the key interdependencies are which should form the basis for the grouping. And there may also exist conflicting demands, which means that one is forced to prioritise among alternative grouping criteria.

Identifying and analysing interdependencies

Unlike the formal reporting relationships depicted on organisation charts, work process interdependencies often remain implicit. Yet it is hard to improve something that is not described or documented. To ensure that work process interdependencies become a part of the decision process regarding the formal structure, they need to be identified and analysed.

There is little disagreement with regard to the definitional framework. As proposed by Thompson (1967), we can distinguish between three levels of interdependency[2] (Figure 5.3). *Pooled interdependency* refers to a low level and indirect form of interdependency, such as when two units rely on the same pool of resources. For example, business units seeking investments may both rely on the same corporate funds; different work processes in the same company may depend on the same computer system. *Sequential interdependency* is a medium level of interdependency and means that two processes or units have a direct connection, so that the output of one process or unit is the input to the other (strictly speaking, in this relationship one unit is *dependent* on the other). The typical example is the relationship between different units along the value chain in a manufacturing firm. Finally, *reciprocal interdependency* means that there is a two-way, iterative relationship, in that the output of one process or unit is the input to another process or unit, and vice versa. Examples include the relationship between a project manager and a project member working on a consulting assignment or between a surgeon and a nurse during an operation. Reciprocal interdependency may sometimes involve ambiguous or uncertain information, making it difficult to use procedures and plans to coordinate the interaction (Donaldson, 2001). Reciprocal interdependency requires what Thompson termed *mutual adjustment* or what some later theorists have described as ad hoc coordination or interactive problem solving (von Hippel, 1990). Mutual adjustment is the most costly form of coordination. It usually requires that two parties are engaged in a direct and continuous dialogue, where each party must be prepared to change its plans and priorities based on the feedback from the other. For this reason it will usually be the first priority to contain reciprocal interdependencies within the same formal unit. Remaining sequential and pooled interdependencies between the units that are formed can then be handled by other means, such as by joint planning, rules, and procedures. In other words, we can restate Thompson's (1967) design principle as that of forming sub-unit boundaries around roles or processes with reciprocal interdependencies.

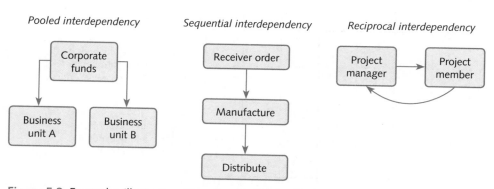

Figure 5.3 Examples illustrating Thompson's (1967) framework for levels of interdependency

Until recently, there was a lack of tools and methods that could help operationalise these concepts. It is one thing to agree on a design principle in theory, but another to ensure that it can be implemented in actual design processes. An important advance in this regard is the introduction of the Design Structure Matrix

(DSM) (Eppinger, 2001; Steward, 1981), sometimes also called Task Structure Matrix (Baldwin and Clark, 2000). The DSM is a square matrix with one row and column per activity. The DSM allows a compact representation of elements and relationships in a system and is useful for representing and analysing work flow interdependencies (Browning, 2009).

To construct a DSM, one first identifies the key tasks or process steps. One then identifies interdependencies between the tasks by asking participants who they interact with: 'Who do you need input from (e.g., physical components, information, approval, etc.) in order to complete your tasks?' And conversely 'To whom do you provide outputs?' This information is normally gathered through interviews with each of the participants in the process, but other data collection methods may also be used, such as electronic surveys or workshops. The information that is gathered is then mapped using the DSM. There are four possible ways to characterise the relationship between tasks by using the DSM (Oosterman, 2001) (Figure 5.4):

● Neither task A nor task B may be involved in an interaction (independence)

● Task A may require the output of task B or vice versa (sequential dependence)

● Task A requires outputs from B, and B requires output from A (comparable to reciprocal interdependency as defined above)

● Task A and B are both dependent upon a shared resource (pooled dependency)

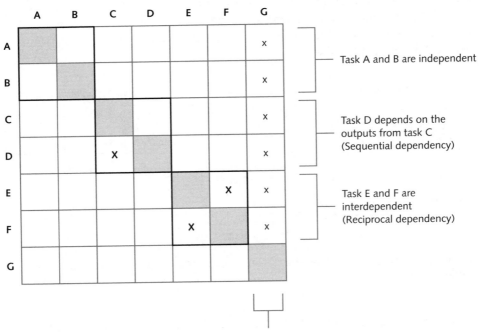

Figure 5.4 Different bilateral relationships expressed in a DSM

Once the interdependencies have been captured, one can consider different ways of clustering the tasks in order to minimise interdependencies across units. Intuitive methods can be used for systems consisting of a small number of elements. In the example provided in Figure 5.5, six elements have been clustered into two units, with no remaining interdependencies across the two units. For more complex processes, there now exist software packages[3] that can assist in identifying the optimal clustering of elements (and thereby the size and number of groups of elements) based on interdependencies.

There are two main types of DSMs. What we have described so far is a 'task-based' DSM where the elements (rows) represent steps in a work process. But the matrix elements may also represent organisational units (this is sometimes called a 'team-based' DSM). The same principles apply, except that a team-based DSM does not imply a time sequence (in a task based DSM, the elements are listed in chronological order, with early activities listed in the upper rows (A precedes B)). A restructuring of a team-based DSM will only indicate an alternative *grouping* (clustering) of roles or sub-units, whereas a restructuring of a task-based DSM will indicate an alternative *task sequence* as well as an alternative grouping.

In Figures 5.4 and 5.5, an 'X' is used in the examples to denote the presence of an interdependency. However, in more sophisticated applications, one also distinguishes between interdependencies of different strength or frequency. For example, members of a work unit may be asked to indicate on a scale from 1–3 *how frequently* they need to receive information from other people in order to complete their tasks.

It is obviously the case that the interdependencies that are identified need to be valid for the subsequent analysis to produce appropriate groupings. If one asks people what information they need to complete their tasks, different people may interpret 'information' in different ways. Various types of information, such as formal data and friendly communication, may be mixed up (Oosterman, 2001). However, this concern may at least partly be mitigated by the fact that the DSM collects information about *bilateral* relations. One asks two people about the same interdependency and may validate the information by evaluating whether the required *inputs* that have been identified by some participants match the *outputs* that other participants state that they feel responsible for providing (see Browning, 2009 for an example).

Locating sub-unit boundaries (interfaces)

To consider in more detail how to group roles and define sub-unit boundaries, let us return to the Subsea Tech example. It will be recalled that Subsea Tech designs and manufactures three main products (pumps, compressors and actuators). In order to illustrate the key concepts, some simplifying assumptions will be made:

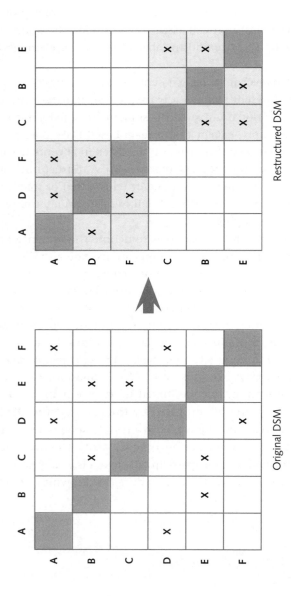

Figure 5.5 Example of clustering of DSM elements

- We focus on two main sub-units: Engineering and Fabrication (we ignore other sub-units such as Sales, Procurement, HR and Accounting)
- We assume that there are 3 employees in each of the 4 sub-units/teams
- We assume initially that the work load is relatively stable over time and similar across the teams
- We highlight work process interdependencies and leave out interdependencies due to the hierarchical structure (i.e., between employees and their managers)

The two main functional requirements of Subsea Tech are to design and manufacture components. The manufacturing operation was further divided into: Machining (fabrication of metal components), welding and assembly, and testing. In the current organisation, each process is carried out by a separate team at the manufacturing plant (see Table 5.2 below and Figure 5.1 above).

Table 5.2 Functional requirements and design parameters for Subsea Tech

	Design parameters			
Functional requirements	Engineering department	Machining team	Assembly team	Testing team
Design components	X			
Perform machining process		X		
Perform welding and assembly process			X	
Perform testing process				X

The work process is by and large sequential, and each worker within the team specialises in a particular procedure. For example, in the Machining team, the first worker receives engineering drawings and raw materials (corrosion-resistant steel), and goes on to set the parameters in computer-assisted machines. The second worker performs the initial turning and milling, and the component is then transferred to another machine where the third worker performs drilling operations. But the three workers also need to coordinate between them as every product is slightly different and may require some adjustment in the procedures used, or even the sequence of different operations.

Let us examine the boundaries between the units. In the DSM shown in Figure 5.6, the four teams are indicated as bold squares. The blocks of 'Xs' in the matrix indicate that the work within each team is interdependent. However, we also see three interdependencies outside the blocks, which represent sequential interdependencies between the teams (e.g., the product must be assembled before it can be tested).

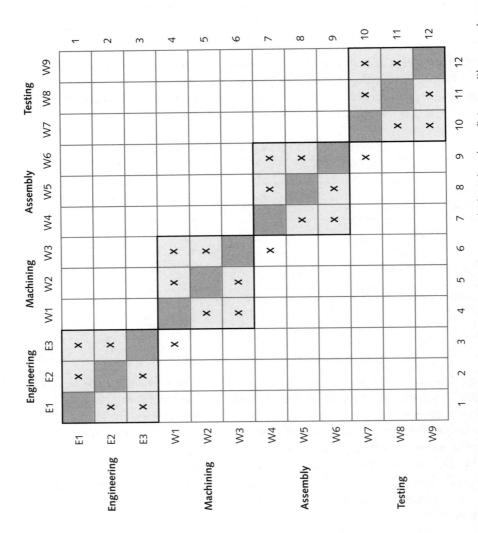

Figure 5.6 Interdependencies between employees belonging to four functional (discipline-based) teams (three engineers and nine workers in the manufacturing plant)

Although this structure represents a well proven, functional (discipline-based) grouping, we may still, as suggested by Baldwin and Clark (2006), ask why the boundaries are located as they are, and the consequences that would follow from altering the boundaries.[4] The first phase of the process is to *design* the products. In this phase, the three engineers (E1, E2, E3) capture the technical specifications, perform calculations and produce drawings and models using computer assisted design tools. The boundary between Engineering and the next team, Machining, is located at the point at which the the physical hand-over of manufacturing specifications occurs (the sequential dependency indicated in Figure 5.6 between Engineer 3 (E3) and Worker 1 (W1)), which provides the information that the Machining team needs to initiate the fabrication of the products. The boundary between the two teams is a natural one, for several reasons. One could imagine, as an alternative, that the boundary was pushed forward and that the Machining team also included Engineer 3 (E3). This would mean that the Machining team would receive unfinished engineering designs as an input, and would have to complete them before initiating the manufacturing process. It would probably also imply more diffuse accountabilities, as the output from the Engineering team would to a lesser degree constitute a distinct, measurable deliverable. How would you monitor and evaluate a partially completed deliverable? On the other hand, moving the boundary downwards, by including worker 1 (W1) or 2 (W2) in the Engineering team, would mean that the deliverable to be transferred would include completed drawings, plus a partially completed mechanical component. In general, the boundaries between units that are linked together by sequential interdependencies are usually located at the junctures with *a measurable output* (Zenger and Hesterly, 1997). By circumscribing activities with a measurable output, one allows monitoring of output levels and evaluation of efficiency. Monitoring and evaluation allows the introduction of performance based incentives – members of the unit can be rewarded based on their productivity. Once you can measure the output you also have the opportunity to introduce a (financial) transaction at the transfer point (Baldwin and Clark, 2006). In a large manufacturing firm, the designs could potentially be valued and sold at an internal transfer price to the internal client (the manufacturing plant). In sum, locating the boundaries around activities with a measurable output allows the creation of 'complete economic entities', even at lower levels of the organisation (Zenger and Hesterly, 1997).

Evaluating alternative grouping criteria

We have confirmed that a functional (discipline-based) grouping may provide logical boundaries between the teams in Subsea Tech's fabrication facility. Yet this is not the only possible grouping under all circumstances. In fact, there exists several possible grouping criteria and the key task for organisational designers is to identify the relative priority of the different criteria.

Let us consider an alternative way in which to group the three manufacturing teams. So far, we have assumed that the fabrication process is largely sequential, and that a team effort is required, in that the three workers in each team need to coordinate with each other in the execution of the process that the team is responsible for (however, each worker specialises in a sub-process, such as milling). We have also assumed that each worker is able to perform his/her particular sub-process to manufacture all of the products (pumps, compressors, actuators). However, let us consider the situation that emerges if the firm decides to introduce multi-task machines that can perform several processes (e.g., turning, milling, drilling, etc.), combined with a 'job enlargement' scheme where each worker is given additional training in order to operate the machines and perform *all of the tasks* that his/her team was previously responsible for. At the same time, let us assume that the scope of work is limited to one of the products (i.e., each worker must now specialise by focusing on either pumps, compressors or actuators). The result is a shift in the interdependencies: Each worker is now independent from the other members of the functionally defined (disciplined-based) teams – no longer providing outputs to, nor receiving inputs from, the other two workers who used to be part of his/her team. (On the other hand, new interdependencies will arise toward the other workers working on the same product.) The component can move from one step of the manufacturing process to the next when one worker has completed his/her job. The three products can also be worked upon in parallel. The interdependencies that arise in this situation are depicted in Figure 5.7.

As we see in Figure 5.7., the interdependencies are in this case poorly aligned with a functional (discipline-based) grouping. To rectify this, one should structure the organisation by *product*. A product-based structure creates 'manufacturing cells' where each cell is made responsible for the fabrication of one product (see Table 5.3 and Figure 5.8). Note that a product-based structure would satisfy the criteria discussed above with regard to boundary definition, to an even greater extent than the functional (discipline-based) organisation. It avoids the sequential interdependencies between the teams. Morever, a finished product – which is the output produced by a team in a product-based structure – is not only measurable internally, but also externally, as it may be valued and priced based on comparison with other offerings in the market.

Table 5.3 Alternative product-based decomposition (compare with Table 5.2)

Functional requirements	Design parameters		
	Pumps team	Compressor team	Actuator team
Manufacture pumps	X		
Manufacture compressors		X	
Manufacture actuators			X

We thus have two alternative groupings. Is the product-based structure the optimal one? Not necessarily. As noted above, the functional (discipline-based) structure implies significant *sequential* interdependencies across the three departments in

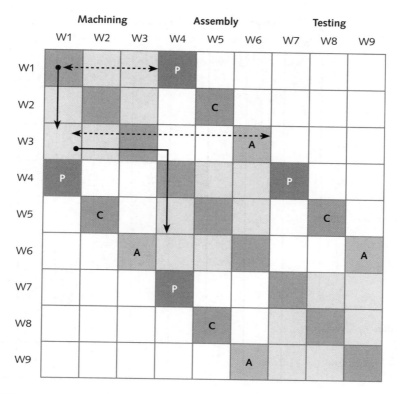

Figure 5.7 Interdependencies created by introducing multi-task machines combined with job enlargement and product focus (compare with Figure 5.6). The letters P, C and A refer to the products (pumps, compressors, and actuators). The solid lines indicate the work flow for the fabrication of pumps. The dotted lines indicate communication between workers. The shaded blocks represent the original functionally defined (discipline-based) teams

terms of the work process. The product must pass through three separate departments in order to be manufactured. A decision in the first team that results in a delay in the machining process will most likely affect the assembly process for all three products. The product-based structure, on the other hand, would contain the work process related, sequential interdependencies within each team. The key advantage of this model is that the product only passes through one department. Decisions regarding a given product can probably be taken more quickly as changes in one team are less likely to affect the other teams.

A product-based structure also has some important limitations, however. It implies that knowledge sharing about working methods would need to occur across the teams, as workers performing the same work process (e.g., machining) are now spread in three different teams, whereas they were together in the same team in the functional (discipline-based) structure. (Note: such interdependencies due to a need for knowledge sharing or coordination about working methods were omitted from

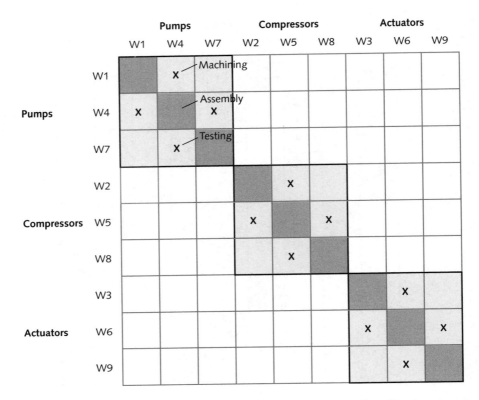

Figure 5.8 DSM of alternative, product-based grouping of manufacturing teams. Compare the grouping of roles (W1, W4, W7 etc.) to that in Figure 5.6

Figure 5.7 and 5.8.) However, the most important limitation is that the model presupposes that each of the sub-units is able to utilise its capacity effectively over time. In a product-based (cell) structure, capacity imbalances may occur at times, such as when the worker performing testing in the Compressor team is idle due to lower demand for its product, while the worker performing the same process in Pumps team is overworked. Empirical research has shown that one of the key obstacles to implementing cell-based manufacturing is identifying part families with enough demand volume and demand stability over time (Johnson and Wemmerlöv, 2004). If demand for the different products fluctuates over time, it may be more cost effective to 'pool' resources; one way to do this is to revert to the more traditional functional (discipline-based) structure.

Resource utilisation is sometimes considered an 'operations management problem' rather than an organisation design problem.[5] Yet, as we see in this case, it is possible to imagine that it may not be economically feasible in some cases to group reciprocally interdependent positions together in the same unit, even if that may be optimal from a work process perspective.

To understand fully the impact that a proposed change in the formal structure of an organisation will have, one thus needs to evaluate the effect of alternative groupings on both work process interdependencies and resource utilisation. A possible outcome of such an evaluation is the introduction of a hybrid model, i.e., a grouping based on a combination of two criteria. Based on such a rationale, the managers at the plant in Subsea Tech might conclude that workers performing one of the processes, such as testing, should be grouped together, while the product-based grouping should be maintained with regards to the other manufacturing processes (see Figure 5.9).

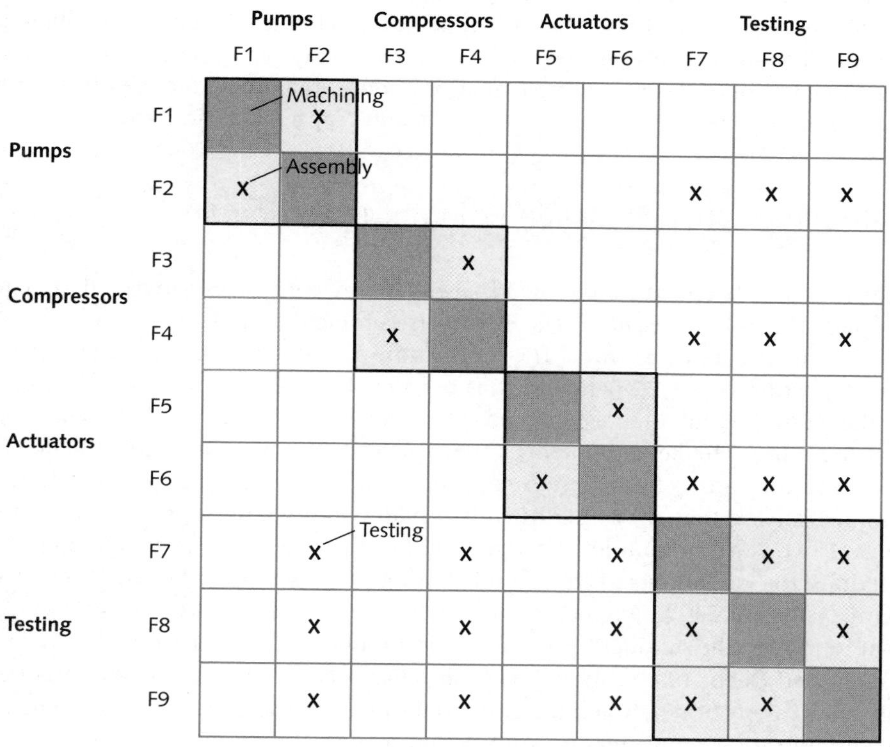

Figure 5.9 Product based grouping of machining and assembly workers combined with functional (discipline-based) grouping of workers performing testing

A unit that is related to a number of other units in the same manner, such as the testing unit in this example, is called a 'bus' in DSM terminology (Sharman and Yassine, 2004). A familiar example is shared services units that provide transactional services to business units in a large firm. As in our example here, shared services units are created by consolidating resources that were previously dispersed in various business units into a common unit that is intended to interact with internal clients in a uniform way.

Even if a hybrid structure is chosen, some weaker, 'residual' interdependencies (Mintzberg, 1979) will often remain that have not been picked up by the grouping criterion chosen as the basis for the formal structure. We already mentioned that there may some interdependencies due to a need for knowledge sharing among workers performing the same process. Such interdependencies will need to be managed by employing different, compensatory means. If a plant selects a product- or cell-based grouping, as in the case just described, workers performing the same process may find other, informal means, such as discussion forums, to share experiences and ideas regarding their working methods. Similarly, instead of reverting to a functional (discipline-based) structure, a plant manager may find alternative ways to compensate for uneven resource utilisation levels across the product-based teams (manufacturing cells). The plant manager may implement a capacity planning system to predict the required resource levels, or implement procedures that allow foremen to 'borrow' resources from each other in order to utilise the total capacity of the plant.

Alternative characterisation of interdependencies

In the example described we assumed that the interdependences between design and manufacturing were *sequential*. The engineers complete a product design and hand it over to manufacturing where the fabrication process takes place. However, this characterisation of interdependence has been challenged by a number of scholars, and the 'design-build' interface has become a classic issue in the technology management literature. The key argument is that this conception of interdependence has led to organisational 'silos'. Design engineers sometimes develop new components without realising that they are difficult to manufacture, and there has often been a lack of two-way communication that could provide feedback to design engineers sometimes the constraints of the manufacturing processes. Manufacturing engineers often have to ask design engineers late in the cycle (sometimes as late as the testing stage) to modify the product so that it can be produced to meet cost or quality goals (Susman and Dean, 1992). The solution that has been advocated has typically been to increase interaction between the two groups by improving the type and frequency of communication or by creating joint design-manufacturing teams. In other words, the design-build interface may in reality be characterised by *reciprocal* interdependencies, thus necessitating closer integration.

However, von Hippel (1990) argued that it would not be appropriate to try to bridge or eliminate the boundary between product design and manufacturing in all firms. The literature has often focused on innovation projects involving new technologies. But the situation is different for more mature technologies and processes. Many firms employ modern manufacturing technologies that are capable of producing a range of new designs. Von Hippel cites book printing as an example. Book authors do not have to write their books with the needs of the printer in mind. Hence, there will not usually be a need for interactive problem solving or two-way communication between printers and authors. (He also notes, however, that a graphics designer trying to do something that pushes the limits of existing printing processes may well find close coordination with the printer to be valuable.)

A firm that experiences problems with the design–build interface should not only consider the boundary between design and manufacturing but also how the process itself may be improved. The product engineers and the manufacturing engineers could work together to agree on *standards for manufacturability* that specify some general rules for how new components are to be developed given the existing manufacturing processes. It may thus be possible to reduce the need for coordination by establishing common standards that the engineers can consult when designing new products (Baldwin and Clark, 2000). These standards essentially remove interdependencies and take the place of on-going coordination between individuals belonging to different teams.

The introduction of software systems sometimes has a similar effect. As an example, consider the task of scheduling a meeting among several participants. If one does not know the other participants' availability, one will usually have to contact each of them in order to find a time suitable for all. With software tools (e.g., Microsoft Outlook), this task is greatly simplified in that the software will indicate the times when all of the participants are available. As long as everybody updates their calendar and has some available time, one does not need to expend much effort to schedule the meeting. Similarly, the need for interaction between designers and manufacturing engineers may be reduced if engineers have access to component databases that list approved components with descriptions of their physical properties, functional characteristics, manufacturing requirements, and so on.

Determining group size

Unit size will, in principle, follow from the decomposition that one arrives at after defining unit boundaries. The basic building blocks of the organisation correspond to the grouping of interdependencies that are identified in the DSM; the optimal unit size from this point of view is the size that maximises intra-unit and minimises cross-unit interdependence. Nevertheless, one still has the option of combining the different building blocks or adjusting the size of a unit by altering the interdependencies that formed the basis for the grouping. For this reason it can be useful to briefly review the main approaches that have been proposed in the literature with regard to the optimal size of sub-units.

At an operational level, the required sub-unit size will in some cases be derived from estimates of 'minimum critical mass'. For example, a consulting firm considering geographical expansion may want to know how large new offices must be in order to justify the cost of establishing and running the office. It may calculate the minimum size of an office based on knowledge of the typical utilisation rate of its consultants, the cost of renting office space and the cost of support personnel to run an office. The conclusion may be that an office must have at least 10 or 15 people in order to justify its costs.

A more strategic approach, mainly relevant to the definition of the main business units, is to match the size of internal units with the size of the market segment

(Christensen, 1997; Eisenhardt and Brown, 1999). A small business unit may not possess the technical or financial resources required to compete in a large market. A large business unit, on the other hand, will have difficulty targeting niche opportunities for growth. (Large and integrated firms often have difficulties justifying investments in emerging technologies because they initially represent only a small fraction of the firm's potential revenues.)

A third approach is advocated by some authors that believe that there are psychological and biological laws governing the efficient size of social sub-systems. This approach is usually based on considerations of cognitive or social psychological constraints to working in large and complex systems. Nicholson (1997; 1998) suggested that there are evolutionary reasons for why human beings prefer to be part of 'herds' of no more than 15–20 people within larger 'clans'. Most studies point to the advantage of small group size on participation and group cohesiveness. Units that reach more than 10 members tend to fraction into cliques (smaller groups). For much of human evolution, individuals lived their lives within a clan system and would rarely if ever encounter a stranger, i.e., someone from outside the kinship network of the clan. Our psychology is as a consequence geared to a known and finite social universe and the social information processing capacity may therefore correspond to what we encounter in a typical clan. The ABB case is frequently cited. In its heyday, ABB was a federation of approximately 1,500 business units, each of which consisted of only 150 people. Eisenhardt and Brown (1999) similarly noted that Microsoft tries to keep its applications businesses at or below 200 people.

On the other hand, some scholars have pointed out that a decrease in the average size of units comes at the price of an increasing number of units overall, leading to a sharp rise in the number of interfaces (see Figure 5.10). The basic trade-off is thus often presented as one of choosing between having a few large subsystems that are in themselves complex but provide few subsystem interfaces, or dividing the system into the smallest possible units, but at the price of having numerous individual units with many subsystem interfaces (Chroust, 2004). A sub-unit manager in a complex organisation may spend half his time coordinating with other units, and may easily become bogged down as the number of interfaces increases (Rechtin, 1991).

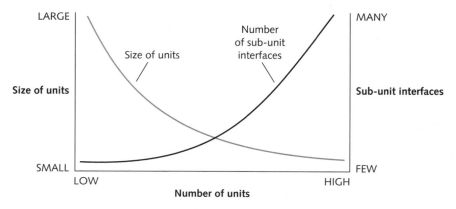

Figure 5.10 Trade-off between size of units and number of units

In reality, the trade-off between size and number of units will depend on the particular nature of the interfaces. It is considerably more time-consuming to handle reciprocal interdependencies than sequential or pooled interdependencies. Sub-unit managers may relatively easily be able to handle a large number of interfaces if they involve standard processes; for example, an internal IT department may be perfectly capable of delivering services to a large number of internal clients, as long as it delivers a standardised service and transacts with each internal client in more or less the same manner (i.e., there exists a *standard interface* between the unit and its internal clients). The internal structure of the unit also influences its possible size. A work unit with a high degree of reciprocal interdependence among its members will require more intense supervision by the unit manager. Consequently, such units will need to be relatively small for the manager to have adequate capacity for supervision (Mintzberg, 1979). On the other hand, a manager may be able to supervise a large number of people – or oversee a large number of sub-units – if the level of interdependency is low. In some retail banks, for example, there are dozens of branch managers reporting to the same divisional executive.

This distinction also partly explains the overall trend toward increasing 'disaggregation' of organisations, that is, downsizing of large firms combined with the introduction of smaller, more autonomous internal units that are treated much like external subcontractors. As explained in Zenger and Hesterly (1997), disaggregation occurs when organisations are able to create semi-autonomous units that are responsible for a complete deliverable and that can be measured on their outputs (as opposed to their resource utilisation or costs). An important enabler for this development is the introduction of enterprise resource planning (ERP) systems that allows precise and timely monitoring of the activities of internal units and that supports transactions between internal customers and suppliers.

Aligning formal structure with work process interdependencies

Effective grouping involves *partitioning* of processes that are characterised by sequential or pooled interdependency, and *integration of* processes with reciprocal interdependences (Figure 5.11). Partitioning entails the creation of one or more structural boundaries (e.g., by dividing a unit into two sub-units), whereas integration involves the removal of one or more boundaries (e.g., merging two sub-units). There are potential pitfalls associated with both options. A lack of coordination (often attributed to organisational 'silos') is often the result if one partitions a process with *reciprocal* interdependencies. The appropriate solution would be to increase interaction across the boundary of the units concerned or to eliminate the boundary altogether. On the other hand, one will usually not obtain any benefit from integrating processes with *sequential or pooled* interdependency into one unit. In fact, it may in some cases produce unwanted costs. Combining two or more different, weakly related units may frustrate efforts at creating a clear group identity around a functional specialisation. The integrated structure may also produce a number of interaction points that result in time being spent on unnecessary and unwanted coordination. Integration increases the size of units and implies that the manager of the combined unit will be responsible for a potentially large set of weakly related processes. Members might be expected to participate in joint meetings and interchange information via e-mail, leading to information overload. Decisions processes may slow down as more stakeholders may have a say in the outcome. Integration may also lead to more diffuse accountability and make it more difficult to assign credit or blame to individuals or teams within the combined unit.

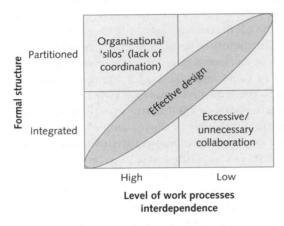

Figure 5.11 The relationship between formal structure (grouping) and work process interdependencies

As indicated in Figure 5.11, the organisational designer has two main levers at his or her disposal. To adjust the formal structure to fit the interdependencies or to manipulate the interdependencies to fit the current organisational structure. The latter option is less frequently discussed but is equally important. As we touched on when discussing the design-build interface, common standards and 'design rules' can be introduced that help participants in a process anticipate interactions and thereby reduce the level of reciprocal interdependence.

This reasoning also points to why ineffective groupings exist or why a grouping that might be perceived as effective today moves out of 'fit' over time. First, the structural design decisions may simply be made without considering work processes. Design decisions are often made by senior managers, who may not be able (or have the necessary data) to identify the actual interdependencies at lower levels of the organisation. However, even if data are available, or a more operational-level manager makes the grouping decision, it will be difficult to make the correct judgement in those cases where people develop new technologies or perform novel processes with unknown interdependencies. In such cases the appropriate strategy is to have a flexible structure that can be adapted as the project evolves. However, even in more stable organisations where it is easier to predict interdependencies, the design can gradually move out of 'fit'. Over time, people document and standardise the different steps of a process, learn to anticipate interdependencies between activities and often develop rules and procedures that reduce the need for coordination or remove the interdependence altogether. This is part of what is referred to as 'process maturity' (Curtis et al., 2002). The formal structure needs to be adapted in step with increasing maturity of the work processes.

In making grouping decisions, one does not need to restrict oneself to the inter-dependencies that are recognised and well understood today. A strategic approach to grouping should include pragmatic ways of considering *potential* interdepend-encies, that is, interdependencies that *can or should be developed* (or removed) to achieve some purpose (e.g., improved organisational performance) (Ensign, 1998). An excellent example is described in McKelvey and Kilmann (1975), who used a statistical technique similar to the DSM approach described here. McKelvey and Kilmann participated in the organisation design of a business school at a large uni-versity. The dean and faculty wanted to change the structure of the school. The key challenge was to identify the right sub-units (which were called study centres, essen-tially groups of researchers). The goal was to maximise the homogeneity of research interests within the group (in order to encourage mutual support and collaborative research projects) while minimising task based interactions across the groups. In accordance with this goal, they developed a questionnaire where the faculty mem-bers were asked to indicate who, among the other faculty members, they would like to collaborate with in their own research activities over the next years (a seven-point scale was used, from 'not at all', to 'none I'd like more'). A statistical technique called factor analysis was then used to identify the optimal groupings. McKelvey and Kilmann also later verified that the the actual organisation that was implemented was in accordance with the suggested grouping. This example demonstrates how the DSM approach can be used to map potential or ideal interdependencies that are required to support a design objective. Moreover, whereas the DSM may be perceived as a purely analytical tool to be used in 'expert driven' processes, this example shows that the DSM can be part of a participatory process that takes into consideration the preferences of individual members of an organisation.

Summary and conclusion

The process of forming sub-units can be viewed from two perspectives. Whereas the decomposition of functional requirements focuses on the ends, the definition of the design parameters (including a unit's operating model) specifies the means. In prac-tice, one often needs to iterate between the two modes of design.[6] One may start by breaking down a high-level mission into functional requirements, but then reverse this process by working bottom up at a later stage in the process in grouping related roles or processes into common units (Mintzberg, 1979).

The key choice facing organisational designers is whether to *partition or integrate* a given set of sub-units (or roles, processes). The general rule is to partition when there is a low level of interdependence and to integrate when there is a high level of inter-dependency. The Design Structure Matrix (DSM) is a tool that facilitates the analysis of interdependencies and the identification of correct groupings. Organisational design-ers may also be able to manipulate the interdependencies themselves by re-designing the process in a manner that reduces the need for coordination.

Competing grouping criteria may sometimes exist. For example, decisions makers may have to choose between a grouping that optimises work process interdependen-cies and one that maximises resource utilisation. There is no universal prescription in such cases, but the recommended approach is to explicitly evaluate all the costs and benefits of a proposed design solution. Once a decision has been taken about the primary grouping criterion, compensatory means should be developed to address the remaining, 'residual' interdependencies between roles or sub-units.

In our discussion in this chapter, we have focused mainly on the relationship between the work process interdependencies and the formal structure. In Chapter 7 we broaden our focus by considering *different types* of interdependencies that arise as a consequence of sub-unit grouping and how these can be managed on a more continuous basis.

Design propositions

Objective   *Create clarity with regards to a sub-unit's functional requirements (FRs)*

5.1   Create an overall mission or mandate for the sub-unit that identi-fies key outcomes, the primary constituent, and constraints

5.2   Involve key stakeholders in interpreting and clarifying the sub-unit mission

5.3   Ensure that the mission is aligned with the higher-level organi-sational architecture of the firm and that it is consistent and complementary to the missions of other sub-units at the same level (i.e., that coupling is avoided)

5.4   Use the mission as the basis for defining lower-level functional requirements for processes, teams, departments, etc.

Objective   *Define an operating model that creates effective working processes within and across different sub-units*

5.5   Identify current and future process interdependencies required to achieve the functional requirements that have been defined

5.6   Define a tentative grouping based on the grouping criterion that partitions the elements (roles, tasks, sub-units) that are lowest in interdependence and integrates elements (roles, tasks, sub-units) that are most highly interdependent

5.7   If an excessive number of interdependencies remain across units in this proposed grouping, consider changing the grouping crite-rion or removing interdependencies (e.g., by establishing common plans, rules or standards)

5.8 Adjust the proposed grouping to reach an adequate group size, depending on the level of interdependency within the group and the number of interfaces overall

5.9 Evaluate the benefit of implementing the proposed grouping against any potential additional costs stemming from e.g., reduced scale or resource utilisation

Review questions

1 Why is it valuable to invest time in clarifying the mission or mandate of a sub-unit as part of the design process?

2 What are the key elements of mission statements according to Haeckel (1999)?

3 What different types of interdependencies exist according to Thompson (1967)?

4 How may these interdependencies be represented in a Design Structure Matrix (DSM)?

5 How may interdependencies between different roles be identified?

6 Why are interdependencies sometimes neglected?

7 How may the formal structure best be aligned with work process interdependencies?

8 What considerations are important when determining the size of units?

9 Try to obtain an organisation chart for a fairly large firm or governmental organisation (e.g., by accessing its internet site). What grouping criteria have been used to define the units? Have consistent criteria been used at the same level, and at different levels hierarchically?

Research questions

1 Managers must sometimes choose between a grouping that optimises work flow and a grouping that optimises resource utilisation or that provides economies of scale. Is it possible to develop a formal, quantitative methodology that could support managers in making such trade-offs?

2 How could we develop better metrics to assess interdependencies, eg., the degree of modularity (sub-unit independence) of a system represented in a DSM?

3 In his doctoral dissertation, Bas Oosterman (2001, p. 57) voiced some concerns about the DSM. He pointed out that the DSM matrix does not clearly distinguish between what needs to be coordinated from the coordination activity itself (an 'X' in a cell may refer to either). How could the conceptual framework underlying the DSM be improved to address this concern?

4 Well-known social psychological studies suggest that people placed in the same groups (even random groups) quickly develop a shared group identity. This may have some implications for the DSM approach, as it assumes that one can restructure the

DSM without affecting the interdependencies between the elements. Is it possible that grouping in itself will lead to the establishment of interdependencies between those that are placed in the same unit/team?

Case study

Merger between Atlantic Life and Dutch Mutual

Atlantic Life and Dutch Mutual are two insurance companies that have merged and are in the process of integrating their organisations. The combined entity will be called Dutch Atlantic Life. As part of the integration process, management must decide how to organise the claims processing unit. A project team has been established to look at this issue.

Dutch Atlantic Life will offer three types of insurance policies:

1 Disability – financial support in the event of the policyholder becoming unable to work because of disabling illness or injury.

2 Pension – benefits that are paid when the member reaches a specified retirement age

3 Life – benefits paid to a designated beneficiary upon the death of the insured

Dutch Atlantic will serve three main market segments: individuals, companies and governmental institutions. In each case, it is an individual (or their descendants) that is being insured. However, the market segments are structured in this manner as employers (in the public and private sector) enter into agreements with insurance companies on behalf of their employees, who are then automatically enrolled in a pension plan or insurance scheme (the Individuals segment includes people who do not work for a company that provides insurance benefits and those who are self-employed).

In insurance companies, *Claims processing units* receive insurance claims, evaluate supporting documentation (e.g., medical records), validate the claim against the policy and calculate the amount to be paid. Resources associated with claims processing are a major cost for insurance companies, consequently higher level management follow up closely the efficiency of the unit's work processes, for example, by monitoring the average number of claims managed per employee (examiner).

Important goals for the unit are to calculate the payments correctly, comply with internal guidelines stipulating the processing time for applications (e.g., 3 weeks for disability insurance), while minimising payments due to fraudulent claims.

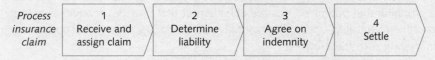

| Process insurance claim | 1 Receive and assign claim | 2 Determine liability | 3 Agree on indemnity | 4 Settle |

Figure 5.12 Mapping done by project team of work process

During the initial phase of the work, the project team reviews the work processes and the existing organisation of both Atlantic Life and Dutch Mutual. A consultant documents the key work processes, and finds that they are similar, at least at a high level (Figure 5.12). However, the two companies have organised the claims processing unit in a diametrically opposed manner (see Figure 5.13): Atlantic Life has a market/customer-based structure, whereas Dutch Mutual has a product-based structure. The members of the project team are uncertain about which of these two models to recommend.

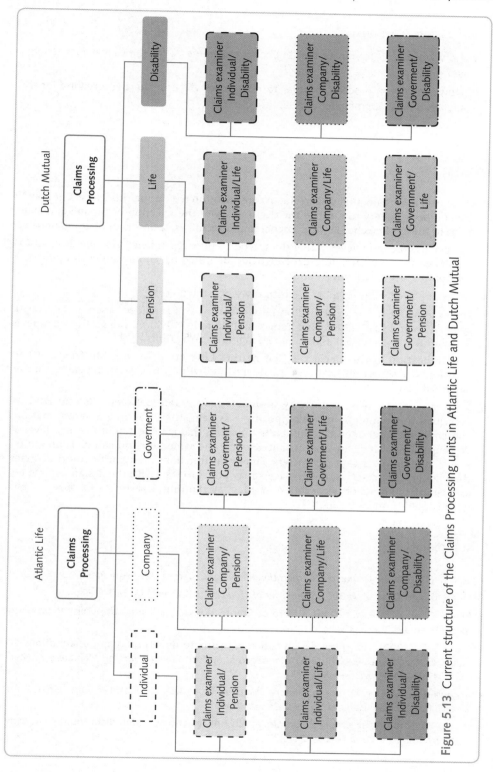

Figure 5.13 Current structure of the Claims Processing units in Atlantic Life and Dutch Mutual

Discussion questions

1 How would you formulate the functional requirements for the Claims Processing unit?

2 How would you proceed in order to determine which of the two organisational models is most appropriate for Atlantic Dutch?

Notes

1 Of course, if fundamental disagreements are encountered during this process, it may in the end be necessary to escalate the decision about the selection of the mission statement to the key stakeholder (e.g., higher level executives, sponsors or board members).

2 We here use the term 'level' rather than 'type' of interdependency as Donaldson (2001) concluded that the three interdependencies identified by Thompson correspond to a scale of increasing task uncertainty.

3 For examples of software tools, see http://www.dsmweb.org/

4 The example in the text is based on Litterer (1973) and extended based on later work by Baldwin and Clark (2006) and Zenger and Hesterly (1997). Although the example is fictitious it reflects several aspects of real manufacturing firms.

5 One indication of this neglect is that neither Litterer (1973) nor Mintzberg (1979) mentioned resource utilisations considerations when discussing the same case as described here.

6 There are several reasons for why designers may iterate between FRs and DPs. As described in Chapter 1, in decomposing a system, the design parameters that are chosen at one level often determine the functions that are relevant at the next level of decomposition. There are also instances where the same function can be achieved by several alternative design parameters. Finally, as functions are typically more abstract than design parameters, some managers may prefer to start with the design parameters and define the function second ('We need an accounting department for sure . . . but what should its mandate be?').

References

Ackoff, R. (1994). *The Democratic Corporation*. New York: Oxford University Press.

Baldwin, C. and Clark, K. (2000). *The Power of Modularity*. Boston, MA: MIT Press.

Baldwin, C. and Clark, K. (2006). Where do transactions come from? Unpublished working paper, Harvard Business School.

Browning, T. (2009). Using the design structure matrix to design program organizations. In Sage, A. P. and Rouse, W. B. (eds), *Handbook of Systems Engineering and Management* (2nd edn), 1401–24. New York: Wiley.

Christensen, C. M. (1997). *The Innovator's Dilemma: When New Technologies Cause Great Firms to Fail*. Boston, MA: Harvard Business School Press.

Chroust, G. (2004). The empty chair: Uncertain futures and systemic dichotomies. *Systems Research and Behavioral Science*, 21, 227–36.

Curtis, B., Hefley, W. E. and Miller, S. (2002). *People Capability Maturity Model: Guidelines for Improving the Workforce*. Reading, MA: Addison-Wesley.

Donaldson, L. (2001). *The Contingency Theory of Organizations*. Thousand Oaks, CA: Sage Publications.

Eisenhardt, K. and Brown, S. (1999). Patching: Restitching business portfolios. *Harvard Business Review*, May–June, 72–82.

Ensign, C. (1998). Interdependency, coordination, and structure in complex organizations. *Mid-Atlantic Journal of Business*, 34, 1, 5–22.

Eppinger, S. D. (2001). Innovation at the speed of information. *Harvard Business Review*, January, 149–58.

Haeckel, S. H. (1999). *Adaptive Enterprise: Creating and Leading Sense-and-Respond Organizations*. Boston, MA: Harvard Business School Press.

Johnson, D. J. and Wemmerlöv, U. (2004). Why does cell implementation stop? Factors influencing cell penetration in manufacturing plants. *Production and Operations Management*, 13, 3, 272–89.

Litterer, J. A. (1973). *The Analysis of Organizations*. New York: John Wiley & Sons.

McKelvey, B. and Kilmann, R. H. (1975). Organization design: A participative multivariate approach. *Administrative Science Quarterly*, 20, 24–36.

Mintzberg, H. (1979). *The Structuring of Organizations*. Englewood Cliffs, NJ: Prentice-Hall.

Nicholson, N. (1997). Evolutionary psychology: Toward a new view of human nature and organizational society. *Human Relations*, 9, 1053–79.

Nicholson, N. (1998). How hardwired is human behavior? *Harvard Business Review*, 76, 4, 134–47.

Oosterman, B. J. (2001). Improving product development projects by matching product architecture and organization. Unpublished doctoral dissertation, University of Groningen.

Rechtin, E. (1991). *Systems Architecting: Creating & Building Complex Systems*. Englewood Cliffs, NJ: Prentice-Hall.

Sanchez, R. (1995). Strategic flexibility in product competition. *Strategic Management Journal*, 16, 135–59.

Sharman, D. M. and Yassine, A. A. (2004). Characterizing complex product architectures. *Systems Engineering*, 7, 1, 35–60.

Sherman, J. D. and Keller, R. T. (2011). Suboptimal assessment of interunit task interdependence: Modes of integration and information processing for coordination performance. *Organization Science*, 22, 1, 245–61.

Steward, D. (1981). The design structure system: A method for managing the design of complex systems. *IEEE Transactions on Engineering Management*, EM-28, 3, 71–4.

Susman, G. I. and Dean, J. W. (1992). Development of a model for predicting design for manufacturability effectiveness. In Susman, G. (ed.), *Integrating Design and Manufacturing for Competitive Advantage*, 207–27. New York: Oxford University Press.

Thompson, J. D. (1967). *Organizations in Action*. New York: McGraw-Hill.

von Hippel, E. (1990). Task partitioning: An innovation process variable. *Research Policy*, 19, 5, 407–18.

Wright, N. J. (2002). Mission and reality and what not? *Journal of Change Management*, 3, 1, 30–44.

Zenger, T. R. and Hesterly, W. (1997). The disaggregation of corporations: selective intervention, high-powered incentives, and molecular units. *Organization Science*, 8, 3, 209–22.

Chapter 6

Structuring vertical layers

Overview

Background

- Defining the accountabilities of key jobs at different organisational levels is a core task in organisation design

- For this purpose one may use Requisite Organisation (RO), a framework originally developed by Elliot Jaques in the 1970s

- RO places the main emphasis on appropriate definition of formal, vertical structures or 'accountability hierarchies'

Challenges

- Some of the assumptions behind RO may seem to be at odds with the realities of modern organisations, characterised by:

  - Work processes that cross formal hierarchical lines of authority

  - Lack of predictability and subsequently lower emphasis on long-term planning

  - Less reliance on predefined positions and greater ability of individual workers to shape their own jobs

- Yet even flexible, project-based organisations need a minimum of structure and clarity with regard to accountability

Key question

- Is it possible to adapt RO to the realities of modern organisations so that it can serve as a framework for defining vertical structures?

Proposed approach

- Clarify RO concepts to avoid common misunderstandings
- Increase applicability of RO by describing jobs in terms of outcomes as opposed to activities
- Combine RO with the concept of the modular organisation to create layered structure in flexible, project-based firms

Introduction

The preceding chapters have mainly focused on the horizontal dimension of organisations, in considering how to design the overall architecture of firms and the interfaces between organisational sub-units. However, one must obviously attend to both the horizontal and vertical dimensions in re-designing large organisations. One does not have an implementable design before one has identified the required number of management layers and defined the responsibilities of key positions at different levels. In this chapter, we will consider how to approach such issues. We will also discuss how an earlier framework for hierarchical/vertical structuring – originally developed for organisations in relatively stable market environments – can be adapted to the demands of today's flexible, project-based organisations.

The ideal hierarchy

Compared to the situation 30 or 40 years ago, it is clear that organisations today rely more strongly on horizontal coordination mechanisms as opposed to hierarchical control (Whittington et al., 1999; Zenger and Hesterly, 1997). Yet all large organisations remain hierarchically structured to some degree. The key question is thus how we can design hierarchies to serve the needs of both the organisation and its internal and external stakeholders.

Let us first consider some of the basic logic for structuring hierarchical systems. It is easy enough to agree on the criteria for an ideal hierarchical system (see Figure 6.1). But it is also true that the structure of most organisations tends to depart somewhat from an ideal hierarchical structure. Over time, roles are added or removed, responsibilities altered and reporting lines changed to accommodate new business opportunities as well as individual preferences, and such adjustments are not necessarily carried out in a coherent or consistent manner. An initial task in a re-design project could be to identify the main logical inconsistencies in the current formal structure. In the subsequent phases, a key priority may be to avoid the introduction of new inconsistencies when developing a new design. A useful list of criteria is Abrahamson's (2002) summary of common deviations from an 'ideal' hierarchical structure (Figure 6.2).

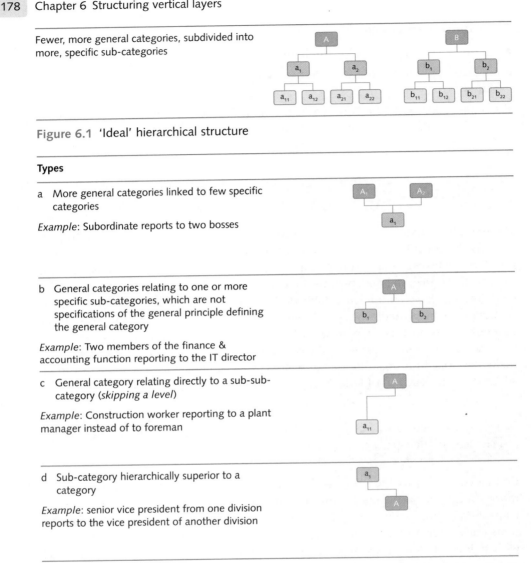

Fewer, more general categories, subdivided into more, specific sub-categories

Figure 6.1 'Ideal' hierarchical structure

Types

a   More general categories linked to few specific categories

Example: Subordinate reports to two bosses

b   General categories relating to one or more specific sub-categories, which are not specifications of the general principle defining the general category

Example: Two members of the finance & accounting function reporting to the IT director

c   General category relating directly to a sub-sub-category (*skipping a level*)

Example: Construction worker reporting to a plant manager instead of to foreman

d   Sub-category hierarchically superior to a category

Example: senior vice president from one division reports to the vice president of another division

Figure 6.2 Deviations from 'ideal' hierarchical structure
Source: Adapted from Abrahamson, 2002.

However, it is not a deviation from an ideal hierarchical structure per se that is a problem, but the consequences that sometimes result from such a deviation. It may be perfectly acceptable for a subordinate to report to two bosses, if the subordinate experiences that there is relative clarity about goals and priorities in his or her job. It may not be acceptable to have two bosses if it results in conflicting priorities and it thus has a negative impact on the subordinate's ability to perform their job. Similarly, it may not be a major problem if a senior vice president reports to a vice president, if this confusion is only due to an idiosyncratic use of titles in different units of the firm. It may be more problematical, however, if the vice president is in fact responsible for more complex tasks than the senior vice president, who may then be unable to provide guidance and support to his direct report (let alone provide the necessary coordination toward other units that interface with the unit managed by the senior vice president). Idiosyncrasies in hierarchical structures also create challenges for large organisations that intend to standardise their operations or introduce common, company-wide processes. A company may be planning a new reward system for all executives at level 1–3 of the company (i.e., those at two levels below the CEO) but may find that the official chart does not reflect the actual job functions and level of responsibility of the different executives, and that people at level 4 in some units carry more responsibility than those at level 3 in other units. Similarly, to ensure compliance with external accounting regulations, a company may need to introduce a clear separation of duties in terms of who requests and who approves financial expenditures. But it may find that the currently defined reporting structure is too ambiguous or incomplete to serve as a basis for defining such responsibilities.[1]

The requisite organisation approach

Of course, correcting errors in the design of the formal structure is not enough to assure that it actually fulfils its purpose. How do we design hierarchies to maximise motivation, productivity and performance? This question was addressed in depth by the late management theorist Elliott Jaques, who, between 1950 and his death in 2003, published a number of works aimed at describing the optimal design of hierarchical structures (Jaques, 1970; 1986; 1989; Jaques and Clement, 1991). He referred to organisations as 'accountability hierarchies', pointing out that they are essentially systems for getting things done. His key purpose was to create designs that enable a large number of people to work together yet preserve unambiguous accountability, place people with the necessary competence at each organisational layer, and ensure that each manager adds value to the work of his or her subordinates.

Although he was trained as a psychotherapist, Jaques concluded that problems in working relationships are often caused by dysfunctional systems rather than by dysfunctional people. He was sceptical of interventions aimed at changing the attitudes and behaviour of individuals. For example, he believed that confusion and mistrust in working relationships (such as between manager and employee, or between members of different internal units) often develop as a result of inappropriate or missing specification of roles and reporting relationships. The key intervention he advocated was thus to create more clarity with regard to accountability and authority. He also proposed that organisations should carefully match the capability of individuals with the requirements of different roles. Jaques initially referred to this approach as *stratified systems theory* (SST) in that it sought to determine the optimal number of layers (strata) in complex organisations and the key individual capabilities required to perform roles at different strata.[2] (Among practitioners today, the approach is more commonly referred to as Requisite Organisation (RO).)

Organisational layers and managerial hierarchies are traditionally defined based on indicators related to size. For example, an organisation may use the number of people reporting to a manager and the magnitude of their sales or profits in order to determine at what level of the organisation the manager's role should be placed. Jaques argued, however, that a more relevant criterion for structuring organisations would be the *complexity of tasks*. More specifically, RO is built on the following assumptions.

1 Tasks that must be performed in an organisation vary in terms of their level of complexity[3]

2 Sharp discontinuities in task complexity exist that separate tasks into a series of steps (or strata)

3 Similarly, the capacity for working at different levels of task complexity differs among individuals, and may also be categorised as a series of steps (or strata)

Solving tasks of low complexity involves the processing of fairly tangible information and only requires the ability to follow an assigned plan or procedure, while tasks of high complexity require the ability to handle ambiguous information, construct alternative routes to a goal, consider multiple, interrelated issues in parallel, and predict the long-term consequences of actions. The essence of RO is to consider the requirements of roles at different levels in relation to the capacity people have for handling the task requirements: 'As [task complexity] gets greater, the feeling of weight of responsibility increases, and the greater the working-capacity you must have in order to cope' (Jaques, 1989, p. 37). Jaques believed that the most effective employees have a capability that matches the requirements at the level they are at. Common sense would lead us to predict that employees faced with tasks that demand higher capacity than they possess will perform poorly and also may experience stress and anxiety. But RO also leads us to predict the reverse: that it may be dysfunctional if individuals have a capability that exceeds the requirements of the work tasks at their level. A lack of challenge in the job may lead to frustration for the individual. The cognitive complexity required at senior levels may be a liability at lower levels where direct judgement and quick action are needed (Popper and Gluskinos, 1993).

To quickly determine the complexity of a given role, Jaques invented the use of 'time span', which is basically the planning horizon required to perform a role successfully.[4] The role of leading a large organisation may require a time span of 10 or more years, while the role of production worker may only require a time span of one day. Jaques concluded that there are at most seven different strata, suggesting that even a large organisation may need no more than seven hierarchical levels, from the shop floor to the CEO role (the key characteristics of the strata are summarised in Table 6.1). Because task complexity is the key criterion for placing roles at different strata, Jaques proposed that certain roles responsible for complex tasks, such as research and development, should be placed near the top of the hierarchy and report to the COO or CEO, even in the case where the individuals holding the roles have no subordinates.

Table 6.1 Summary of the organisational strata proposed by Elliott Jaques

Domain	Level	Typical title	Time span	Key tasks
Systems/ strategic	VII	Chief Executive Officer	20 years or more	Interpret environmental trends, understand impact of alternative scenarios, conceptualise long-term mission and strategy, initiate structural changes
	VI	CFO; COO etc.	10–20 years	Set broad direction for entire systems/ organisations, build consensus among internal and external constituents for required changes
General management	V	Executive vice president; business unit president	5–10 years	Manage uncertainty, make continual adjustments to changes in the business environment
	IV	General manager; department manager	2–5 years	Handle several interacting projects, manage interdependencies between sub-units
Operations	III	Unit manager	1–2 years	Make trade-offs between short-term and long-term goals; interpret trends (e.g., quality data)
	II	Supervisor	3–12 months	Exercise diagnostic judgement and initiate actions to deal with identified problems/ obstacles
	I	Production worker; operators; clerk	1 day – 3 months	Perform well-defined tasks

An absolute condition set by Jaques was that *managers should always be in the next higher strata* from their subordinates in terms of their working capacity. If a manager is at the same level as the subordinates he predicted that they would be unable to provide effective leadership:

Such a manager cannot set adequate context; gets involved in too much detail; breathes down the subordinate's neck; seems to be comfortable doing work that the subordinate ought to be doing; does not add any value; is inclined to take all the credit for what goes well, and to blame subordinate for everything that goes wrong . . . It is the exact opposite of what managerial leadership ought to be.

(Jaques & Clement, 1991, p. 42)

It is interesting to note that the phenomenon that Jaques describes is essentially an example of *coupling* as defined in Chapter 2 (Table 6.2). The only difference from the cases discussed in Chapter 2 is that we are here talking about vertical as opposed to horizontal relationships. The solution to remove the coupling in this case is to ensure that individuals with the right working capacity are selected, and that roles and responsibilities are properly defined.

Table 6.2 Consequence of a lack of separation in strata

	Design parameters	
Functional requirements	Manager	Subordinate
Perform managerial tasks	**X**	x
Perform subordinate tasks	x	**X**

Jaques claimed that the actual organisation often would work according to the strata defined in RO, even if the formal organisation chart suggested otherwise. For example, he observed that if the manager of a group of employees does not possess a cognitive capacity superior to his or her employees, the employees will frequently consider another manager, at the level (stratum) above their own, to be 'the real manager'. In contrast, what Jaques termed 'requisite' organisation is one where the extant (actual) organisation is aligned with the formal structure of the firm (Dive, 2004). The number of levels in such an organisation reflects the actual differences in task complexity across the different levels. Promotion is a move from one level of accountability to another, and the manager who appears on the organisation chart is the person that the direct reports actually turn to for advice and supervision.

Application of requisite organisation concepts in re-design processes

In determining the shape of the formal structure, one will, for obvious reasons, need to consider the vertical and horizontal dimension simultaneously. An organisation with broad spans of control (i.e., a higher number of direct reports for each manager) will have few vertical layers. Conversely, an organisation with narrow spans of control will have more vertical layers (Figure 6.3) (Littener, 1973). The key is to find an appropriate balance. Increasing the span of control implies a lower cost, as the number of managers is reduced, but it may also decrease the overall effectiveness of the organisation if it results in insufficient capacity for supervision and coordination of the work of employees. Increasing the span of control by removing management positions also reduces the opportunities for promotion, which in turn may impact motivation and effort. On the other hand, Jaques and other proponents of RO have often argued that the span of control is generally too narrow in most organisations (i.e., there are unnecessary layers). When the span of control is too narrow, people with seemingly distinct titles in fact perform work at the same level of complexity; which limits the accountability of each individual manager and slows down the speed of decision making.

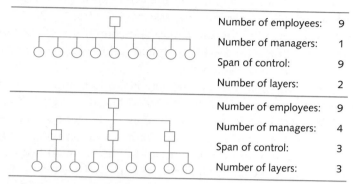

Number of employees:	9
Number of managers:	1
Span of control:	9
Number of layers:	2
Number of employees:	9
Number of managers:	4
Span of control:	3
Number of layers:	3

Figure 6.3 Comparison between broad and narrow span of control

Dive (2004) describes the case of Unilever plc, a firm with 170,000 employees and 20,000 managers, which during the 1990s, used the RO concepts[5] to simplify its hierarchical structure. In order to verify the required number of levels, interviews were conducted with managers in several units. The aim of the interviews was to identify the unique accountabilities at each level. This was done by asking the managers what decisions they made, that their subordinates could not make, and also what decisions the managers made, that their boss did not need to make. Based on these results, 17 existing job grades were reduced to only five work levels, which became the basis for performance management, compensation and leadership development (Dive, 2004).

The applicability of requisite organisation concepts in modern organisations

Stratified systems theory remains popular among some consultants and HR managers. By and large, however, it receives little attention today and is almost completely ignored in the mainstream literature.[6] This paucity of interest in Jaques' work is perhaps not surprising. With its focus on deliberate planning and hierarchical structure, it does not seem to be a good fit for those seeking methods and frameworks for managing flexible, project-based organisations. Nevertheless, Jaques addressed some fundamental managerial challenges and offered innovative and intriguing solutions to problems faced by many – if not most – organisations. To identify the potential value and the possible imitations of RO it is worthwhile examining some of the core assumptions in more detail and consider to what extent these depart from current assumptions about organising large firms.

Requisite organisation is essentially a system for defining and structuring jobs. But the concept of a job has changed over time as a result of the introduction of new organisational forms. Organisations used to be fairly stable and well-defined entities, which made it possible for managers to carefully design all key aspects of the job before hiring a new employee: identifying the tasks and responsibilities of the job, defining the required skills to perform the tasks, and positioning the job at the right organisational level depending on the nature and complexity of the tasks. Indeed, there is a whole discipline, with specific tools and techniques, dedicated to the issue of job design (e.g., Parker and Wall, 1998).

In large organisations today, however, there is typically much less specification of jobs than before; more depends on the individual holding the role. The typical output of job design – a job description – may no longer be a meaningful tool. Haeckel (1999) noted that collaboration and communication processes in organisations basically revolve around negotiation and fulfilment of ad hoc commitments (see Chapter 7). To improve clarity in terms of what is expected of the individual job (role) holder, he suggested that each employee maintain an updated list of commitments that he or she has made to other employees, a list of the commitments that others have made to him or her, and the status of both. Compared to the tasks and responsibilities in the typical job description, such commitments will usually be more specific, focused on a concrete deliverable or goal, rather than on a repetitive task or permanent area of responsibility. Moreover, whereas job descriptions represent vertical agreements (between a subordinate and his/her manager) commitments are usually made horizontally, between people accountable for producing specific business outcomes (Haeckel, 1999).

Even in organisations where formal job descriptions still exist, the scope and content of the roles that people perform gradually expand, contract or change focus. Some authors have proposed that employees are *architects of their own jobs* (Wrzesniewski and Dutton, 2001). Employees influence both the number and nature of tasks that are performed, exercise discretion in terms of selecting who they should interact with, and even alter the very purpose and identity of their own role. An employee with energy and initiative will be able to craft his or her own role.

The changing concept of jobs also affects career structures and employment relationships more generally. RO included frameworks for creating career trajectories (career paths) and systematic methods for assessing future potential and defining criteria for promotions (i.e., succession planning). Similar frameworks and methods have been popularised by other authors[7] (e.g., Charan et al., 2001) and form the basis for the HR and leadership development processes in many large firms. The goal for many of these firms was to create long-term succession plans to ensure that they had the leadership talent ready when they needed it. As an example, Exxon Mobil reportedly had already hired its CEO for the year 2010 in 1988, in order to develop, assess and prepare the candidate for the top job (McManis and Leibman, 1988). Current authors, however, are sceptical of the ability of firms to create long-term career plans for their people or develop specialised skills that fit future strategic needs. It is difficult to predict who will have relevant skills in the future if the business environment is undergoing rapid change. Capelli (2008), for example, noted that the uncertainty faced by many companies necessitate frequent updates and changes to the succession plans, as strategies and jobs change (and as individuals leave the organisation). Rather than attempting to align people with a particular strategy, some authors have suggested that one should instead develop a broad skill base that allows the company to create the capability to implement a wide range of strategies (Snow and Snell, 1993).

Discussion

Few would contest that jobs, career paths and leadership development processes have undergone change as a result of the emergence of new and more flexible ways of working. But do these observations necessarily invalidate the key assumption behind requisite organisation systems?

We should note first that although the concept of jobs has changed, it has not vanished. The reality is that organisations are still structured around jobs (Sparrow and Cooper, 2003). However, the general emphasis among practitioners and management thinkers has shifted to a more individualistic and 'people-oriented' view. Some modern management thinkers even seem to believe that structures may emerge as they may, if one only has the right set of people.[8] Such a view does contradict Jaques, who strongly favoured 'structure first' – mission followed by structure followed by selection and education. He defined an organisation as a set of roles, not as a collection of people, although roles are occupied by people. He argued that unless structure comes first, there would be no consistent way of identifying who should lead whom or ensure that those who do not fulfil role requirements are removed, if necessary (Jaques and Clement, 1991).

Yet it is easy to misunderstand the purpose of systems of vertical structuring such as RO. For example, Jaques in no way assumed that information would only flow along the formal reporting lines of the organisation, or that actual working relations would be perfectly aligned with the formal structure of an organisation. On the contrary, Jaques acknowledged that many employees would participate in cross-functional projects, work with and for managers at several levels and possibly in several internal units of the organisation. In fact, Jaques outlined principles for structuring a range of role arrangements, including those related to advisory relationships between colleagues and temporary assignments for managers in other parts of the organisation.

On the other hand, it is precisely the complexity of such work processes and working relationships that often lead to a deterioration of accountability and a lack of clarity with regard to goals and priorities. One symptom is that employees in large organisations sometimes find it difficult to name an individual manager that they report to. They may be uncertain whether the boss is the project manager, the internal client, the functional manager or some other, hierarchically superior manager. But Jaques insisted that one should be able to define a clear, coherent and consistent *accountability hierarchy*, even in large and complex organisations. In other words, one could argue that the concepts in RO are all the more relevant, the more complex the overall organisational structure is.

Although the RO concepts may at first sight appear to be an elaborate excuse for a 'top-down' management philosophy, Jaques actually saw RO as a prerequisite for achieving fair treatment of employees and for implementing systematic people development processes. He recommended that managers should be judged not only on their ability to attain business related outcomes (e.g., sales and profits targets) but also on their effectiveness as leaders, including their ability to create an effective working environment, utilise the existing skills and competencies, and develop their people.

The definition of a manager is the key premise. A manager, according to Jaques, is someone who is held accountable for the outputs of others. Instead of asking who a given employee 'reports to', he suggested that one should turn the question around by asking who is accountable for the performance of the employee. One may work with and for many managers, but only one should be held accountable for the effectiveness of any given employee – and that person is the employee's manager. (And, as already mentioned, to handle the complexity inherent in his or her own role, and provide effective leadership to subordinates, the manager should have a cognitive working capacity one level above the subordinates whom he or she leads.)

Jaques believed that people's working-capacity would mature throughout life, although the rates of progression would be different from person to person. (In general, the higher a person's potential working capacity, the faster is the rate of maturation and the later in life it continues to grow.) Thus in addition to placing people in the right strata based on their current working capacity, an important additional task is periodically assessing their future potential. Jaques offered an important and intriguing idea for how this process should be carried out. He suggested that one should follow what is sometimes called the 'grandfather principle', namely that the manager's manager, rather than an employee's direct manager, should be responsible for assessing the employee's future potential. The manager's manager works at a higher stratum and thus has a broader overview of the requirements at different levels and the future opportunities that may exist in the organisation. Although the practice is widespread, Jaques deemed it illogical asking a line manager to assess the potential of his or her current subordinates. If the potential of a subordinate is deemed high and the employee is promoted, he or she will, in many instances, become a subordinate of the manager's manager. (The line manager's favourite employee may not be the one that the manager's manager judges to be the most qualified to join his or her team.) According to RO, it is also the manager's manager who should monitor the manager's leadership performance. In sum, a proper implementation of RO would *make leaders accountable for developing their people.*

We mentioned above that whereas RO presupposes that there are predefined roles in an organisation, there is typically a low level of specification of jobs in fast-changing organisations, such as project-based firms. The more dynamic the organisation, the greater the need to periodically reassess the purpose of different roles; in many role relationships it may also be up to the job holders themselves to agree on the boundaries between their roles and their respective responsibilities. But even if we accept that it is harder to design jobs in advance, and that creative employees in any case will (and should) shape their own roles, we may simultaneously acknowledge that there needs to be 'minimal critical specifications' of roles and accountabilities in a hierarchical system. However, it may be possible to bridge these seemingly contradictory concerns.

One may increase the applicability of RO in dynamic organisations by modifying how individual jobs are designed. It is customary to define individual jobs by listing the *activities* that the individual is supposed to perform. For example, a job description for a Chief Financial Officer (CFO) may contain lists of activities such as 'prepare budgets', 'oversee accounting practices', and 'analyse financial performance'. Such job descriptions are often quite detailed and lengthy, which means that they are difficult to maintain. Traditional job descriptions also do surprisingly little to clarify the purpose of the job or even why the role exists at all (Haeckel, 1999). An alternative is instead to define jobs in terms of accountabilities and outcomes. Outcome-oriented job descriptions focus on the desired results, while leaving it to the job holder to decide which activities are required to attain the outcomes that have been agreed.

Haeckel (1999) maintained that accountabilities only exist in connection with commitments between people: A person must be accountable to someone, which means no one can be generically accountable for sales, manufacturing, or quality. He proposed the following format for specifying accountabilities: '*In the role as [role name], [name of person] is accountable to [customer] for [outcome]*' (Haeckel, 1999, p. 146).

The desired outcome may be more fully described by adding the customer's conditions of satisfaction, i.e., criteria for acceptable performance, such as delivery time or quality level. Often it is possible to substitute a long list of activities with one or two sentences that express the purpose of the job in this manner (see Table 6.3 for examples). Evaluation of performance will then be based on the ability to deliver the specified outcomes rather than on the ability to carry out tasks skilfully, which is the likely focus when jobs are defined in terms of activities. Outcome-oriented job descriptions provide management with a tool for the definition of jobs, while at the same time allowing the individual job holder to shape the content of the job and create new ways to respond to unexpected events.

Table 6.3 The difference between activities and outcomes, exemplified by excerpts from three job descriptions

Role	Activities/tasks	Outcomes
Sales executive	• Develop sales and marketing strategy • Oversee development of sales and marketing materials • Plan customer visits • Develop proposals • Negotiate contracts	• Acquire two new major accounts • Increase customer retention • Ensure customer satisfaction
Manager responsible for Health, Safety and Environment	• Develop HSE policy • Communicate HSE guidelines to business unit staff • Conduct audits to ensure compliance with HSE policy • Monitor and report HSE incidents • Regularly review HSE performance in leadership team	• Create proactive HSE culture, as measured in HSE attitude survey • Minimise frequency and severity of incidents
Payroll clerk	• Compile employee time, production and payroll data from time sheets and other records • Record employee information, such as exemptions, transfers and resignations, to maintain and update payroll records • Compute wages and deductions and enter data into computers	• Salary and benefits paid without errors or delays

The relevance of RO is not limited to traditional line organisations. In fact, RO can support the design of highly flexible, project-based organisations. One example is firms where employees are organised in a resource pool (Figure 6.4). (This is a key feature of the modular organisational form described in Chapter 4.) This is a model that traditionally has been used by many professional services firms, but there are also examples of its use in other industries. Some project-based engineering firms use resources pools to organise its engineers, and some hospitals organise nurses in 'float pools' (Worren, 2008).

As an internal service provider, the resource pool assigns people to projects based on requests from internal clients (e.g., projects or business units). Once an employee has been assigned to a project initiated by a product unit, the employee works for a project manager in the product unit on a day-to-day basis. However, the permanent reporting relationship of employees is to a *people manager* belonging to the resource pool. A larger resource pool may be divided into several skills groups, each led by a skill group leader (people manager). A manufacturing company may define skill groups representing different technical and commercial disciplines, such as marketing, engineering, and operations. There will usually be slightly different roles and competency requirements within each skill group, leading to a set of career paths.

It is common to define role/career levels in a resource pool based on competence requirements for the different career paths. The competence requirements that are defined for each layer support selection decisions, assessment of performance and also provide criteria for promotion within the career track (or transfers to other skill groups). For example, in a consulting firm, consultants may enter the firm as junior consultants, and advance to consultant and project manager once they demonstrate that they perform according to the requirements defined for those levels. In an engineering firm, there may be different career levels such as junior and senior engineers, chief engineer, and so on. The role/career levels may have a structure similar to the strata defined in RO. The main difference is that the role structure and the competence requirements in a resource pool will relate to the type of tasks that one will be responsible for in temporary projects, rather than the more permanent tasks of a line management role in the organisation. One example would be the requirements for project managers, which are usually defined based on the size and complexity of projects that one is able to manage (Table 6.4).

Table 6.4 Example of roles and competence requirements used to define levels (strata) of resource pool

Level	Role	Requirements
V	Project director/ programme manager	• In-depth knowledge and skills of tools and processes used to plan, organise and control projects • Able to lead large, complex projects, often involving several technical disciplines, or programmes of longer duration consisting of multiple, interrelated projects
IV	Project manager	• In-depth knowledge and skills of tools and processes used to plan, organise and control projects • Able to lead projects of small to medium-size and low to moderate complexity
III	Project team member	• Familiar with basic project management tools and processes • With increasing experience, able to take responsibility for separate deliverables/work streams within a project

Applying RO principles in the design of the resource pool means that it becomes possible to maintain a layered role structure even in a flexible, project-based firm (Figure 6.4). This also means that systematic people development processes can be implemented. The resource pool is the 'home base' and a stable core in an otherwise changeable structure. The people managers in the resource pool are responsible for supporting staffing decisions, providing feedback to the individual employee and creating individual development plans based on the employees' own preferences and development needs. It may not be possible in such an organisation to develop detailed and long-term succession plans, but a resource pool should, at a more aggregate level, be able to forecast the overall demand for different role categories, which can form the basis for longer term recruitment and development plans.

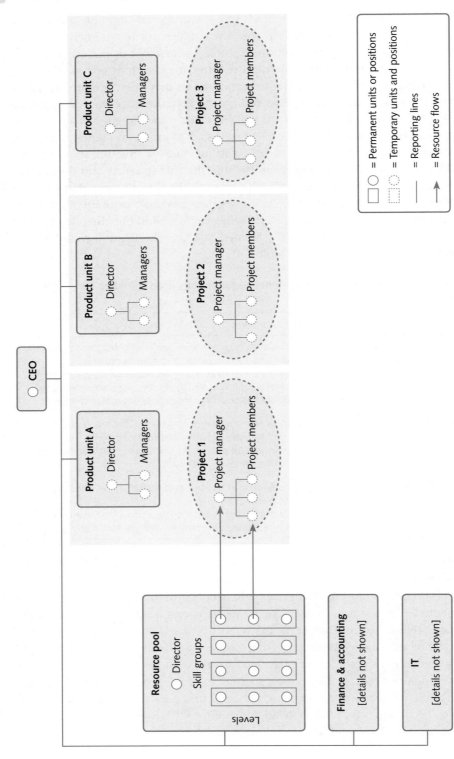

Figure 6.4 Resource pool structured according to RO principles in project-based organisation

Summary and conclusion

The key concepts of Requisite organisation provide a useful 'lens' through which to view an organisation, and a clear set of normative criteria for structuring vertical relations, which complement the other design tools and frameworks described in this book. But RO is largely ignored by academics today and is often associated with the design of traditional, 'hierarchical' organisations. Yet we have seen in this chapter that it may be possible to adapt and extend RO to the demands of modern organisations. By specifying jobs in terms of outcomes rather than activities, one creates a structure for accountability while at the same time providing job holders with the autonomy to define the best way to perform their tasks. Another alternative is to combine RO with the concept of the modular organisation described in Chapter 4, by applying RO in defining the vertical structure of resource pools. This makes it possible to maintain a well defined role structure even in dynamic, project-based organisations. In conclusion, with some modifications, RO remains a relevant framework for structuring the vertical dimension of organisations.

Design propositions

Objective   Achieve clarity with regards to accountability, allow each manager to add value to the work of his or her subordinates, and ensure that people with the required competence are placed at each organisational level

6.1   Remove deviations from an 'ideal' hierarchical structure that negatively affect organisational effectiveness (cf. Figure 6.2)

6.2   Design the vertical structure in line with the principles in the Requisite organisation approach (Jaques, 1989; Jaques and Clement, 1991), i.e.:

a   Define a requisite number of organisational strata (maximum 7)

b   Place people into each strata that have the required working capacity to handle the level of task complexity encountered at that level

c   Ensure that each role reports to a role located in the stratum above

d   Hold managers accountable for the results of their immediate subordinates

e   Ensure that managers have minimum managerial authority, including the right to veto appointments of new subordinates and the removal from role

f   Designate the manager's manager as accountable for assessing future potential and evaluating the manager's leadership effectiveness

6.3   In project-based organisations, apply the same principles as above but with the following modifications:

   a   organise people who perform ad hoc activities or temporary projects in a resource pool

   b   structure the role /career levels of the resource pool according to the RO principles

Review questions

1   One of the basic assumptions in RO is that managers should be one level above their subordinates in terms of ability to handle task complexity. How does this compare with the assumptions made in theories of leadership advanced by other authors?

2   What concerns would you expect that managers and employees might have with regard to the application of RO concepts in their organisation? To what extent are these concerns well founded? To what extent may they be addressed by revising some elements of RO?

3   Draw a diagram of the hierarchical layers of an organisation that you know or can obtain information about (e.g., your employer or your university). To what extent does the formal structure correspond to an ideal structure according to RO?

4   What does the word accountability entail? To what extent are managers in the average organisation accountable, in the sense of the word used by Jaques?

5   Are large organisations able to place the right people at the right level? What indications do we have to suggest that this may or may not be the case?

Research questions[10]

1   What are the effects, on individuals and organisations, of mismatches between individual working capacity and task requirements?

2   What is the reliability and validity of time span as a proxy for task complexity?

3   What are the most reliable and most convenient methods for assessing individual's working capacity?

4   To what extent does the introduction of a structure based on RO improve the perceived fairness of key HR processes related to appraisals, succession plans, reward and promotions?

5   What are the key prerequisites for institutionalising the role of the manager's manager as advocated by Jaques?

6 Did Jaques pay sufficient attention to the non-cognitive aspects of leadership, such as emotional intelligence?

7 To what extent is individual working capacity as defined by Jaques correlated with organisational capabilities? To what extent may strong institutional processes and systems compensate for either low individual working capacity, or mismatches between person and role?

Notes

1 Sherman (2005) describes a company that was using the organisation chart to analyse existing reporting relationships. Out of 17,000 people, it had 400 people who did not report to anybody and 35 who reported to each other.

2 Jaques did not limit his analysis to the *manifest* organisation (the organisation as officially presented on the organisation chart) but considered the *extant* organisation as well (how the organisation actually functions). For example, an organisation chart may depict four different hierarchical layers while a closer analysis of the real authority relationships would suggest that only three exist.

3 It is important to distinguish this notion of task complexity (related to individual roles and job requirements) from the notion of organisational complexity (a characteristic of an entire organisation) used in Chapter 2 of this book.

4 More specifically, the level of a role can be assessed by considering the time span of discretion of the longest task in the role (Jaques, 1989).

5 More precisely, Dive (2004) used the 'Levels of work' approach, which is derived from Jaques' RO approach (Kinston and Rowbottom, 1989).

6 For example, SST is not even mentioned in Mintzberg (1979), Pfeffer (1997) or Morgan (1998), three well-known books reviewing organisation theory. (Morgan (1998) does mention earlier works of Jaques unrelated to SST.)

7 According to Craddock (2007), Charan et al. (2001) do not cite Jaques, but the concepts they present are largely based on General Electric's management structure and leadership competencies, which were defined by a consultant who was influenced by Jaques' work.

8 For example, Jim Collins (2001), the author of the best-selling management book *Good to Great*, stated that leaders should first 'get the right people on the bus', and only then decide where to drive it (i.e., what strategy and structure to pursue).

9 This case is based on a real company. Some details have been changed to preserve confidentiality.

10 One should note that these research questions are not entirely new; a number of empirical studies on RO were conducted during the 1960s, as documented in the annotated bibliography of RO research by Craddock (2007). However, I believe the issues mentioned deserve renewed attention as there has been very little systematic research in this area during the last couple of decades.

The staff function in Scandic Consult[9]

Scandic Consult is a project management and consulting firm with around 250 employees. The firm is organised geographically with offices in four different cities.

The Managing Director initiates a re-design project to improve the internal staff function in the firm. The staff function comprises 15 people responsible for various internal administrative services such as accounting and billing, IT and HR, and they also support the sales and marketing process. The Managing Director of the firm works out of the main office, together with the managers in the staff function. One member of the staff function reports to the Finance & accounting (F&A) manager in the main office, while eight other staff employees report to the director (partner) of the local office. The Quality Assurance manager reports directly to the Managing Director. The formal reporting structure for staff employees is shown in Figure 6.5.

The Managing Director is particularly concerned about the quality of the finance and accounting processes. The management team has complained that the F&A manager reports operating data, such as utilisation rate, with little analysis and interpretation of trends. The board of the firm has voiced concerns about unreliable earnings forecasts, and the external auditor has also delivered a critical report to the board about the firm's accounting processes.

The F&A manager on his side feels that it is difficult to devote sufficient time to analysis as he is forced to spend considerable time manually correcting errors in the time sheets and financial accounts. He also explains that although the staff at the local offices have the same title ('administrative assistant'), they do not perform tasks of equal complexity – while some largely perform secretarial work, four of them in fact perform finance and accounting tasks such as budgeting, invoicing and financial reporting. He acknowledges that there is a need to raise the quality of the finance and accounting processes. Yet he finds it difficult to properly involve the staff organised locally, as they do not report to him but to the office partner/director. The same picture emerges from interviews with the staff members, who say that they feel 'disconnected' from the work being done at the main office.

To evaluate the administrative costs, Scandic Consult performs a benchmarking analysis against a similar firm in a neighbouring country. The analysis concludes that Scandic's costs are about 10 per cent higher per employee than the comparison firm (Scandic has more staff employees as well as higher IT costs due to expensive outsourcing agreements.) Despite the higher costs, the analysis shows that only 20 per cent of Scandic's staff employees have a university degree whereas the situation is the reverse in the comparison firm, where 70 per cent of the staff employees have completed higher education programmes.

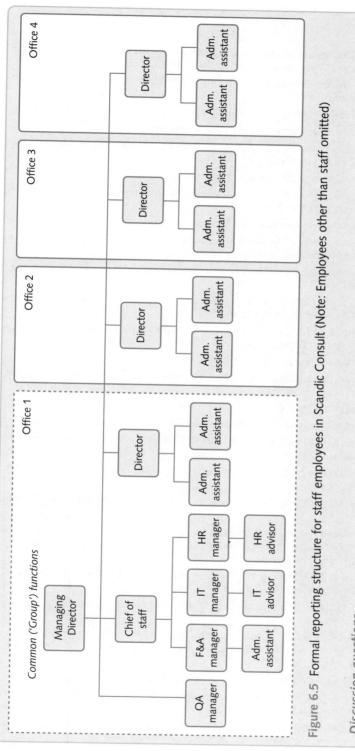

Figure 6.5 Formal reporting structure for staff employees in Scandic Consult (Note: Employees other than staff omitted)

Discussion questions

1 At which stratum (cf. Table 6.1) would you place the roles described above (i.e., the level that the employees in the staff function *actually* perform at)?

2 How could one use the principles proposed by Jaques to create a 'requisite' staff function in Scandic Consult?

References

Abrahamson, Eric (2002). Disorganization theory and disorganizational behavior: towards an etiology of messes. *Research in Organizational Behavior*, 24, 139–80.

Capelli, P. (2008). *Talent on Demand: Managing Talent in an Age of Uncertainty.* Boston, MA: Harvard Business School Press.

Charan, R., Drotter, S. and Noel, J. (2001). *The Leadership Pipeline.* San Francisco, CA: Jossey-Bass.

Collins, J. (2001). *Good to Great.* New York: HarperCollins Publishers.

Craddock, K. (2007). *Requisite Organization – Annotated Bibliography* (4th edn). Available online: http://globalro.org/pick-up/RO-Intro.pdf.

Dive, B. (2004). *The Healthy Organization.* London: Kogan Page.

Haeckel, S. H. (1999). *Adaptive Enterprise: Creating and Leading Sense-and-Respond Organizations.* Boston, MA: Harvard Business School Press.

Jaques, E. (1970). *Work, Creativity and Social Justice.* London: Heinemann.

Jaques, E. (1986). The development of intellectual capability: A discussion of stratified systems theory. *Journal of Applied Behavioral Science* 22, 361–84.

Jaques, E. (1989). *Requisite Organization: The CEO's Guide to Creative Structure and Leadership.* Arlington: Cason Hall & Co.

Jaques, E. and Clement, S. D. (1991). *Executive Leadership: A Practical Guide to Managing Complexity.* Arlington: Cason Hall & Co publishers.

Kinston, W. and Rowbottom, R. (1989). Levels of work: New applications to management in large organisations. *Journal of Applied Systems Analysis*, 16, 19–34.

Littener, J. (1973). *Organizational Analysis.* New York: Wiley

McManis, G. L. and Leibman, M. S. (1988). Succession planners. *Personnel Administrator*, August, 24–30.

Mintzberg H. (1979). *The Structuring of Organizations.* Englewood Cliffs, NJ: Prentice-Hall.

Morgan, G. (1998). *Images of Organization.* Thousand Oaks, CA: Sage Publications.

Parker, S. K. and Wall, T. D. (1998). *Job and Work Design: Organizing Work to Promote Well-being and Effectiveness.* Thousand Oaks, CA: Sage Publications.

Pfeffer, J. (1997). *New Directions for Organization Theory: Problems and Prospects.* New York: Oxford University Press.

Popper, M. and Gluskinos, U. (1993). Is there an inverse 'Peter Principle'? *Management Decision*, 31, 4, 59–64.

Sherman, E. (2005). Tweaking HR information systems can help HR stay in compliance with Sarbanes-Oxley rules. *HR Magazine*, online edition: http://www.shrm.org/Publications/hrmagazine/EditorialContent/Pages/0505hrtech.aspx

Snow, C. C. and Snell, S.A. (1993). Staffing as strategy. In Schmitt, N. and Borman, W. C. (eds), *Personnel Selection in Organizations*, 448–78. San Francisco, CA: Jossey-Bass.

Sparrow, P. and Cooper, C. L. (2003). *The Employment Relationship: Key Challenges for HR.* London: Butterworth-Heinemann.

Whittington, R., Pettigrew, A., Peck, S., Fenton, E. and Conyon, M. (1999). Change and complementarities in the new competitive landscape: A European panel study, 1992–1996. *Organization Science*, 10, 5, 583–600.

Worren, N. (2008). Managing the company's resource pool. *People & Strategy*, 31, 3, 42–49.

Wrzesniewski, A. and Dutton, J. (2001). Crafting a job: revisioning employees as active crafters of their work. *Academy of Management Review*, 26, 2, 179–201.

Zenger, T. R. and Hesterly, W. (1997). The disaggregation of corporations: selective intervention, high-powered incentives, and molecular units. *Organisation Science*, 8, 3, 209–22.

Chapter 7

Configuring interfaces

Overview

Background

- After grouping roles and activities into sub-units, some interdependencies toward other sub-units in the organisation will still remain
- Managing these interdependencies is a core task for managers of sub-units

Challenges

- The task of managing interdependencies is becoming more challenging as organisations grow more complex:
  - Sub-units are increasingly engaged in multiple projects or working 'laterally' across vertical lines of control
  - Several internal stakeholders may influence a sub-unit's ability to take decisions or access resources
- In considering interventions to improve coordination, there is a tendency among managers to focus on one particular type of interdependency while ignoring others
- Similarly, both the practitioner and the academic literature tend to focus on one type of interdependency at a time

Key question

- How should one manage the multiple types of interdependencies that may exist between sub-units in complex organisations?

Proposed approach

- Identify different types of interdependencies that may exist and anticipate where they are likely to arise
- Evaluate the kinds and degrees of interdependencies that will best support effective functioning of sub-units and the achievement of a sub-unit's goals

Introduction[1]

Unit grouping – as we discussed in Chapter 5 – facilitates coordination within the groups that are formed at the expense of coordination across groups (Mintzberg, 1979). Once sub-units have been formed, a key challenge is thus to consider how to create effective interfaces between the different sub-units.

Managing the relationship toward other organisational units has always been a core task for managers of sub-units. However, this task is becoming more challenging as organisations grow more complex. Sub-units are increasingly engaged in multiple projects or working 'laterally' across vertical lines of control. In a networked, decentralised organisation, there is a myriad of stakeholders that may influence the performance of the processes that the sub-unit is engaged in, the resources that it controls, or the decisions that it is formally authorised to take.

Consequently, the key question addressed in this chapter is how managers in complex organisations can design effective interfaces. How can managers identify the different types of interdependencies that exist – or anticipate where they are likely to arise? How can managers decide the kinds and degrees of interdependencies that will best support effective functioning of sub-units and the achievement of the unit's goals?

To address this issue, this chapter expands on the concept of interdependency introduced in the previous chapters. We here consider not only the existence (or lack) of an interdependency, but the relative *degree* of interdependency and different *types* of interdependencies between sub-units. Compared to the previous chapters, we also shift the 'level of analysis' by formulating a set of design propositions that should be relevant for sub-unit managers. Defining the overall architecture (Chapter 4) and re-designing the structure of sub-units (Chapters 5 and 6) usually require senior management support and occur relatively infrequently. In this chapter, we focus on more frequent, incremental design improvements that leaders of sub-units may themselves initiate once the overall design choices have been made.

Case example: ProTech

To illuminate the nature of different types of interdependencies, we describe a simplified case of an IT department in a firm called ProTech, a pseudonym for a multi-divisional engineering company[2] (see Figure 7.1). Until 1999, IT staff in ProTech were organised within the engineering departments in different business units (the IT manager would typically report to the head of engineering in each unit). In 1999, the company decided to introduce the shared services concept, and IT staff were transferred to shared services together with staff performing transactional processes such as accounting and payroll. The key rationale behind this decision was to derive economies of scale and scope. By consolidating administrative functions into one unit, the company sought to standardise processes, reduce costs, increase its resource flexibility and also (over time) increase the quality of services. Today, the Shared Services IT unit comprises two teams: Application management and Service delivery (i.e., IT support). These teams serve users employed in the business units. Within a business unit, the engineering department is the main user of the IT department's services, as engineers make heavy use of computer-aided design tools and document management systems. As part of the staff functions at the headquarters, there is also a Corporate IT unit, which develops and implements IT policy for ProTech. In addition, the IT department interacts with external software vendors that develop application programmes to meet the needs of ProTech's business units. The functions of the different sub-units are listed in Table 7.1.[3]

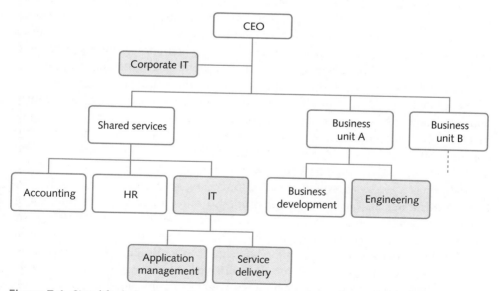

Figure 7.1 Simplified chart showing organisational structure of ProTech (units described in text highlighted)

Table 7.1 Key functions of IT units in ProTech

	Design parameters			
Functional requirements	Corporate IT	Application management	Service delivery	Software vendor
Develop and implement IT policy	X			
Provide applications		X		
Provide IT support			X	
Develop applications				X

Degrees of work process interdependency

Interdependency exists when actions in one sub-unit of the organisation affect important outcomes in another sub-unit – for example, quality, cost or customer satisfaction. Consider the IT department and the Engineering department within ProTech's business unit. To what extent is Engineering dependent upon IT, or vice versa? To determine the *degree* of interdependency, we consider two factors. The first is *criticality*, in other words, do actions taken in the IT department affect important outcomes in the Engineering department? This may be the case if engineers make heavy use of software applications to do their work, and if IT is the only provider of those applications. Similarly, IT may be dependent upon Engineering for internal funding for its activities or for support for continual software application development. The second factor is *uncertainty*, which is related both to *dependability* and to *ambiguity*. For example, can the IT department be relied upon in terms of keeping promises with regard to service levels? To what extent do Engineering and IT have the same understanding of their respective roles and responsibilities?[4] Sub-units enjoy stable and isolated conditions if interdependencies are of low uncertainty and importance. As uncertainty and importance increase, the intensity of communication and collaboration between sub-units increases (as does the potential for conflict) (Miles, 1979). Interdependencies that are very high in both importance and uncertainty are likely to produce situations that are perceived as chaotic (Figure 7.2).

Traditionally, the key recommendation for coping with an interdependency has been to introduce a *coordination mechanism* (also called integration mechanism or integration device in some texts) (Galbraith, 1993; Lawrence and Lorsch, 1967). The appropriate coordination mechanism depends on the degree of criticality and uncertainty. For interdependencies that are relatively low in criticality and uncertainty, it may suffice that managers in the sub-units affected interchange information (e.g., via e-mail or phone). For interdependencies that are considered at least moderately critical and uncertain, it may be necessary to set up regular meetings to allow managers of sub-units to coordinate between them. Another approach is to create a 'liaison' or integrator role by making one employee responsible for coordinating

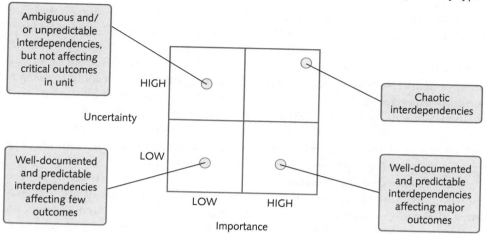

Figure 7.2 Framework for characterising degree of interdependency between organisational sub-units

work between the two sub-units. With higher degrees of interdependency, more extensive integration may be needed. Proponents of business process re-engineering (Hammer and Champy, 1993/2001) and, more recently, some Six Sigma experts, have proposed that one should create cross-functional teams with end-to-end responsibility for processes (Hayler and Nichols, 2005). The intention is to minimise the number of 'hand-offs' between sub-units involved in a work process.

The establishment of coordination mechanisms to integrate the work of interdependent units remains a key organisation design option. However, as argued in Chapter 5, it is also possible to intentionally change the degree of interdependency between sub-units – and thereby reduce the need for coordination in the first place (von Hippel, 1990). In addition to introducing coordination mechanisms, three options exist for managing interdependencies between sub-units. One may: a) eliminate an interdependency; b) add a new interdependency; or c) change the degree of an interdependency (i.e., alter its uncertainty or criticality). In this chapter, we examine these options in more detail.

Interdependency types

Traditionally, when using the term interdependency, authors have often referred to what we shall here call *activity interdependency*. (An activity is a step in a work process that transforms an input to an output.) Yet interdependencies between activities are only one of several types of interdependencies that sub-unit managers must manage. To configure an effective interface, one may need to take into consideration four other interdependency types – activities incur costs and must be resourced, creating *resource interdependencies* toward other units. Moreover, activities within an organisation are performed in an 'accountability hierarchy', leading to what we call *governance interdependencies*. However, formal authority is not enough to assure actual performance of activities: Activities are often performed to fulfil either semi-permanent or ad hoc commitments (promises) toward internal or external customers – leading to *commitment interdependencies*. Finally, activities are performed by people who form informal relationships with each other while they are working. When these social relationships affect the decisions made or the performance of work processes, they create what we call *social network interdependencies*. (The five types of interdependencies correspond to the five layers of design parameters introduced in Chapter 1.)

There is an extensive literature on each of these types of interdependencies. However, in most cases, the existing research examines one type of interdependency in isolation. There is a similar tendency among managers when selecting an approach to address a performance problem. In dealing with a lack of coordination between two departments, some managers will tend to focus on governance (and may suggest changing reporting lines as a remedy); others will tend to focus on commitments (and may suggest creating joint goals or agreements between the departments), and so on. Indeed, each interdependency type may represent a *frame* (Bolman and Deal, 1997) that managers use in diagnosing coordination problems and in designing interventions. Being aware of several types of interdependencies may thus provide a potential for reframing the situation by bringing to the fore elements that would otherwise go unrecognised.

Activity interdependencies

The activity type encompasses interdependencies that are directly related to the flow of work across sub-units. Activity interdependencies may exist due to the need for physical inputs from another sub-unit or – more frequently today – a need for *information*. To describe the current activity dependencies one must first identify the different tasks or activities involved in a given work process. One then maps activity dependencies by asking the participants in the process who they rely on for information to complete their tasks and who they in turn provide outputs to. These data may be summarised by using a design structure matrix (Figure 7.4). Activity interdependencies are often surprisingly complex. A typical sub-unit in a large organisation may be engaged in several work processes, may receive inputs from multiple other sub-units, and may in turn provide outputs to several internal (and possibly external) clients.[5]

The Application management team in ProTech has a dependency toward the external software vendor, which licenses applications to ProTech. Application Management in turn provides applications as an internal supplier to users in the Business Unit (see Figure 7.3). Service Delivery provides user support to end users; while also receiving information from Application Management about application functionality, on-going upgrades, common errors, known software bugs, etc. In Figure 7.4, these interdependencies are indicated by an X in the appropriate cells of the matrix.

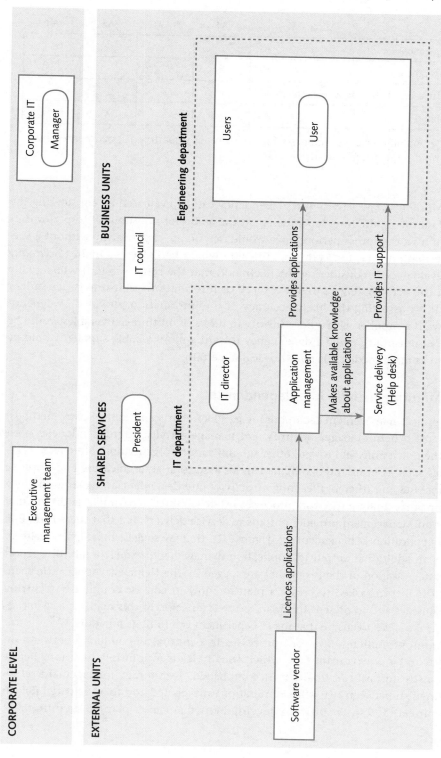

Figure 7.3 Activity interdependencies for the IT department at ProTech

		A1	A2	A3	A4
Licence applications	**A1**				
Provide applications	**A2**	X			
Make available knowledge about applications	**A3**		X		
Provide support	**A4**			X	

Figure 7.4 Activity interdependencies for ProTech's IT department documented by means of a design structure matrix (DSM)

The *criticality* of an activity interdependency can be evaluated by considering the effect of removing the interdependency on the ability of the sub-unit to perform its function: If work process performance would deteriorate significantly without a specific information flow, for example, criticality would be judged as high. *Uncertainty* can be evaluated by considering the likelihood that the other sub-unit will actually perform the activity (e.g., provide a piece of information) that one is dependent upon and by assessing the likely accuracy of the information provided. A dependency toward a supplier with a poor history in terms of on-time deliverables would be considered uncertain, while a dependency toward a more reliable supplier would be perceived as more predictable and thus less uncertain.

Configuring activity interdependencies

Several project management techniques (e.g., PERT charts and critical path methods) exist that can help managers identify and manage activity interdependencies both within their own units and toward other sub-units in the organisation. Moreover, methodologies such as Lean and Six Sigma can be used to analyse, measure and improve work processes and (thereby) reconfigure activity interdependencies. As an example, a consultant may analyse the work processes in ProTech's IT department and note that Application Management provides outputs to Service delivery, but that there is no link back to Application Management (cf. Figure 7.3). He may suggest that Service delivery provides an additional output to Application management, namely a monthly report with a categorisation of the issues that are logged by the HelpDesk. Application management is in turn asked to create a plan for how to address commonly recurring technical issues and to present this plan to the IT director. In this manner, *new interdependencies are added* to ensure that the IT department can fulfil its function.

A common challenge in work processes is a mutual dependency between an upstream and a downstream task, which usually leads to multiple iterations before the downstream task can finally be accomplished. Technology management scholars distinguish between two types of iteration: anticipated and unanticipated (Smith and Eppinger, 1993). A software development team may plan to reconfigure a software application based on feedback from users testing a beta version. However, they may also be forced to completely re-design the application if unexpected problems are discovered during the testing. It has been documented that unanticipated iteration may account for as much as 70 per cent of the lead time in product development projects (ibid.). Using tools such as the Design Structure Matrix, it is often possible to lessen the need for and length of iterations by re-ordering activities. But it may also be necessary to *remove interdependencies* that create delays or add coordination costs. As described in Chapter 5, as processes become more mature, it is possible to introduce common standards that remove the need for coordination between workers, as long as the standards are complied to. The removal of interdependencies is the essence of *modularity*, the partitioning of a product design (or work process) into modules separated by standard interfaces (Baldwin and Clark, 2000; Sanchez, 1995; Sanchez and Mahoney, 1996).

In integrating the processes of different sub-units, an important design principle is to define *transfer-points* (Jastram, 1974). As already mentioned, it has been observed that process breakdowns often occur during 'hand-offs' between different sub-units engaged in the same overall process. One approach to avoid this outcome is to create a mutual agreement regarding the deliverables (inputs and outputs) to be contributed by the respective sub-units. For example, in ProTech, Applications Management and Service delivery may define at precisely which point the responsibility for handling software errors for a new application is transferred to the Service Delivery team (e.g., only after an application has been rolled out and appropriate documentation have been made available to the team).

Commitment interdependencies

The basic source of a commitment interdependency is the existence of (or need for) an agreement between actors or sub-units involved in a work process. For example, suppliers agree to deliver specific products or services and clients accept responsibility to pay once the deliverables have been received.

The role of *contracts* in commercial relationships has been studied extensively by economists. The term may cover so-called spot contracts regulating an immediate exchange (e.g., a purchase), classical (formal and written) contracts, or relational contracts, which are implicit agreements between two parties (Kay, 1995). Although formal contracts are usually made only with external customers or suppliers, organisational sub-units may still have written agreements with other sub-units.[6] Typically, such agreements define the services to be delivered, the quality level, and costs. They may also define governance structures for managing inter-sub-unit relations, for example, the mechanisms to be used to monitor performance or to resolve issues that may arise.

However, a sub-unit may hold a large number of commitments that are not formalised in a contract or even a written agreement. Researchers studying communication processes within organisations have considered how commitments are conveyed between actors holding roles such as customer and supplier in a work processes (Scherr, 1993; Winograd and Flores, 1986). They argue that practically all communication in organisations may be reduced to a small set of basic communication acts, such as 'requests' and 'promises'. According to this view, an interdependency is created when an actor makes an explicit promise to produce a certain action (e.g., deliver a service fulfilling the customer's requirements). Commitments are thus formed in a process of negotiation; the key medium is conversations about requirements and deliverables. As the term 'conversation' suggests, these agreements are not static: The responsibility to deliver a service or perform a certain role is not 'allocated' once and for all; it is formed in an on-going, 'authorising' process (Kahn and Kram, 1994) in which people request and agree to perform actions.[7] People may also re-negotiate their commitments if unexpected events occur along the way.

> In managing dependencies toward its external software vendors, the IT department at ProTech relies on a formal contract that regulates costs and support levels (see Figure 7.5). With its internal clients, ProTech enters into Service Level Agreements (SLAs) that specify service levels, prices, support availability, etc. The SLAs are renegotiated annually. However, within the framework of the SLA, commitments are exchanged between IT employees and users/clients several times a day. For example, every time a user reports an application error, the Help Desk confirms that a software engineer will address the issue and thus commits to delivering a service.[8]

Commitment interdependencies vary in *criticality* and *uncertainty*. Commitment interdependencies are high in criticality if they have direct and significant impact on key work outcomes that a sub-unit is responsible for. For example, commitments regarding reliability and quality made by an IT vendor may be critical for an IT department in terms of its own ability to provide services to internal users according to agreed standards. The uncertainty of a commitment interdependency will tend to be reduced (for the client) when a supplier (internal or external) faces and accepts *consequential accountability* for delivering a product or service – i.e., when a supplier will suffer significant negative consequences if it fails to perform as promised. Commitment interdependency may also become less uncertain if a supplier not only guarantees the delivery of a service or product as specified, but also guarantees a positive outcome for its customer as a result of using the service or product (e.g., a 'no cure, no pay' commitment). For example, a real estate agent may make its fee contingent upon obtaining a certain price for the house its client is trying to sell.[9] Similarly, managers may ask internal suppliers to commit to producing a positive outcome for an internal client (e.g., 'reduce the time engineers use to search for information in the engineering database').

However, as several authors have noted (Ford and Ford, 1995; Haeckel, 1999; Scherr, 1993) communication between members of an organisation often falls short

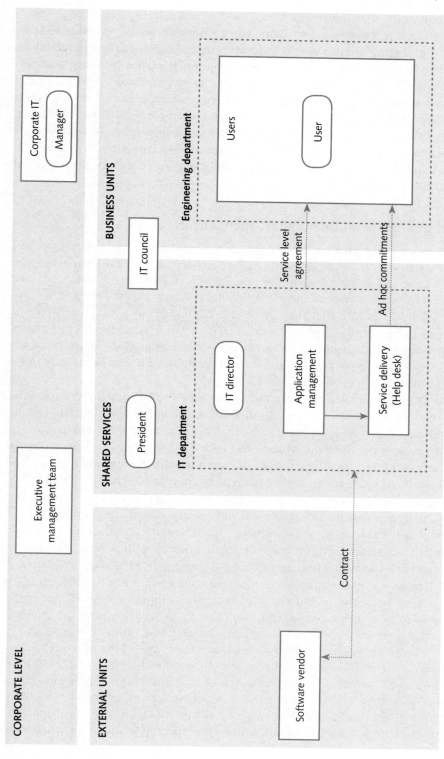

Figure 7.5 Key commitments between the ProTech IT department and other units

of providing explicit commitments to deliver specified actions or achieve predetermined goals. It is more common to define fairly unspecific, activity-based goals (e.g., 'provide engineering applications'). Moreover, there is also frequent uncertainty about whether a decision or act of communication signals a 'binding commitment' or not. For example, a customer may not clearly understand whether a price quoted by a supplier is just an estimate or a real commitment. Employees may similarly wonder whether management decisions represent broad guidelines or intents, or whether they represent non-negotiable policies and principles. To address such issues, techniques have been proposed to 'test' the level of commitment and negotiate more explicit agreements among people collaborating in a work process (Ford and Ford, 1995; Smith, 1999).

Configuring commitment interdependencies

In a work process involving a customer and a supplier, the process of forming a commitment starts with the customer requesting a service. An offer from the supplier may then prompt a negotiation over requirements, timing of deliverables, etc. The intention is to produce an agreement that implies not only that the supplier is committed to deliver but also that the customer is committed to paying upon receipt (or any other mutually acceptable schedule) (Scherr, 1993). A similar process occurs in the 'performance dialogue' between managers and employees: Managers ask for actions (i.e., make request) and negotiate with employees to clarify what is to be achieved, when, and by whom (Ford and Ford, 1995).

Several design principles have been proposed for establishing effective commitments. Two key principles are to establish explicit *conditions of satisfaction* and to clarify *upstream dependencies*. 'Conditions of satisfaction' are the criteria that are to be used to evelute the outcomes (the agreed deliverable or action) – commitments without any conditions of satisfaction are highly uncertain, because they are ambiguous. However, in order for a supplier to credibly commit to achieving satisfactory outcomes, the supplier must also ensure that the sub-suppliers that it depends on itself (i.e., upstream dependencies) can and will actually deliver their inputs. A third design principle is to focus on the *reduction of risks* inherent in relying on a sub-unit's commitment. An important function of formal contracts is to define and manage each party's risk in a relationship by spelling out the specific obligations created in a commitment, as well as the consequences of non-conformance of these obligations.

Clearly specifying the lateral chain of customer–supplier roles will generally reduce ambiguity and role conflicts. In the example of ProTech, roles designating internal customers and suppliers already exist. In large and complex organisations, however, it is not always clear 'who owes what to whom'; specifying who one's internal customers are is often a surprisingly complicated task (Haeckel, 1999). Scherr (1993) proposed a technique – the Commitment Protocol – for mapping customer-supplier roles and commitments at various points in a work process from initial request to final deliverable and acceptance by client (see Figure 7.6). Applying this technique to map processes in organisations, he typically found cases where the customer role was missing or where an individual who performed the role of customer early in a work process would reappear downstream in the role as supplier. In some cases there may even be conflicting demands that prevent a clear definition of customer-supplier roles: Some members of corporate staff functions, for example, may be service providers (e.g. as advisers to business units), while at the same time overseeing policy compliance. However, techniques such as those proposed in Scherr (1993) may be used to re-design work processes to separate responsibilities of different individuals in ways that avoid role conflicts. (We shall examine this issue in more detail in Chapter 8.)

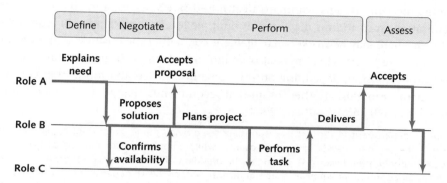

Figure 7.6 Example of a commitment protocol showing customer and supplier roles (this format for visualising commitment interdependencies was proposed by Scherr (1993) based on the earlier work by Winograd and Flores (1986))

Governance interdependencies

The Governance type concerns interdependencies related to authority relations in organisations. Governance dependencies arise because of a need for formal approval of a sub-unit's plans or activities by some party or because of a requirement to conduct an activity in conformance with a policy set by superiors. In most cases, managers with a superior position in an authority hierarchy have the right to define tasks, allocate resources, monitor and reward performance, hire or fire, and so on with regard to sub-units occupying lower positions in the hierarchy. Work outcomes at one level are therefore to a significant extent dependent upon decisions made (or not made) by managers or sub-units at higher authority levels in the organisation. However, only in the simplest of cases can the issue of governance be reduced to the formal, vertical relations in an organisation. One consequence of the increasing use of projects and cross-functional business processes is that decision authority may be distributed among a number of entities. It is common practice, for example, to establish steering groups for larger projects. Whereas the initial ratification of the project proposal is usually the responsibility of line management, the steering group's charter is to monitor and evaluate that the project fulfils its mandate, ensure adequate

use of resources, and occasionally, to assist the project manager in resolving particular issues that require senior management support or intervention. The steering
group is usually composed of managers drawn from different functions and departments (sometimes customer or supplier representatives may also be included) (Earl,
1996). In addition, there may also be technology boards, user forums, reference
groups, etc., that may be able to make certain decisions (or at least provide advice
and thus influence decisions) regarding service delivery or functionality. There may
also be forums for consultation such as worker–management councils consisting
of employee representatives who meet with line managers to discuss business conditions, the working environment, health and safety issues, and so on. In a large
organisation, such forums may exist at multiple levels. For example, in a divisionalised firm, there may be worker–management councils at the business unit, divisional
and corporate levels. There may also be multiple decision forums within the same
function or division, depending on the domain; one decision forum that considers
investment proposals, another forum that recommends changes to company policy,
and so on (Weill and Woodham, 2004).

> The IT department in ProTech is responsible for providing and supporting applications that
> serve the business needs of internal clients, while complying with the company's IT poli-
> cies.[10] Although the head of IT reports to the president of Shared Services, there are two other
> governance interdependencies that significantly affect the IT department (see Figure 7.7):
> Corporate IT develops IT policies to which the IT department must conform, and individual
> business units like the Engineering department define the user requirements that the IT depart-
> ment must fulfil. The latter governance relationship is mediated by an IT council, which consists
> of representatives from both IT and the Engineering department. The IT council escalates larger
> investment proposals to the Executive management team. If approved, the IT council then
> monitors and reports on implementation of projects in evaluating whether the expected busi-
> ness benefits of each project are being realised.

The *criticality* of a sub-unit's governance interdependencies will depend on the
potential effects of decisions made by other sub-units on the work process of the
sub-unit. Interdependencies toward sub-units whose decisions determine whether
a sub-unit can begin, continue, or terminate a work process are obviously the
most critical. The *uncertainty* of governance interdependencies is determined by
their degree of stability and ambiguity. Governance uncertainty is affected by
the individuals that lead the sub-units toward which one is dependent. As March
(1988) observed, decision makers may not always have stable preferences; in fact,
preferences may shift or even be erratic. Ambiguity with regards to governance
interdependencies may arise due to unclear role definitions, or because of gaps and
overlaps in decision rights allocated to various sub-units. One would expect to find
the strongest – and least ambiguous – authority relations between sub-units occupying different vertical positions in a hierarchical organisation. In project-based
organisations that rely on multiple decision forums, however, a sub-unit may face
a combination of different governance interdependencies of varying importance.
The more complex an organisation becomes, the more uncertainty will typically be

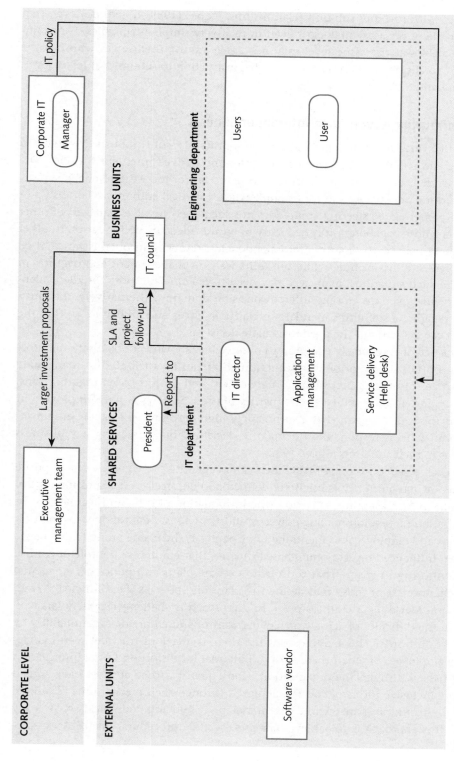

Figure 7.7 Governance interdependencies between ProTech's IT department and other units

associated with role and sub-unit relationships. Jaques (1989) noted, however, that considerable uncertainty may exist even in relatively simple hierarchies. For example, executives at the same level may not agree among themselves who has the authority to allocate certain resources or give instruction to sub-units at lower levels in the organisation.

Configuring governance interdependencies

In practice, managers of organisational sub-units are continuously involved in defining and redefining governance structures and derived interdependencies. The interdependencies affecting a sub-unit may be too few or too weak to enable a process to perform adequately – as for example when a vertical authority relationship or a laterally interrelated steering group does not adequately involve managers of other sub-units whose collaboration is necessary to ensure adequate performance. In other cases, there may be too many interdependencies, resulting in open issues that go unresolved or a loss of time while sub-units wait for management approval for an action. In such situations, managers may need to redefine authority interdependencies to reduce overlaps among different decision domains. Alternatively, they may seek to redefine a sub-unit's mandate to clarify its goals and guidelines so that the sub-unit can act without the need to escalate decisions.

In practice, it is relatively common to observe breakdowns in organisational processes and other organisational dysfunctions that can be attributed to inadequate governance. In today's increasingly 'networked' and project-based organisations, authority and accountability are frequently blurred. Surveys among employees in large organisations suggest that a surprisingly high percentage of people are uncertain about who is responsible for making decisions or for solving key business problems in their sub-units (Shaw, 1992).

However, a second type of breakdown can occur when one goes to the opposite extreme – when authority is minutely defined and enforced. A demand for control can result in increasing formalisation (the introduction of rules and regulations) or centralisation of decision-making power, resulting in a loss of autonomy for sub-unit managers and employees. As mentioned in Chapter 1, theorising around governance has been influenced by economics-based theories that emphasise the role of control and monitoring to ensure that those who execute plans and policies (i.e., agents) act in the interest of those that define the plans and policies (i.e., principals) (e.g., Jensen and Meckling, 1976). However, this approach is challenged by scholars who focus on the difficulty of actually achieving control and enforcing accountability by means of authority. This may occur when there is a lack of trust between managers and employees or when there exists a potential for distortion of the information that is passed through the organisation. Consequently, some authors have argued for more inclusive forms of control, achieved through such mechanisms as mutual monitoring and transparency in decision making (Child and Rodrigues, 2003). A key goal of this approach is to achieve 'fair process' (i.e., procedural justice) by clearly communicating expectations, soliciting employee's views before making decisions and providing explanations for the rationale behind decisions (Kim and Mauborgne, 1996). Some authors have gone even further, in recommending the establishment of democratic organisational structures consisting of governance bodies that include employee representatives (e.g., Ackoff, 1994).

In sum, then, there are three key design principles that sub-unit managers may consider when establishing governance interdependencies. The first is to ensure that governing bodies include adequate *representation*. Second, one may *define roles and responsibilities* in a manner that clarifies accountability while avoiding gaps or overlaps in decision rights. Finally, governance should be exercised in a manner that *maintains or increases trust* between the actors involved.

Resource interdependencies

Resource interdependencies arise when units share resources or transact with each other (McCann and Ferry, 1979; Pfeffer and Salancik, 1978). In the following, we focus on interdependencies that relate to *financial* resources; however, resources may be of many kinds, including knowledge, personnel and machines. One important source of interdependency among organisational sub-units is budgets developed to allocate limited financial resources and anticipate revenues. Financial resource budgeting in large companies is often a complex and political process that creates interdependencies between sub-units that control the budgeting process and those that receive budgeted resources (Bower, 1970). Indirect interdependencies are created between sub-units competing for resources in the budgeting process.

Sub-units with profit and loss responsibility usually receive income directly from sales made to external customers. Sub-units that provide internal services may receive their funding from the corporate centre or from the business unit that they belong to. Alternatively, they may also receive revenues or charge costs to other sub-units within the organisation, particularly if the company has adopted an internal client–supplier model or has instituted a transfer pricing scheme. To understand the resource inter-dependencies for a particular unit, one must ask where its revenues come from, how costs are allocated (e.g., overhead charge or usage based fees), how any deficits would be covered, where any profits accrue, and how profits may be used.

In ProTech, the IT department pays yearly license fees to the software vendor who provides software. Because the IT department at ProTech is organised as a Shared Services unit, it invoices the business unit depending on the level of usage (e.g., the number of users per application) (see Figure 7.8). In other words, there is a standardised financial transaction – with monthly billings – in the same manner as would occur between any supplier and client. As a Shared services function, the IT department is only supposed to cover its costs, and for this reason, does not generate profits that are transferred to the corporate level. However, it has received investment funds (a loan) from corporate to cover procurement of new IT infrastructure.

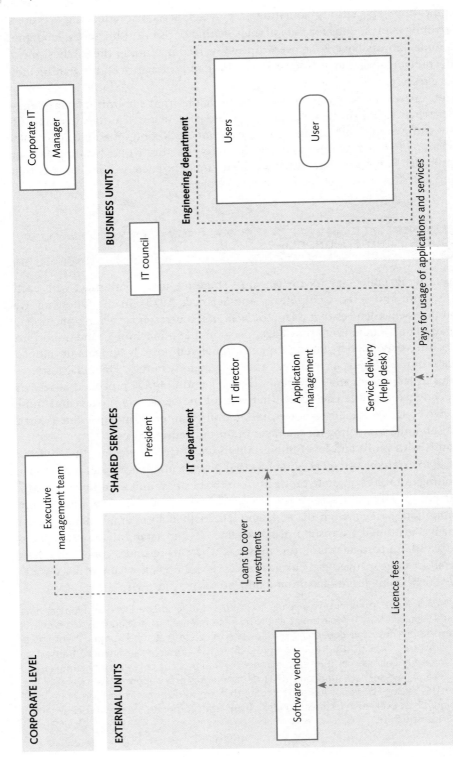

Figure 7.8 The most important resource interdependencies for the IT department at ProTech

The *criticality* of a resource interdependency will depend on the relative share of the sub-unit's resources that is provided by a contributing sub-unit. In the simplified example shown in Figure 7.7, the income is received from one internal client (resource provider), but in a real company there will often be a variety of sources of income; any sub-unit that controls a budget may become a resource provider. The *uncertainty* of the interdependency will increase to the extent that the resource flow fluctuates or is subject to competitive pressures from other (potential) suppliers, but may decrease if resource providers lack the ability to switch suppliers (McCann and Ferry, 1979; Pfeffer and Salancik, 1978). For example, business units may be bound by company policy to use only internal suppliers or use a fixed amount of resources for a given activity. If this is not the case, uncertainty may be decreased by identifying alternative resource providers to offset the potential loss of income from current internal clients (e.g., one may consider selling to external clients). In other words, the highest degree of resource interdependency exists when resource providers supply a great portion of a sub-units' (internal supplier's) critical resources that cannot easily be substituted by other resource providers. A sub-unit (internal supplier) will have a low degree of interdependency with a resource provider when the resource provided is not essential to the sub-unit's activity or can be obtained from other resource providers.

Configuring resource interdependencies

A key task of managers is to ensure that their sub-units have the resources needed to perform their mandated activities and that resource flows are as predictable as possible in order to avoid a sudden interruption of activities. Another key concern may be to reduce asymmetries in the exchange relationship, that is, altering an interdependency where the exchange is not equally important to both parties. Asymmetry may arise when the units that transact are unequal in size. An application development team consisting of five people in ProTech may use 100 per cent of its capacity on developing a specialised software application for one of ProTech's large engineering departments, yet the team may only be responsible for a small fraction of the department's entire application portfolio (cf. Pfeffer and Salancik, 1978). There are several organisational strategies for adapting to and balancing resource dependencies (ibid.). A manager may attempt to increase the share of the sub-unit's essential resource transfers that derive from reliable resource providers. If an IT unit serves several business units, it may expand the scale and/or scope of services to those sub-units/resource providers that are seen as most reliable in terms of keeping their commitments. It may remove resource interdependencies with high uncertainty – for example, with an unpredictable resource provider whose budget is shared among several units competing for the same budget means. The effect is to increase the criticality of some interdependencies, but reducing their uncertainty. Moreover, managers may try to counterbalance an asymmetrical resource relationship by introducing new resource interdependencies where the power advantage is reversed. The small application development team may utilise its knowledge of ProTech's business processes to develop a software application that has a unique feature that will be difficult for the engineering department to substitute with other alternative applications. It may also reduce dependency by attempting to add alternative internal or external clients or suppliers (i.e., thereby reducing the criticality of each of the existing resource interdependencies).

Social network interdependencies

Social network dependencies exist whenever the performance of a work process is affected by informal ties among sub-units. Ties between organisational sub-units are created by individuals, such as the leader, who represent the sub-unit in his/her interactions with other organisational members (Bonacich, 1991). These ties aid sub-units in obtaining or sharing knowledge across the organisation (Hansen, 1999), in influencing decisions related to governance, resources, and activities that may affect the unit (Pfeffer, 1992) and also in developing trust toward individuals in other sub-units, which may increase willingness to form commitments when collaborating in the future.

As with the other types, the *criticality* of social network interdependencies is determined by the effect that these interdependencies have on the outcomes that the work unit is responsible for. *Uncertainty* is related to perceived dependability and reliability of informal ties, which in turn are related to the level of trust that exists between the parties. If the level of trust is low, one does not expect to receive valid or accurate information from the other party, or one may suspect that the other party's support may not be consistent over time (hence, the interdependency would be characterised as uncertain). Some authors also point out that the particular type of uncertainty differs depending on the form and depth of the relationship. For example, Sheppard and Sherman (1998) proposed a continuum ranging from non-critical or 'shallow dependency' to 'deep interdependency' between two or more parties.[11] For non-critical interdependencies, the key uncertainty is related to whether the other party will behave in an unreliable or indiscrete manner. As the importance of the interdependency increases, other, more serious uncertainties and risks appear, such as cheating, neglect and abuse. Sometimes another party may also exploit dependencies by using the risks of such negative consequences as a lever in negotiations. High trust, on the other hand, leads to the expectancy that one will attain positive outcomes based on the actions taken by the other party.

> ProTech's IT director enjoys close relations with his boss (the President of Shared services) and with the head of Corporate IT (see Figure 7.9). At one point the Executive Management Team was drafting a plan to outsource the entire IT department; however, the IT manager received early warning of this plan from Corporate IT and was able to convince his superiors to change their minds. The IT manager also has informal ties with employees elsewhere in the company that prove useful to the IT department. For example, in order to gauge the quality of services seen from the users' point of view, he solicits feedback from a former colleague with whom he frequently socialises and who now works in the business unit that the IT department serves.

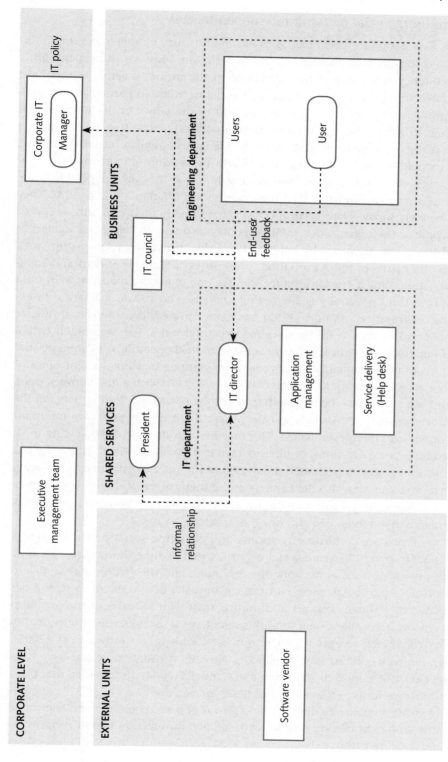

Figure 7.9 Social network interdependencies between the IT department and other sub-units of Pro-Tech

Configuring social network interdependencies

There are several ways in which managers of sub-units may be able to develop informal ties and thereby improve their ability to maintain, improve and expand other interdependency types should the need arise in the future. Several authors have demonstrated that a manager's position in a social network, in particular, the proximity to influential people, is a key determinant of the power of the sub-unit that one belongs to within the organisation. From a political perspective, the key design principle is thus to achieve *network centrality*. Managers establish informal ties (i.e., add interdependencies) in important networks by seeking out interactions strategically, even social interactions, and making sure that they are 'plugged into the structure of communication' within the organisation (Pfeffer, 1992, p. 123). They may deliberately lobby for projects and tasks that provide their unit with access to senior people of the organisation. Managers may also seek to *enlarge the number* of informal ties. As pointed out by Kaplan (1991), by cultivating relationships with people in other parts of the organisation, one creates 'a reservoir of trust and goodwill' that can become a crucial resource the day one requires support or help from other units. A third possibility is attempting to *bridge otherwise disconnected networks* inside the organisation. As Burt (1992) has demonstrated, considerable influence flows to a person who can bridge so-called structural holes. For example, if corporate staff functions in a firm are disconnected from field operations, a corporate staff manager may initiate a quality improvement programme that involves members of corporate staff with operations engineers, and thereby establish a link between operations and staff functions. Finally, managers will be concerned with enhancing the *quality of relationships* (particularly in cases where there already exists an important activity or resource interdependency). This may involve attempts at enhancing trust, aligning values or expectations, or offering favours to build goodwill. Following our framework above, this may change the degree of the interdependency by reducing its uncertainty; one may also deliberately strengthen the criticality of the interdependency, if one manages to turn a distant and infrequent relationship (i.e., a 'weak tie') into a closer and more frequent one (i.e., a 'strong tie').

Most managers are continuously adding and changing social network interdependencies. However, there are social norms as well as time limitations that may constrain how wide a social network one can build, and with whom one is able to establish ties. In particular, these constraints limit the development of strong ties characterised by frequent contact and mutual trust. Not all parts of the organisation are equally accessible: Some sub-units may have a strong sense of territoriality and effectively block access to their resources or knowledge (Brown et al., 2005). Moreover, network building and influencing activities consume time and have costs (Hansen et al., 1999). Indeed, McFadyen and Cannella (2004) documented that there are diminishing returns as the number of ties is increased.

Yet the greatest challenge may be the removal of a social interdependency. One may simply stop maintaining contact with people; however, norms of reciprocity, loyalty and stability within networks make social relationships inherently 'sticky'. As pointed out by Walker (1997) we know little about how social networks are dissolved and one of the few theoretical models that includes the dissolution stage adopts the metaphor of marital divorce to explain how it happens. In other words, reconfiguring social network interdependencies may be a difficult and protracted process.

Discussion and conclusion

In large and complex organisations, significant opportunities for performance improvement are often to be found at the interfaces between sub-units. However, one often focuses on a single type of interdependency, usually activity interdependencies, when considering options for sub-unit performance improvement. In this chapter we have therefore proposed a broader framework that encompasses five different types of interdependencies (Figure 7.10).

An important consideration is whether the different interdependencies that we have described are independent or not. In other words, is the degree of interdependency between two sub-units equal with regard to the different types of interdependencies (commitments, resources, activities, governance, and networks)? There are several examples that would suggest that different interdependencies are independent and that they for this reason may be in misalignment with each other. We may again return to the example of ProTech. In the description above, we explained that the IT department is an independent cost centre that charges out its costs to the different business units. In other words, the resource model is decentralised – it follows the Shared Services model intended to supplant hierarchical and functionally oriented departments with customer-driven service provider units. However, consider the situation that emerges if ProTech introduces a governance model where application development choices are centralised to Corporate IT, or a second 'matrix' reporting structure where the IT manager reports to the vice president of Corporate IT in addition to the head of Shared services. In these cases, the governance model would become more centralised, but ProTech may not necessarily centralise the resource model, that is, transfer IT costs to a central, corporate budget. The same possibilities exist with regard to other interdependencies, for example, social network structures do not always match the formal authority relations, work processes do not necessarily match the resource flows, and commitments do not always match the activities being performed, and so on. In fact, instances of misalignment are probably very common. To some extent, this may reflect the added – and perhaps unavoidable – complexity that arises when organisations try to move from a functionally oriented to a more project- or network-based structure, or when organisations introduce matrix structures that combine e.g., product- and market-based reporting lines. However, we would also speculate that misalignment may be due to a form of 'coordination neglect' (Heath and Staudenmayer, 2000), that is, a failure on the part of managers to effectively coordinate the different design parameters that need to work in concert to sustain effective organisational functioning.

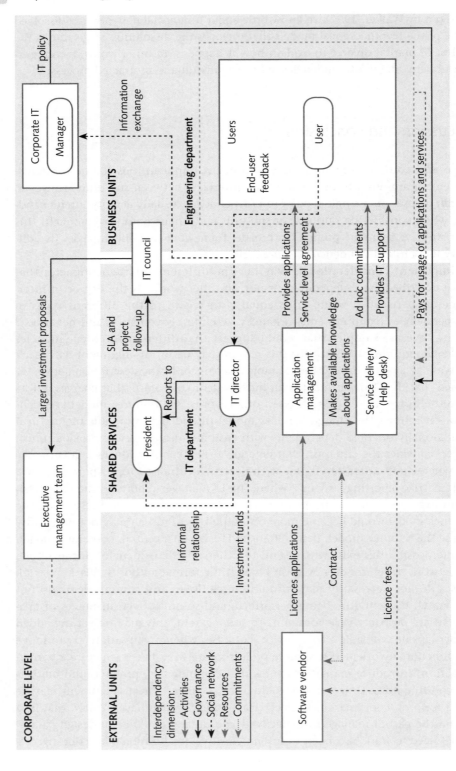

Figure 7.10 Dependencies between the IT department and other units in ProTech

Acknowledging the independence, and possible misalignment, of different interdependency types also has some potential implications for management research. The approach that we have outlined can help interpret some of the conflicting empirical results obtained by the so-called structural contingency school. As described in Chapter 1, this line of research, which was the dominant perspective within organisation theory in the 1960s and 1970s, sought to establish connections between structural factors, such as organisational size and form, and various internal and external factors, such as strategy, technology and market environment. The empirical studies aimed at supporting contingency theory have in some cases failed to produce consistent results, for example, regarding the relationship between environmental uncertainty and the degree of centralisation of an organisation. Pfeffer (1997) concluded that this was largely due to an oversimplification of the meaning and measurement of organisational structure. From the perspective developed in this paper, it seems clear that an organisation may be centralised on one interdependency type (e.g., governance) and decentralised on another (e.g., resources). This may partly explain why different studies have failed to converge: They may simply have measured different aspects of constructs such as centralisation, formalisation, and differentiation, etc. The implication is that structural contingency research might yield different results if it employs less abstract constructs.

In sum, this chapter has described five interdependency types and proposed a set of generic design propositions for addressing common challenges related to sub-unit interdependencies (see summary below). This framework may serve as a basis for managerial practice as well as for academic research aimed at improving the performance of work processes within complex organisations.

Overall design propositions

Objective   *Enhance organisational functioning by improving sub-unit interfaces*

7.1   Identify *current* interdependencies (cf. Table 7.2)

7.2   Identify the interdependencies that *should be* created, removed or reconfigured to ensure that the functions of the organisation or sub-unit can be fulfilled (cf. Detailed design propositions below)

7.3   Implement the required changes to close the gap between the current and the required interdependencies (cf. Detailed design propositions below)

Table 7.2 Diagnostic questions that may be used to describe current interdependencies

Type	Question
Activities	• Which other sub-units provide inputs to the activities performed in this sub-unit? • To which other sub-units does the sub-unit provide outputs? • What is the criticality and uncertainty of these interdependencies?
Commitment	• To which other sub-units does the sub-unit hold commitments (and vice versa)? • What is the criticality and uncertainty of each of these interdependencies?
Governance	• Who makes decisions that may affect the sub-unit? • What is the criticality and uncertainty of each of these interdependencies?
Resources	• Who provides resources to the sub-unit? • What is the criticality and uncertainty of each of these interdependencies?
Social network	• What informal ties exist toward other actors/sub-units in the organisation that may affect decisions or outcomes in the sub-unit? • What is the criticality and uncertainty of each of these interdependencies?

Design propositions

Objective	*Configure activity interdependencies*
7.1	Add interdependencies that are required to fulfil the function of the unit/organisation
7.2	Remove activity interdependencies that create delays or add coordination costs (e.g., by standardising processes, interfaces)
7.3	Define transfer points to avoid breakdowns during hand-offs
Objective	*Configure commitment interdependencies*
7.4	Establish explicit conditions of satisfaction at start of process
7.5	Clarify downstream dependencies before committing to a client
7.6	Manage risks in important projects (e.g., by formalising mutual obligations)
7.7	Remove conflicting customer/supplier roles in processes
Objective	*Configure governance interdependencies*
7.8	Ensure that governance bodies include key stakeholders
7.9	Clarify roles and responsibilities to reduce ambiguity around accountability
7.10	Establish trust by implementing decision processes satisfying criteria for procedural justice

Objective   *Configure resource interdependencies*

7.11   Obtain an increased share of the sub-unit's essential resource transfers from reliable resource providers to reduce uncertainty

7.12   Remove resource interdependencies with high uncertainty to increase predictability of resource flows

7.13   Reduce the risk in asymmetrical exchange relationships by developing counterbalancing asymmetries

7.14   Add alternative internal or external suppliers or clients to reduce dependency on one or a few resource providers

Objective   *Configure social network interdependencies*

7.15   Act to achieve network centrality to increase sub-unit power

7.16   Enlarge the number of informal ties to build options for future support

7.17   Increase influence by bridging unconnected networks

7.18   Enhance quality of important relationships

Review questions

1   How do you evaluate the criticality and uncertainty of an interdependency?

2   What are the key characteristics of the five types of interdependencies described in this chapter?

3   What may managers do to ensure that the members of their sub-units are aware of, and effectively manage, interdependencies toward other units?

4   Select a sub-unit that you are familiar with (e.g., a team in the company where you work, a university department, etc.). Interview a member of the unit and use the questions above to identify the key interdependencies between this unit and other units within the same organisation. Draw a diagram to summarise your findings. Comment upon any 'disconnects' that you may observe.

5   From the business press or your personal experience, select a case where a company is attempting to resolve a performance problem involving one of its sub-units and its relations to other units within the organisation (or toward external constituents). Can you think of alternative ways of resolving this problem, invoking the five interdependency types?

Research questions

1   To what extent could the consideration of current and potential interdependencies sensitise sub-unit managers or employees to uncertain interdependencies and improve the ability to predict interdependencies that may affect them in the future?

2   How could interdependency misalignment be operationalised and measured?

3   What are the performance implications of interdependency misalignment?

4   Thompson (1967) assumed that interdependencies were strongly linked to work processes, yet in many settings one may be able to alter the work processes in order to change the degree of interdependency. What implications does this insight have for Thompson's framework?

Case Study

TowerTech

TowerTech is an engineering firm designing and manufacturing components such as pumps used in chemical plants. TowerTech has a traditional functional organisation comprising departments for sales & marketing, engineering, production, and staff (see Figure 7.11).

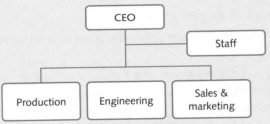

Figure 7.11 Organisational structure of TowerTech.

TowerTech is experiencing severe problems in delivering what it has promised. Projects are running behind schedule and are over budget. Customers are complaining. The management team asks a team of consultants to identify the root causes and to design a process that will be more predictable in terms of cost and time and that will result in higher customer satisfaction.

The consultants first speak with the CEO. He draws a diagram on a sheet of paper (see Figure 7.12) to explain the work process. He notes that the company has two types of customers. The primary customers are the chemical firms and TowerTech delivers to these firms when they are in the process of building or modifying their plants. But TowerTech also designs some components that it does not manufacture itself but that are manufactured by other firms that target companies in other industries.

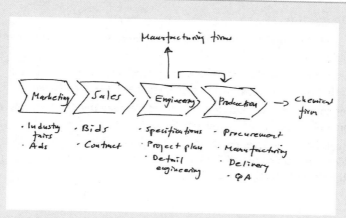

Figure 7.12 CEO's drawing of TowerTech's main work processes

TowerTech's Engineering department is a *profit centre* with regard to its external customers but is also a *cost centre* in that its internal customer (Production) is only charged the cost of the engineering hours used to design a particular product.

The consultants also interview the three department managers. The following is an excerpt from the interview transcripts:

Sales and Marketing manager:

> When I took on this position, the main goal that the CEO asked me to focus on was increasing sales. That is something we have delivered on: Our backlog is up 35 per cent compared to last year. As for the delivery problems . . . it's difficult for us when Production make changes to the spec that we included in the bid. We have tried to voice our concerns . . . but it's the CEO and the Engineering manager who seem to make the decisions here . . . they're former colleagues and often form an opinion about things before we are consulted . . . as you can see we're also housed in a building on a separate site, so we have to make a deliberate effort every time we want to interact or communicate with the Engineering and Production guys.

Head of Engineering:

> The new Sales and Marketing manager is inexperienced and sends away bid proposals with no idea whether we can deliver or not. If we win the project, we often have to drop whatever else we are doing to deliver what he has committed us to do. We can't go on like this so we're implementing a new resource allocation process in our unit to formalise how we plan and resource projects . . . I am also telling the CEO that we must change the way we develop the bids . . . we need to work in a more coordinated way.

Production manager:

> Our activity level is very high, and that's a big improvement . . . but the challenge now is that we're not prepared when the engineering drawings arrive . . . at times Engineering change the materials requirements without our knowledge . . . in addition we're not always happy about the quality of the drawings . . . some of the engineers seem to be more motivated to work for external clients, they earn no margin for working for us, and don't pay a penalty, either, for any screw-ups.

→

Discussion questions

1 Draw an illustration of some of the key interdependencies between the units described.

2 Identify how some or all of the five perspectives described in this chapter may shed light on the issues described by the managers that were interviewed.

3 Consider some tentative solutions that could improve performance. Try to apply at least three of the five interdependency types described in this chapter.

4 If you feel that some information is missing, what questions would you have asked the three managers or the CEO of TowerTech in order to confirm your hypotheses about the current situation or challenges?

Notes

1 *Acknowledgement*: Parts of this chapter draw heavily from a working paper that was developed in collaboration with Ron Sanchez of Copenhagen Business School.

2 The author was engaged as a consultant in re-designing the IT function of the company used as an example in this chapter.

3 The case example has been simplified in that only a small set of sub-units is included, moreover, each sub-unit only performs one function.

4 These constructs may be operationalised and measured. It is possible to ask members of organisational sub-units to rate the importance of interdependencies and to pool their assessments into a variable that can be evaluated for reliability and validity.

5 One indication of this complexity is that it frequently requires several iterations to arrive at a description that all members can agree correctly represents the way work is actually done in their unit.

6 The main difference compared to contracts made with outside partners is that internal agreements are either 'self-enforced' or enforced by means of hierarchical authority.

7 A supplier may also issue a generalised commitment to all customers in the form of a *service guarantee* ('we will resolve all technical issues within 24 hours after notification').

8 In a highly customer-focused organisation one would expect the supplier to commit to a certain time for resolving the issue (e.g., within 12 hours for errors with significant impact).

9 Such commitments are relatively rare, however. Doctors normally do not commit to curing diseases (only to deliver treatment) and university professors normally do not commit to produce learning (only to provide teaching).

10 The purpose of an IT policy is usually to ensure that IT management and development are aligned with overall business strategies and that different units follow a consistent set of practices. More specifically, it may include general IT principles, infrastructure strategies, standards regarding IT architecture and processes for prioritisation of investment proposals (see Weill and Woodham, 2004).

11 For simplicity we only describe two of the four levels of interdependency described in Sheppard and Sherman (1998).

References

Ackoff, R. L. (1994). *The Democratic Corporation: A Radical Prescription for Recreating Corporate America and Rediscovering Success*. New York: Oxford University Press.

Baldwin, C. and Clark, K. (2000). *The Power of Modularity*. Boston, MA: MIT Press.

Bolman, L. G. and Deal, T. E. (1997). *Reframing Organizations: Artistry, Choice, and Leadership*. San Francisco, CA: Jossey-Bass.

Bonacich, P. (1991). Simultaneous group and individual centralities. *Social Networks*, 13, 155–68.

Bower, J. L. (1970). *Managing the Resource Allocation Process*. Boston, MA: Harvard Business School Press.

Brown, G., Lawrence. T. B. and Robinson, S. L. (2005). Territoriality in organisations. *Academy of Managemenet Review*, 30, 577–94.

Burt, R. S. (1992). *Structural Holes: The Social Structure of Competition*. Cambridge, MA: Harvard University Press.

Child, J. and Rodrigues, S. B. (2003). Corporate governance and new organisational forms: issues of double and multiple agency. *Journal of Management and Governance*, 7, 337–60.

Earl, M. J. (1996). *Information Management: The Organisational Dimension*. Oxford: Oxford University Press.

Ford, J. D. and Ford, L. W. (1995). The role of conversations in producing intentional change in organisations. *Academy of Management Review*, 20, 3, 541–71.

Galbraith, J. (1993). *Competing With Flexible Lateral Organizations*. Reading, MA.: Addison-Wesley.

Haeckel, S. H. (1999). *Adaptive Enterprise: Creating and Leading Sense-and-respond Organisations*. Boston, MA: Harvard Business School Press.

Hammer, M. and Champy, J. (1993/2001). *Reengineering the Corporation*. London: Nicholas Brealey Publishing.

Hansen, M., Pfeffer, J. and Podolny, J. (1999). Too much of a good thing? Social networks, influence behaviors, and team performance. Paper delivered at the Academy of Management Conference, 6–11 August.

Hansen, Morten T. (1999). The search-transfer problem: The role of weak ties in sharing knowledge across organisation subunits. *Administrative Science Quarterly*, 44, 82–111.

Hayler, R. and Nichols, M. (2005). *What is Six Sigma Process Management?* New York: McGraw-Hill.

Heath, C. and Staudenmayer, N. (2000). Coordination neglect: how lay theories of organizing complicate coordination in organizations. *Research in Organizational Behavior*, 22, 153–91.

Jaques, E. (1989). *Requisite Organization: The CEO's Guide to Creative Structure and Leadership*. Arlington, VA: Cason Hall & Publishers.

Jastram, R. W. (1974). Notes: organization by sequential responsibility: transfer points. *California Management Review*, 17, 1, 124–5.

Jensen, M. C. and Meckling, W. H. (1976). Theory of the firm: managerial behavior, agency costs and ownership structure. *Journal of Financial Economics*, 3, 305–60.

Kahn, W. A. and Kram, K. E. (1994). Authority at work: internal models and their organisational consequences. *Academy of Management Review*, 19, 1, 17–50.

Kaplan, R. E. (1991). *Beyond Ambition: How Driven Managers can Lead Better and Live Better*. San Francisco, CA: Jossey-Bass.

Kay, J. (1995). *Foundations of Corporate Success.* Oxford: Oxford University Press.

Kim, W. C. and Mauborgne, R. A. (1996) Procedural justice and managers' in-role and extra-role behavior: the case of the multinational. *Management Science,* 42, 2, 499–515.

Lawrence, P. R. and Lorsch, J. W. (1967). *Organization and Environment: Managing Differentiation and Integration.* Boston, MA: Harvard University Press.

Malone, T. W. et al. (1999). Tools for inventing organisations: Toward a handbook for organisational processses. *Management Science,* 45, 3, 425–43.

March, J. (1988). *Decisions and Organizations.* Oxford: Basil Blackwell.

McCann, J. E. and Ferry D. L. (1979). An approach for assessing and managing inter-unit inter-dependence. *Academy of Management Review,* 4, 1, 113–20.

McFadyen, M. A. and Cannella, A. A. J. (2004). Social capital and knowledge creation: diminishing returns to the number and strength of exchange relationships. *Academy of Management Journal,* 47, 735–46.

Mintzberg, H. (1979). *The Structuring of Organizations.* Englewood Cliffs, NJ: Prentice-Hall.

Miles, R. M. (1979). Organizational conflict and management. In Miles, R. H. and Randolph, W. A., *The Organisation Game,* pp. 204–21. Santa Monica, CA: Goodyear.

Pfeffer, J. (1992). *Managing with Power.* Boston, MA: Harvard Business School Press.

Pfeffer, J. (1997). *New Directions for Organisation Theory: Problems and Prospects.* New York: Oxford University Press.

Pfeffer, J. and Salancik, G. R. (1978). *The External Control of Organisations: A Resource Dependence Perspective.* New York: Harper & Row.

Sanchez, R. (1995). Strategic flexibility in product competition. *Strategic Management Journal,* Vol. 16 (summer special issue), 135–159.

Sanchez, R. and Mahoney, J. T. (1996). Modularity, flexibility, and knowledge management in product and organization design. *Strategic Management Journal,* 17 (winter special issue), 63–76.

Scherr, A. L. (1993). A new approach to business processes. *IBM Systems Journal,* 32, 1, 80–98.

Shaw, R. B. (1992). The capacity to act: creating a context for empowerment. In Nadler, D. A. et al. (eds), *Organizational Architecture,* 155–74. San Francisco, CA: Jossey-Bass.

Sheppard, B. H. and Sherman, D. M. (1998). The grammars of trust: A model and general implications. *Academy of Management Review,* 23, 3, 422–37.

Smith, D. K. (1999). *Make Success Measurable! A Mindbook-Workbook for Setting Goals and Taking Action.* New York: Wiley.

Smith, R. B. and Eppinger, S. D. (1993). Characteristics and models of iteration in engineering design. *Proceeding of the International Conference on Engineering Design (ICED'93),* The Hague, The Netherlands, 564–71.

Thompson, J. D. (1967). *Organizations in Action.* New York: McGraw-Hill.

Von Hippel, E. (1990). Task partitioning: An innovation process variable. *Research Policy,* 19, 5, 407–18.

Walker, O. C. (1997). The adaptability of network organisations: Some unexplored questions. *Academy of Marketing Science,* 75–82.

Weill, P. and Woodham, R. (2004). *IT Governance: How Top Performers Manage IT Decision Rights for Superior Results.* Boston, MA: Harvard Business School Press.

Winograd, T. and Flores, F. (1986). *Understanding Computers and Cognition: A New Foundation for Design.* Norwood, NJ: Ablex Publishing Corporation.

Chapter 8

Rooting out complexity

Overview

◉ Background

- Organisational complexity is increasingly regarded as a key managerial challenge
- Practical tools and methodologies are needed that can be used to manage and/or reduce organisation designs that stakeholders perceive as excessively complex

◉ Challenges

- Organisational theory is frequently criticised for being too abstract to provide guidance to practitioners intending to improve the design of their organisations
- The practitioner-oriented literature has so far failed to produce effective advice due to inadequate definitions and generalisation of simplistic solutions

◉ Key question

- How can we develop a more rigorous approach that can lead to the development of specific tools and methods that practitioners can use to simplify organisational designs?

◉ Proposed approach

- Use specific cases of complex organisation designs as the starting point
- Identify possible generic causes that create complexity in these cases based on a mapping of functional requirements and design parameters
- Propose generic solutions (Design Propositions) that can be translated into specific solutions for handling similar challenges in other organisations

Introduction

Organisational complexity is increasingly regarded as a key managerial challenge. One implication is that we need to consider practical tools and methodologies that can be used to manage and reduce complexity. Unfortunately, neither the academic literature nor the practitioner literature provides much guidance to practitioners on this issue. As noted in Chapter 1, current theories in the organisational sciences are generally too abstract to serve as a basis for designing specific managerial interventions. The practitioner literature has recently started to focus on complexity reduction, but the actual prescriptions do not always address the underlying causes of complexity. One issue is the definition of complexity that is used. A common recommendation is to *reduce variety* that create internal complexity, for example, cutting the number of product variants, centralising operations, or reducing management layers (e.g., Ashkenas, 2007). In some cases, these may well be relevant options to consider. Yet it is not variety per se but the *interdependencies* between elements (units, levels, products, etc.) that create complexity (cf. Chapter 2). There is also a tendency to prescribe general principles for simplification rather than on developing diagnostic frameworks that can help practitioners analyse the particular problem they are confronted with and identify the most appropriate approach to resolve it. Moreover, recommendations for how to simplify organisations tend to focus on structure in isolation, instead ofconsidering what the structure exists to do – that is, its *function*. What are the key outcomes or results that the organisation, its sub-units and individual roles are accountable for? The question is not how to simplify organisational structures, but how we can reduce organisational complexity *while at the same time* maintain or even improve the 'functionality' – the ability of the organisation to attain key business goals (related to financial results, process performance, costs, customer satisfaction, etc.).

This chapter builds on the key assumptions in Axiomatic Design theory (AD). As the majority of other similar approaches, AD assumes that *problem definition* is the key to successful design. This means that we first need to find ways to *identify and characterise* complex organisational designs, before we can consider how to simplify them. As described in Chapters 1 and 2, Suh (2001) has demonstrated how it is possible to capture the structure of a particular design solution by mapping functional requirements against design parameters. Moreover, he has indicated how one can identify common features *across* different concrete instances and identify generic design solutions that can be applied to reduce complexity for different categories of designs. The approach is similar to that developed by Altshuller (1985), a Russian inventor, who analysed thousands of patents in order to identify common problem–solution relationships. Altshuller identified approximately 200 patterns common to the patents that he studied, and he termed these patterns 'standards'. These standards are now being taught as inventive principles to designers facing similar problems (the approach is called TRIZ, which is an acronym for a Russian term meaning 'The theory of inventor's problem solving') (see Figure 8.1).

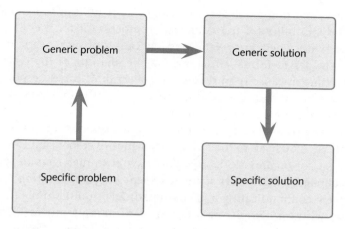

Figure 8.1 The TRIZ problem solving method

Altshuller's (1985) approach was intended for engineers designing physical products, yet may also serve as a guide for developing similar frameworks in other design disciplines. The approach has already been used by marketing researchers who have identified 'inventive templates' that can be used by marketing professionals to generate ideas about new products attributes and business models (Goldenberg and Mazursky, 2002).

This chapter is built around a set of brief case examples, drawn from consulting projects with firms in different industry sectors.[1] Each case describes the particular challenges associated with a particular organisation design. It shows how each case can be described using the AD design matrix and formulated as a generic problem, and then considers a generic solution (summarised as Design Propositions at the end of the chapter). The cases are tentatively grouped into five categories, based on the most salient issue in each: 1) responsibility overlaps; 2) role inconsistencies in horizontal processes; 3) excessive interfaces; 4) conflicting requirements; and 5) interdependency misalignment.

The main purpose of this chapter is to introduce a systematic approach to complexity reduction that is pragmatically valid (i.e., usable by practitioners) as well as testable (i.e., that contains design propositions that may be confirmed or disconfirmed by observing the outcome of interventions in organisations). The chapter concludes with a brief discussion of how the approach may be further refined and improved.

Responsibility overlaps

Central to all organisations is the concept of division of labour: In all large organisations, the responsibility for performing different tasks is allocated to different internal units (or individuals). But the allocation of responsibility is rarely perfect.

One frequently occurring problem is that two or more units or individuals may have been given responsibility for the same task or process (or for the same set of decisions or objectives). There are several possible causes of such overlaps. Those with the authority to design formal structures may be unaware of the issue or may not have had the time or capacity to remove the overlap. At times, responsibility overlaps emerge gradually and may be difficult to prevent before they begin to cause friction between the units or individuals concerned.

To what extent should we be concerned about responsibility overlaps? Up to a certain point, we may have to tolerate the existence of responsibility overlaps as an unavoidable fact of organisational life, and leave it to managers to sort them out. Much of a manager's daily work is indeed spent on compensating for such overlaps, by actively communicating and coordinating with other units that they share responsibility with for completing a task or performing a process. (There are also cases where responsibility overlaps are the result of a deliberate effort to 'force collaboration' between individuals or units by creating joint goals.) On the other hand, it also seems clear that responsibility overlaps negatively affect performance in some cases. A company may have ignored to define the dividing line between sales teams responsible for two different products, resulting in internal competition and uncoordinated marketing efforts toward potential clients. The head of the IT department and the head of the Finance department may both believe that they have the required authority to select a new software package supporting finance and accounting processes. Such disagreements may slow down decision making, and often require escalation to higher level managers for resolution. If this happens intermittently, it may be deemed acceptable, but if it occurs more frequently, it may be a source of concern. Responsibility overlaps can also make it difficult to make individual managers accountable, and to reward them appropriately: poor performance may always be attributed to the lacking effort or capability of others who participate in the same process. For this reason, it should be a general design principle to minimise responsibility overlaps as much as possible.

Let us consider the situation in an oil services company of around 500 employees. This company design and manufactures process equipment used on oil platforms, such as modules for water injection, hydrate inhibition, water/oil separation and water treatment. It carries out engineering and production in each of its five country subsidiaries (in Canada, France, Norway, Malaysia and the UK). The original strategy was to allocate geographical territories to each subsidiary. For example, the unit in Malaysia would serve Asian clients, the French unit would serve southern European clients, and so on. However, over time, clients had become more global, and no longer perceived the ability to carry out engineering projects locally as a prerequisite for awarding a contract to a supplier.[2] This in turn led to increasing competition among the five country subsidiaries.

A team of managers from each subsidiary were asked to participate in a project team facilitated by an internal consultant.[3] The team identified seven common product categories across the units. A key observation was that most of the subsidiaries would deliver the entire product/technology portfolio (see Table 8.1).

Table 8.1 Product categories delivered by different subsidiaries in oil services firm

	Country subsidiary				
	Norway	Canada	UK	France	Malaysia
Deliver oil treatment systems	X	X	X	X	X
Deliver gas treatment systems	X	X	X	X	X
Deliver produced water systems	X	X	X	X	X
Deliver seawater treatment systems	X	X	X	X	X
Delivery utility equipment	X	X	X	X	X
Deliver internals (components)	X	X	X	X	
Deliver hydrate inhibition systems	X	X	X	X	

The main solution that was recommended was to allocate responsibility so as to minimise overlaps (Table 8.2). The subsidiaries were asked to concentrate on those technology areas in which they had demonstrated technological and commercial capabilities, and to drop technologies for which they did not have sufficient capabilities to gain a strong competitive position. The proposed solution had two key advantages. It would capitalise on the strengths of each unit while eliminating competition between the units.

Table 8.2 Product categories delivered by different subsidiaries in oil firm after re-allocation of responsibility

	Country subsidiary				
	Norway	Canada	UK	France	Malaysia
Deliver oil treatment systems		X			
Deliver gas treatment systems		X		X	
Deliver produced water systems	X				
Deliver seawater treatment systems	X				
Delivery utility equipment					X
Deliver internals (components)			X		
Deliver hydrate inhibition systems	X				

The re-allocation of responsibility only concerned the design and engineering processes in the company. It was recommended that the sales function in each country would continue to offer the entire product range and interface with the client. (This solution is consistent with the organisational models described in Chapter 4, with sales units defined geographically, or by market segment, while product units are defined in terms of product or technology.)

A key prerequisite for splitting or re-allocating areas of responsibility in this manner is obviously that the underlying processes for which different actors or units are made responsible are in fact separable. It is assumed that the seven technology areas shown in Tables 8.1 and 8.2 are relatively independent, so that each country subsidiary may develop, design and manufacture products related to the technology without too many operational dependencies toward the other country subsidiaries.[4] (If there is uncertainty about whether this assumption holds, one may employ the techniques discussed in Chapter 5 in order to map interdependencies and find an appropriate grouping of activities.)

In this particular case, the solution that was selected was to *re-allocate* responsibilities among the units. However, responsibility overlaps can be resolved in several different ways. We should therefore review the options that exist *in principle* for handling similar cases. For this purpose, let us consider a simplified example of a technology company with a somewhat different structure (Figure 8.2).

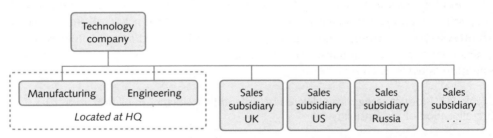

Figure 8.2 Structure of the technology company discussed in text

Unlike the oil services company discussed above, this company had maintained engineering design and manufacturing activities at its home base, while expanding its activities by establishing pure sales subsidiaries in various countries. The products were sold based on bids submitted in response to RFQs (Requests for Quotations). Initially, both the central engineering unit and the sales subsidiary shared responsibility for the sales and marketing process. The main reason for the shared responsibility was that the sales subsidiary was highly dependent upon the engineering unit's participation in terms of evaluating technical specifications, developing a proposed solution and estimating a price taking into account the production cost. A decomposition of the high-level functions against design parameters would look like the one shown in Table 8.3.

Table 8.3 Design matrix for sales process in the technology company

	Design parameters	
Functional requirements	Engineering unit	Sales subsidiary
Perform sales and marketing process	X	X

The initial strategy to deal with a perceived overlap of responsibility is often *specification*. One may attempt to describe the processes and areas of responsibility in more detail to see whether it is possible to isolate the more specific areas affected by overlap. In this particular case, it was found that the sales representatives in the country subsidiary were the ones that called on potential clients, identified leads and received the RFQs; however, that the RFQs were channelled to sales engineers in the engineering unit, who developed proposals based on the client's requirements. The engineering unit and the sales subsidiaries collaborated in developing the marketing plan, and representatives from both units participated in trade fairs, distributed brochures and placed advertisements in industry magazines. This leads to the decomposition shown in Table 8.4.

Table 8.4 Specification of responsibilities

	Design parameters	
Functional requirements	Engineering unit	Country subsidiary
Develop marketing plan	X	X
Identify new prospects		X
Develop proposals based on RFQs	X	
Set prices	X	X

As one specifies in more detail how responsibility is defined, one does not remove the overlaps themselves, but one may at least create some clarity regarding where the overlaps actually occur. Instead of simply stating that sales and marketing is a shared responsibility, it allows the company to allocate the responsibility for identifying new clients to the country subsidiary, while the engineering unit could be made accountable for developing proposals. One may not approve of this particular split of responsibilities, but it would probably be fairly effective in terms of creating clarity of accountability. One can imagine separate (and relatively independent) indicators being developed to measure performance, such as the number of new leads identified by the country subsidiary, and the 'hit ratio' (sales made to proposals developed) for the product unit.

A second approach, which can be termed *standardisation*, could be applied to handle the overlapping responsibilities with regard to pricing (cf. Table 8.4). If there are frequent disagreements between the country subsidiary and the engineering unit regarding pricing, one could develop standard guidelines or norms for how pricing decisions are to be made. For example, it is common among car manufacturers to centrally develop price guidelines for car models, while national car importers or dealerships are able to adjust prices within a certain range based on the local market conditions.

One responsibility overlap listed in Table 8.4 remains to be clarified, namely the shared responsibility for the marketing and sales plan. This overlap could be handled in the same manner, by detailing different aspects of the plan (e.g., focused on the global, regional, segment level) and specifying what aspects of the plan each unit would be responsible for. On the other hand, the development of a marketing and sales plan is often an annual event. For this reason, an approach we may call *sequential separation* is possible. The two units may jointly participate in this activity, if it can be conducted prior to – and be considered an input to – the other activities that they are responsible for. It may therefore be treated differently from the other, more continuous processes that are listed in Table 8.4.

The possibility of *re-allocating* the responsibilities remains (that is, changing which unit or actor is responsible for a given activity, process or decision). In this case, sales subsidiaries interfaced with clients yet the engineering unit developed the actual proposals to them. This may work well in some companies where client needs are expressed as written, technical requirements. Splitting the initial sales and the subsequent proposal development process would be less appropriate in firms where customer needs are more implicit, so that direct client interaction is required, or where clients for other reasons prefer to interact directly with the technical experts. Different options for re-allocating responsibilities exist in such cases. One option is to give the responsibility for the entire sales process to the market unit (i.e., the Sales subsidiary). (This would not necessarily involve the transfer of technical personnel from the engineering unit to the subsidiary. The technical experts in the engineering unit could be considered internal suppliers to the country subsidiary's sales staff in the proposal development process.) It would then be the country subsidiary that would request assistance and also be held accountable for sales revenues.

One also has the option of re-drawing the formal boundaries between units, an option we could call *restructuring*. For example, if two units are jointly responsible for the same activity, one has the option of merging the two units into one. A country subsidiary and a product unit may be merged. This could be an appropriate option if the product in question is only produced for one national market. By merging two units, one also removes the responsibility overlaps, viewed at the top level, as shown in Table 8.5. Of course, the issues will remain *within* the units that are merged, unless one follows the same process as above in terms of clarifying responsibility at a more detailed level.

Table 8.5 Design matrix for merged units

	Design parameter
Functional requirement	Engineering unit and country subsidiary
Perform sales and marketing process	X

Role inconsistencies in horizontal processes

The sales and marketing process that we have described above is one example of a 'horizontal' business process that depends on collaboration and negotiation between units performing different roles in the internal value chain. A number of processes that were once managed by means of vertical hierarchical governance are now managed in this manner. Another example is IT. Whereas IT staff in large companies used to be organised in IT departments within different business units, many companies have consolidated IT departments into Shared Services organisations that provide services to business units based on service level agreements (SLAs) that stipulate quality levels and costs. Although this model has gained widespread adoption, many firms encountered – and still encounter – significant challenges in the attempt to transform hierarchical relationships into effective customer-supplier processes underpinned by formal commitments such as SLAs. One important challenge is to appropriately define the role of customers, responsible for requesting services and monitoring service delivery, and internal suppliers, who are supposed to perform the work needed to deliver the services.

Table 8.6 Design intent behind the shared services model

	Design parameters	
Functional requirements	Business units	Shared Services
Define, request and approve services	X	
Provide services		X

In this section, we will consider the situation confronting the Chief Information Officer (CIO) of a large engineering firm with a global IT function of altogether 500 people. A couple of years before the CIO took on this role, the IT function had been split into two parts. The responsibility for hardware (servers, networks, etc.) and IT support was allocated to an IT department organised within the firm's Shared Services unit, whereas the responsibility for software related to core processes (application management and maintenance) had been allocated to IS departments, organised within the business units. The rationale behind the model was that the software teams needed to be organised as part of the line organisation, as their work typically involved configuring software to the unique needs of engineering projects. When establishing the Shared Services unit, the leaders of the business units had been sceptical of introducing another boundary between the application developers and the users, and had argued that the people providing software that supported core processes should remain in the line organisation.

Table 8.7 Design matrix for the firm that split IT and IS

	Design parameters	
Functional requirements	IT (Shared Services)	IS (Business unit)
Perform IT operations	X	
Provide core applications		X

At first sight, this particular split of responsibilities does not appear to be illogical (see Table 8.7). However, when examining how this design intent had been decomposed further, several problematical areas were discovered.

In order to evaluate the model, both IT managers and the internal clients were interviewed. The overall finding was that the Shared services unit generally failed to deliver services to the expected level. Representatives from the engineering projects complained that it was unclear who they should contact in order to fix problems and that it took an inordinate amount of time to respond to change requests (i.e., requests for changes in the features or functionality of applications). An IT manager that was interviewed remarked that the organisation was 'messy'. Meetings with representatives from IT, IS and the business units were characterised by 'fire fighting' to resolve technical issues, and little time was left to discuss how to address more longer-term needs. There were also concerns about high costs due to inefficient work processes and a lack of standardisation of applications across different internal units.

It was concluded that the mess was caused by several interconnected problems, such as unclear goals and performance standards (i.e., the SLA), inappropriate grouping (i.e., suboptimal boundaries) and lack of effective governance (including diffuse and overlapping accountabilities). A large restructuring project was initiated by the CIO to address these issues.

A particularly interesting implication of the split between IT and IS was the effect that this design decision had had on horizontal customer and supplier roles. It was found that the particular allocation of responsibilities in this company meant that IS sometimes was a supplier to IT, a client of IT, a joint supplier, or a link or mediator between IT and the line organisation. This is represented in the design matrix shown in Table 8.8.

Table 8.8 Actual design that was implemented (cf. Table 8.6)

	Design parameters	
Functional requirements	Business units	Shared Services
Define, request and approve services	X	
Provide services	X	X

Just as the same individual may have more than one role assigned to him or her (e.g., the same person may be manager and sales representative), an organisational unit may also perform multiple roles. One challenge in conceptualising this problem is that the roles may be logical when considering a single work process separately, yet they may be inconsistent when considering how they have been defined *across* different work processes. Three examples are illustrated in Figure 8.3a–c using the visual format of the so-called commitment protocol described in Chapter 7. When establishing or revising the service level agreement, it was IS, on behalf of the line organisation, who would negotiate the terms (Figure 8.3a). (There was no service level agreement that covered the services that IS provided to the business units.) In other words, in this case IS performed the role as 'customer', which was natural, in that IS departments were organised within business units. At other times, however, IS would be a kind of supplier to IT, for example, in resolving a software application error (Figure 8.3b) or creating access to applications (Figure 8.3c). It was also observed that the help desk, which was organised within IT, would log requests (and thereby allocate capacity by assigning the task to an IT specialist) not only for its own personnel but also for personnel belonging to IS. In other words, the purported supplier (IT) 'managed' the client's (IS) resources in this case.

As pointed out in Scherr (1993), the existence of multiple roles sometimes occurs legitimately, but it can also be a source of confusion and even represent a conflict of interest. In this particular case, end users were uncertain about who to contact for help and they also experienced that IS and IT were poorly coordinated. As illustrated in Figure 8.3c, both units would independently send a message to the user confirming that requested software had been installed or that access had been created. As already mentioned, responsibility overlaps not only creates unnecessary hand-offs, but may also make it difficult to create clear accountability for process performance. One example in this company was that the unit performing the customer role (IS) was asked – in its role as 'SLA manager' (Figure 8.3a) – to monitor, evaluate and approve outcomes that it itself has been an active participant in producing (Figure 8.3b–8.3c).[5]

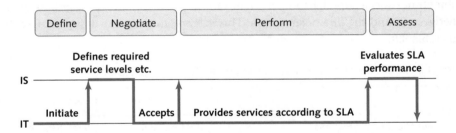

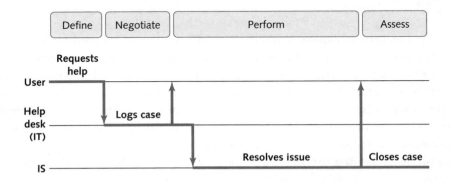

Figure 8.3a Commitment protocol for SLA management process

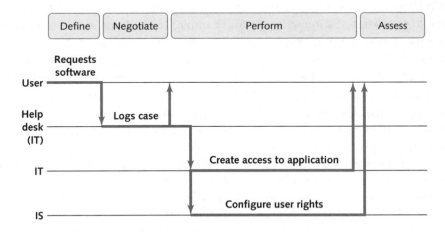

Figure 8.3b Commitment protocol for software error resolution process

Figure 8.3c Commitment protocol for process used to create access to application

The solution proposed by the restructuring team was to integrate the IT and IS units, that is, transfer the IT personnel to the Shared Services organisation. By implication, the services provided by both units would then be included in the service level agreement. Moreover, a new role of 'customer manager' was defined that would be responsible for all IS/IT deliveries to a business unit. To create a clear customer role it was also proposed that each customer manager should relate to a Business Information Officer (BIO) in the business units responsible for defining requirements based on the unit's current operations and business plans. Finally, more detailed process mapping was undertaken to remove overlapping responsibilities in the various work processes that IT and IS were engaged in. In some cases, the responsibility for performing work tasks was transferred from the IS to the IT sub-unit, removing the need for escalation of issues from IT to IS. The design matrix for the new organisation is shown in Table 8.9. (Note that this decomposition preserves the design intent shown in Table 8.6 above.)

Table 8.9 Revised allocation of responsibility between business units and IT/IS

	Design parameters		
	Business unit	Shared Services	
Functional requirements	(BIO role)	IT	IS
Define, request and approve services	X		
Perform IT operations		X	
Provide core applications			X

We can view inconsistent roles in horizontal customer-supplier processes as a special case of overlapping responsibilities as described in the case in the first section of this chapter. In addition to the overlap of responsibility, however, we are here also dealing with an in-built *conflict* between two roles performed by the same person or unit. As mentioned in Chapter 7, Scherr (1993) developed a methodology that can be applied in such cases. The first step is to define the internal suppliers and customers. By creating a chart that shows the requests and the commitments made in a work process involving suppliers and customers (cf. Figure 8.3a–c) one can then 'test' the consistency of the design by considering the roles at various steps in the same process as well as across different work processes. As we have seen in this example, if inconsistent roles are identified it may require a regrouping of tasks/roles, the creation of new roles, and/or the transfer of responsibilities between internal units.

Excessive interfaces – 'Everybody connected to everybody'

Organisation design methodologies have traditionally placed a strong emphasis on the importance of effective coordination and integration. As discussed in Chapter 7, one frequently discovers 'disconnects' in large organisations, that is, poorly functioning or lacking interfaces between sub-units (i.e., there are latent interdependencies that are not identified and/or enacted). Yet the emergence of higher levels of internal complexity has also created the opposite phenomenon – the existence of too many interdependencies. The question in such cases is not how to introduce more or better coordination, but how to expend less effort on unnecessary coordination.

A telecom company with around 9,000 employees created a team to deliver strategic HR services to the organisation. Ten strategic HR advisors were recruited, whose main roles were to serve as project managers in developing and rolling out various HR systems and initiatives, such as leadership development programmes, performance management tools and employee surveys. The company was comprised of eight different divisions. In addition to serving as project manager for a particular initiative, each strategic HR advisor had therefore been asked to take on an additional role, that of client relationship manager, in which they each served as the advisor to one of the divisions. The key responsibility in this role was to build and maintain effective relations with the internal clients in the divisions (line managers and HR managers) and ensure that programmes, tools or processes were adapted to the current needs in the divisions. The key responsibilities of the ten HR advisors are summarised in Table 8.10.

One of the initial observations[6] was that members of the unit seemed to spend quite a lot of time in meetings. It was also noted that many different members of the strategic HR team seemed to be involved in the same process, and that it was difficult to identify who the real 'owner' was of a given process or activity. To understand the organisational design of this team, it is helpful to map interdependencies of the various members of the team against each other (see Figure 8.4).

Table 8.10 Allocation of responsibilities in the Strategic HR team

	Strategic HR team									
	Advisor 1	Advisor 2	Advisor 3	Advisor 4	Advisor 5	Advisor 6	Advisor 7	Advisor 8	Advisor 9	Advisor 10
Plan and implement employee survey	X									
Plan and implement performance management process		X								
Plan and implement leadership development process			X							
Plan and implement competency management process				X						
Plan and implement succession planning process					X					
Assist in planning and development of performance management process						X				
Assist in planning and implementing leadership development process							X			
Assist in planning and implementing employee survey								X		
Assist in planning and implementing employee survey									X	
Assist in planning and implementing competency management process										X
Serve as client manager for Division 1	X									
Serve as client manager for Division 2		X								
Serve as client manager for Division 3			X							
Serve as client manager for Division 4				X						
Serve as client manager for Division 5					X					
Serve as client manager for Division 6						X				
Serve as client manager for Division 7							X			
Serve as client manager for Division 8								X		

	Advisor 1	Advisor 2	Advisor 3	Advisor 4	Advisor 5	Advisor 6	Advisor 7	Advisor 8	Advisor 9	Advisor 10
Advisor 1		X	X	X	X	X	X	X	X	
Advisor 2	X		X	X	X	X	X	X		
Advisor 3	X	X		X	X	X	X	X		
Advisor 4	X	X	X		X	X	X	X		X
Advisor 5	X	X	X	X		X	X	X		
Advisor 6	X	X	X	X	X					
Advisor 7	X	X	X	X	X					
Advisor 8	X	X	X	X	X				X	
Advisor 9	X							X		
Advisor 10				X						

Figure 8.4 Work process interdependencies between members of strategic HR team

When looking at Table 8.10 and Figure 8.4 it becomes apparent that the dual roles had created a complex structure with a high number of interdependencies. For example, the project manager for the annual employee survey (Advisor #1 in the matrix) would need to communicate with the HR advisor representing each of the divisions (Advisors #2–#8) in order to perform his/her role. (Typical issues to coordinate with the divisions would include how to communicate the purpose and timing of the survey, how to provide feedback about the results to different leadership teams in the division, and so on.) The project manager is herself the customer contact for one division, so there are seven other HR advisors to coordinate with, in addition to the colleague who assists in the project (Advisor #9). Advisor #1 thus has dependencies toward all but one of the unit's members, and the situation is similar for the other advisors – the distribution of roles is one that ensures that 'everybody is connected to everybody'. (This situation was exasperated by the unit's norm of always communicating with a division through the customer contact.) This design leads to a high coordination cost. There are 56 interdependencies in the matrix (out of 90 potential bilateral interdependencies), or 5.6 on average per advisor, and that is counting only the strongest, most critical interdependencies between the advisors – the matrix does not show potential, weaker interdependencies that may exist between the advisors or dependencies toward entities such as external service providers, other corporate functions, etc.

There are two main approaches that one can take to reducing the number of interdependencies in such a case. The most obvious solution is to remove the dual roles, which we could call *specialisation*. The distribution of roles would depend on the expected work load for each role, but as an example, we could create two teams. The first would be six process owners or specialists, each working on only one strategic HR process: the employee survey, performance management, leadership development, succession planning or competence management. The second team would consist of four customer contacts, each responsible for two divisions (Table 8.11). The resulting matrix (Figure 8.5) shows that this structural change would reduce the number of interdependencies by around 25 per cent (from 56 to 42). Such a change implies a considerable decrease in coordination cost – which translates directly into added capacity that can be used on the core tasks that the unit is responsible for. It is important to note that this improvement does not come not at the cost of added dependencies at the other end – each business unit will still have one common interface toward the strategic HR team.

	Advisor 1	Advisor 6	Advisor 2	Advisor 3	Advisor 4	Advisor 5	Advisor 7	Advisor 8	Advisor 9	Advisor 10
Advisor 1		X					X	X	X	X
Advisor 6	X									
Advisor 2							X	X	X	X
Advisor 3							X	X	X	X
Advisor 4							X	X	X	X
Advisor 5							X	X	X	X
Advisor 7	X		X	X	X	X				
Advisor 8	X		X	X	X	X				
Advisor 9	X		X	X	X	X				
Advisor 10	X		X	X	X	X				

Figure 8.5 Work process interdependencies after revising the allocation of responsibilities

This solution has the additional advantage of creating greater role clarity for the individual advisor. One would be either a specialist, focusing on a certain service or initiative (at least for a period of time), or a generalist, consulting with the internal clients and planning how to roll out the programmes and processes.

The disadvantages of this solution are that it may reduce task variety for the individual and that it increases the distance between the specialists and the internal clients that the specialists serve in the divisions. This may be a concern among some HR professionals, who would prefer a model that places them in direct contact with their internal clients more often (Kates, 2006). An approach which would address this concern would be to step outside the matrix, so to speak, and distribute the roles among the eight divisions. The strategic HR team would then be reduced in size (or even disbanded) and the 10 HR advisors would instead be transferred to the divisions, where they might report to the divisional HR manager. This solution could be appropriate as part of an initiative to decentralise resources. It adds capacity to roll out the programmes and processes in the divisions at the expense of capacity in the corporate centre dedicated to the development of common new programmes

Table 8.11 Revised allocation of responsibilities within the Strategic HR team

	Strategic HR team									
	Advisor 1	Advisor 2	Advisor 3	Advisor 4	Advisor 5	Advisor 6	Advisor 7	Advisor 8	Advisor 9	Advisor 10
Plan and implement employee survey	X									
Plan and implement performance management process		X								
Plan and implement leadership development process			X							
Plan and implement competency management process				X						
Plan and implement succession planning process					X					
Assist in planning and implementing employee survey						X				
Serve as client manager for Division 1 and 2							X			
Serve as client manager for Division 3 and 4								X		
Serve as client manager for Division 5 and 6									X	
Serve as client manager for Division 7 and 8										X

and processes. Distributing the strategic HR roles among the divisions will be more problematical in the absence of such a rationale. If the company requires new programmes and processes, or intends to maintain a common approach to strategic HR, it will probably increase coordination costs as the advisors will be forced to coordinate across formal boundaries (i.e., across the eight divisions). An already high coordination cost will increase even further. It is possible, though, to envisage that advisors spend some of their time in cross-divisional projects to develop new HR programmes and processes even if they are organised within divisions. On the other hand, once they have been transferred to a division, the division may be reluctant to see the experts work on projects outside the division (as long as the division is allocated the cost for the HR heads) (Kates, 2006).

Conflicting requirements due to resource dependency

Dependency on a common resource – such as production facilities or distribution channels – is a common source of coupling in functional requirements. We will use a key dilemma facing a seismic surveying company to illustrate this form of complexity. Seismic surveying companies basically help oil companies in the search for oil by collecting seismic data (both offshore and onshore) that are then analysed and interpreted by geologists in the oil companies. In the particular company that we will examine, offshore (marine) surveys were conducted by a fleet of around 12 specialised vessels, while the onshore surveys were carried out by a separate business unit with field crews, working on projects around the globe. The CEO initiated a review of the organisational structure of the company. One important design criterion that was identified was to differentiate more strongly between two parts of the offshore business. Offshore seismic surveys are done either on the request of a particular oil company, which then becomes the sole owner of the data collected (so-called 'contract' surveys), or as an investment by the seismic survey company itself, in building up a library of data that can be sold to multiple clients over time (so-called 'multi-client surveys'). The income from contract surveys are received upon completion of the survey, whereas the income from multi-client surveys are spread over several years, depending on the sales of the library data. Historically, these two areas had been combined in the company both in terms of managerial accountability and operations. The same senior managers would be accountable for both contract and multi-client work, and would often try to schedule multi-client work in between contract work in order to utilise vessel capacity effectively (however, at lower levels of the organisation, one would find sales teams dedicated to either product). Yet the CEO had come to believe that these two areas in fact represented fundamentally different business models. Consultants working for the company had observed that contract work had a tendency to drive out multi-client work in the short term, hurting the company's longer-term prospects. They recommended a stronger separation of the two areas, in fact, they had tentatively drawn a new organisational chart showing an entirely product-based organisation, with 'Contract' and 'Multi-client' as two separate business units.

The key managers in the company were intrigued by this idea, but wanted to spend some time clarifying what the objectives of a re-design should be and to evaluate the implications of a possible change in structure. During interviews with managers in the different business units, it quickly became clear that there were some challenges related to a possible split between contract and multi-client. The simple reason was that both relied on the same production resource, namely the vessels. Although contract and multi-client clearly represented two different business models, they were highly interdependent from an operational point of view, in that the same vessels, with the same crews and equipment, would do both types of work. In times of high demand for both products, and limited vessel capacity, management would have carefully to allocate capacity between the two product areas.

Table 8.12 Allocation of functions with product line organisation

	Design parameters			
Functional requirements	Management	Vessels	Contract business unit	Multi-client business unit
Allocate vessel capacity	X			
Perform contract surveys		X		
Perform multi-client surveys		X		
Maximise revenue from contract projects			X	(x)
Maximise revenue from multi-client projects			(x)	X

The proposed organisation design would lead to a decomposition of functions as shown in Table 8.12. It is indicated (with an 'x' in parenthesis) that there may be coupling with regard to the revenue goals. One cannot maximise revenues for multi-client projects without considering whether there is capacity to carry out the surveys, which depends on how many contract projects that are sold and scheduled, and vice versa. The underlying challenge is thus related to the shared use of the production resources (vessels). It is similar, in principle, to the case where two product lines are manufactured in the same factory. In a seismic surveying company, the additional challenge is that the 'factory' – the vessels carrying out the seismic survey – are moving objects and that it requires considerable time and cost to switch a vessel from one region to another.

There are three generic solutions to this challenge. First, a company may simply separate the production resources. The seismic survey company may divide its vessel fleet into two groups, one handling contract, and the other multi-client projects (see Table 8.13).

Table 8.13 Design matrix showing allocation of functions with separation of production resources

	Design parameters				
Functional requirements	Management	Vessels 1–6	Vessels 7–12	Contract business unit	Multi-client business unit
Allocate vessel capacity	X				
Perform contract surveys		X			
Perform multi-client surveys			X		
Maximise revenue from contract projects				X	
Maximise revenue from multi-client projects					X

This is an uncoupled design according to axiomatic design principles, in that it does allow the achievement of each functional requirement without compromising the other.[7] Other factors being equal, an uncoupled design is clearly preferable. It not only removes the production resource interdependency but also creates a situation where the two business units can sell their respective products in an autonomous fashion. Removing the resource interdependency removes the need for complex internal coordination mechanisms, such as matrix reporting structures.

On the other hand, there may be design criteria or constraints on the desired solution that will need to be met. For example, minimisation of costs could be one constraint. Separating a manufacturing process by product may result in higher costs due to slack (one may not be able to utilise the production facilities fully), in addition there is the initial investment of creating the extra assembly line. Since the production resources in this case are moving objects, operating around the globe, this solution would imply a significantly higher fuel cost, as one would need to cover a lot more distance with only 6 vessels at one's disposal compared to 12.

A second option would be not to split the company into two business units, but instead create one unit responsible for the sales of both products (Table 8.14).

Table 8.14 Design matrix showing the allocation of functions if the two product lines are combined

	Design parameters		
Functional requirements	Management	Vessels	Contract and multi-client business unit
Allocate vessel capacity	X		
Perform contract surveys		X	
Perform multi-client surveys		X	
Maximise revenue from contract projects			X
Maximise revenue from multi-client projects			X

With this option, vessel capacity is shared between the product areas, and one avoids the conflicting interdependencies described above (Figure 8.12).

Rather than structurally merging the two sales units (contract and multi-client), the same effect may be achieved by *aligning the incentives* of the two units. The intention would be to ensure that the sales units focus simultaneously on sub-unit performance and overall corporate performance, by finding a production mix that maximises overall profitability. However, it is important to note that neither of these two alternatives would solve the underlying problem, they simply delegate the resolution of complex trade-offs to managers further down in the organisation.

Finally, a third alternative is to use market mechanisms to increase access to production resources. Namely, one or both business units may be allowed to outsource production (i.e., lease vessel capacity), either for all projects or only in times of high demand (obviously, a key assumption is that adequate vessels would be available on the market). This may be an uncoupled design (see Table 8.15).

Although this approach should be effective from a structural perspective, there are some potential disadvantages as well. Market sourcing is often more expensive than using internal production facilities. In a cyclical industry like the seismic surveying business, the rates for hiring a vessel move in step with overall demand, and when the market is at a peak, rates are at their highest level, and there may not be any additional capacity available. Moreover, one may not be able to remove the interdependency entirely as suggested in Table 8.15. For example, if one business unit chooses to outsource production, while the other continues to source internally, the latter may have to tolerate a higher unit cost (as the overall volume decreases). A potential solution to this problem may be to allow the production resource to also produce for other companies, when there is available capacity. (This would be akin to adopting a full internal market where units may both sell and buy externally.)

Table 8.15 Design matrix showing the allocation of functions with market sourcing

Functional requirements	Management	Own vessels	Leased vessels	Contract business unit	Multi-client business unit
Allocate vessel capacity	X				
Perform contract surveys		X			
Perform multi-client surveys			X		
Maximise revenue from contract projects				X	
Maximise revenue from multi-client projects					X

However, a company is likely to consider such a move only if it does not consider its production technologies to be a core competency (in addition to its design, project execution, and marketing capabilities). In many industries, production resources often become gradually more commoditised over time. This is partly the case in the seismic surveying business; recently, geophysical companies have emerged that do not own any vessels but rely entirely on market sourcing, i.e., hired vessels. However, so far, these are mainly low-end vessels that are not fitted with the latest technologies used by the seismic surveying companies operating their own fleet.

Misalignment of interdependencies

In Chapter 7, we discussed five different types of interdependencies that may exist between organisational sub-units, related to activities, governance, resources, commitments and social networks. We also noted that these interdependencies may not always be in alignment with each other. This creates a special form of complexity that often presents managers with considerable challenges. Misalignment of this form may occur for a number of reasons, but a fairly common cause is the partial transfer of responsibility or the establishment of dual reporting lines.

The Chief Operating Officer (COO) in a large multidivisional company is planning the development and roll-out of several new quality improvement programmes, such as Lean manufacturing and Six Sigma. To succeed with these initiatives, he believes he needs the support of the internal consulting team in the company. However, this team is not part of the corporate staff, but organised within the Shared Services unit, a separate, legal entity in the company. The COO believes he needs several full-time project managers for the quality initiatives and therefore considers merging the consulting group with the corporate staff group at the company's headquarters. However, the CFO of the company is concerned about the (appearance of) overhead costs and is sceptical about any increase in the number of corporate staff. As a compromise solution, the COO announces that the head of the internal consulting unit will report directly to him, with only a dotted-line relationship to the pre-existing line manager (i.e., the head of the Shared services unit). No other formal changes are made to the design of the unit, which continues to appear on the organisation chart as a sub-unit within Shared services.

In reality, a 'hybrid' model is created by this change (Figure 8.6). According to the organisation chart, the internal consulting team is a sub-unit within Shared Services. Yet it becomes a corporate staff function in terms of its governance interdependencies (the formal reporting relationship). For example, after the change, all hiring decisions were authorised by the COO rather than the head of the Shared Services unit. In terms of its resource interdependencies, the internal consulting unit remained an internal supplier unit, like other Shared Services units, as its costs were still expected to be covered from fees generated from internal clients, rather than from the corporate staff budget. (The funding for the quality programmes was partially created by charging the business units a fee for the use of various quality improvement tools, participation on training courses, etc.)

Although this change was implemented simply by drawing a new reporting line crossing two legally separate units, it increases complexity in some subtle ways.

Table 8.16 Coupling due to introduction of new reporting line

	Design parameters	
Functional requirements	Shared Services director	COO
Increase corporate support for quality improvement programmes		X
Balance internal revenues and costs	X	(X)

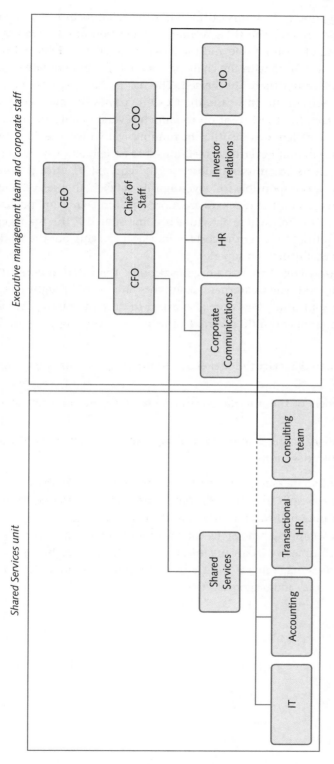

Executive management team and corporate staff

Shared Services unit

Figure 8.6 Organisation chart depicting new reporting line (black line) for internal consulting team

The change creates asymmetry in terms of the reporting relationship as well as misalignment between the resource and the governance dimension of the organisation, which carries the risk of creating role and incentive conflicts (see Table 8.16). The Shared Services director is faced with the challenge of having a subordinate who reports to a manager more senior than him/herself. The risk is that the more powerful manager on one dimension (in this case, the COO) bypasses the manager on the other dimension. In fact, the COO went on to launch several quality improvement programmes for which there was insufficient funding, yet which the director of the Shared Services organisation nevertheless felt forced to accept, and which consequently led to a deficit in its accounts. (It subsequently required significant time and energy to clarify who was responsible for covering this deficit.) Alternatively, in a scenario where the managers on the two axes are more equal in status and power, one can easily imagine a situation where activities become stalled if the manager controlling the resources refuses to cover the costs involved in carrying out the work mandated by the unit's formally defined superior.

It was eventually acknowledged that the organisation of the internal consulting team was suboptimal, and when external consultants later were brought in to reorganise the corporate staff unit, they were also asked to develop a new organisational model for the internal consulting team. In this process, three options were considered:

- Reverting to a pure Shared Services model (i.e., eliminating the dual reporting relationship)
- Transferring the members of the internal consulting team to the corporate staff unit
- Transferring the members of the internal consulting team to other parts of the organisation (i.e., the business units)

A combination of the last two measures was eventually chosen by this company. The internal consulting team was split in half, with some consultants transferred to the divisions, while the remaining half was transferred to the corporate staff.

This case shows how a seemingly innocuous change in formal reporting lines may introduce considerable complexity in an organisation. In addition to the contradictory functional requirements (Table 8.16) it also led to power asymmetries and ambiguity with regards to roles and responsibilities.

Conclusion

In this chapter, five cases have been described that all exemplify different forms of complexity, but the causes and the consequences differ. Table 8.17 summarises some key features of the cases described.

The cases demonstrate how complex organisation designs may be described and analysed by considering the relationship between different functional requirements and/or design parameters as suggested in Suh (2001). The solutions that have been proposed illustrate various ways of simplifying the designs. The intention has been to maintain or improve the system's functionality (i.e., the ability of a sub-unit or an entire organisation to realise its goals and strategies) while minimising internal complexity by de-coupling functional requirements and/or design parameters. Put differently, the proposed solutions are intended to serve as directions for simplifying the structure of the system that delivers an outcome, not to change or simplify the outcome itself.

The proposed approach may be further developed and validated in different ways. As the cases were derived from a limited number of consulting projects, it is necessary to confirm, and if necessary, revise the framework proposed here. One question is the validity of the categorisation. The cases were tentatively grouped into five categories; further analytical and empirical work may extend or revise this conceptualisation. Second, the consequences of complexity that have been described (and summarised in Table 8.17) were mainly based on the author's own observations. More systematic research may identify in a more precise manner the consequences of complex designs on organisational functioning. Finally, it is important to verify that replicable *solutions* have been identified, in other words, that the design propositions that are proposed can be used to resolve similar issues encountered by managers in other organisations. This may be done by collecting data from organisation re-design projects where the design propositions are employed and where data are collected to evaluate the outcome. It is also possible to use experimental methods (see Goldenberg and Mazursky, 2002), by asking one group of participants in an experiment to re-design a structure by applying the design propositions, and comparing this with the results from a second group that uses another, alternative approach (or purely intuitive means).

Although we are far from having a system as rigorous as that developed by Altshuller (1985) in the physical domain, the approach that has been outlined will hopefully serve as a starting point for managers in selecting interventions and for scholars in further developing theory, methods and tools that address the challenge of organisational complexity.

Table 8.17 Summary of cases representing complex organisational design

Case	Main issue	Consequences
1 Overlapping accountabilities	• Lack of definition or separation of responsibilities between two or more roles, units	• Competition among sub-units, roles • Unclear accountability • Frequent escalation of issues
2 Role inconsistencies in horizontal processes	• Inconsistent unit mandates • Role conflicts (e.g., same person performs and approves outcome of process) • Missing customer or supplier role	• Poor service quality as perceived by customers • General lack of oversight, accountability • Interdepartmental conflicts
3 Excessive interfaces	• Excessive number of work process interdependencies due to dual roles	• Information overload • Excessive time and effort used to coordinate work • Low productivity
4 Conflicting functional requirements	• Coupling between strategic or operational goals due to resource dependency	• Competition for resources • Interdepartmental conflicts • Suboptimal performance compared to similar systems without coupling
5 Interdependency misalignment	• Misalignment of different interdependencies (such as those relating to governance and resources)	• Unclear governance; accountability • Conflicting priorities • Power asymmetries

Design propositions

Objective *Reduce or eliminate responsibility overlaps between units, roles*

8.1 Depending on the specific design goals and circumstances, select one or more of the following actions:

a *Specify* responsibilities for individual process steps or decision areas

b *Standardise* processes, for example, by establishing common guidelines for resolving issues

c *Sequentially separate* activities in time, to allow units to reach a joint decision or form a policy together

d *Re-allocate responsibilities* to ensure that related activities are conducted within the same unit

e *Restructure* formal boundaries to merge units responsible for interdependent activities together

Objective   *Ensure that customer and supplier roles in horizontal business processes are consistently defined*

    8.2   Depending on the specific design goals and circumstances, select one or more of the following actions:

        a Ensure that lower level grouping is in accordance with higher level design intent (i.e., avoid coupling when decomposing the design)

        b Establish explicit customer and supplier roles

        c Analyse processes as a series of commitments between customers and suppliers

        d Redesign processes to remove inconsistent roles and ensure that there are 'complete' commitment protocols (see also Chapter 7)

Objective   *Reduce the number of interfaces between different roles within a unit (or between different sub-units that form part of a larger unit)*

    8.3   *Specialise* roles by removing dual responsibilities

Objective   *Reduce or remove coupling between functional requirements that is due to dependency on shared resources*

    8.4   Depending on the specific design goals and circumstances, select one or more of the following actions:

        a *Separate resources* by splitting them into independent groups

        b *Restructure* formal boundaries between sub-units

        c Introduce *market sourcing* to increase flexibility and the range of resources accessible to the firm

Objective   *Avoid interdependency misalignment*

    8.5   When considering a change in one design parameter of the organisation (e.g., governance), assess the impact on other design parameters (e.g., resources, commitments, activities, and social network) and evaluate whether there exist design options that preserve interdependency alignment

Review questions

1   In general, how can one map the structure of a design that stakeholders perceive as excessively complex?

2   Why do responsibility overlaps emerge in many large organisations?

3   How can horizontal customer–supplier roles be consistently defined?

4   How can you reduce the number of interdependencies between individuals or teams?

5   What options are available when one wants to simplify an organisation where functional requirements for different sub-units (e.g., business goals) are in conflict?

6   Why does misalignment between different interdependency dimensions sometimes emerge?

Research questions

1 What would be an appropriate research methodology to verify that the categorisation of issues proposed in this chapter is representative, or alternatively, identify an improved conceptualisation?

2 How could one more systematically test out, and further improve, the proposed interventions aimed at reducing complexity (i.e., the design propositions)?

Case study

Defining EVP responsibilities in Royal Bank

Royal Bank is a large European bank with around 15,000 employees. During a recent restructuring the bank is divided into seven separate profit centres:

- Retail banking – banking products and financial services delivered via online banking and branches to individual customers and small businesses
- Capital Markets & Savings – development of savings and capital markets products such as mutual funds
- Transaction services – Royal Bank's credit card business
- Corporate banking – banking solutions to medium-size and large businesses
- Wealth management – investment management services
- Royal Insurance – insurance company providing life and non-life insurance products
- Royal Bank Africa – the bank's emerging network of branches in five different African countries offering retail banking services

The retail banking unit develops and distributes everyday banking products such as savings accounts, loans and cash management services. In addition, it also distributes products developed by several other units, such as credit cards, non-life insurance (e.g., accident and travel), as well as savings products. Royal Bank Africa mainly distributes products developed by the Retail banking unit. The Corporate banking and Wealth management units interface directly with clients and do not distribute their products via the retail banking unit. Although the Retail banking unit distributes non-life insurance products, Royal Insurance also has its own sales force that sells life insurance products (as well as non-life insurance).

In addition to the seven profit centres, there are six staff and support units: Operations, IT, HR, Marketing, Credit & Risk Control and Group Strategy. The staff and support units serve all seven profit centres. Administrative services are charged according to use at cost.

The CEO would like to have a small executive team with three or four executive vice presidents (EVPs) and is thus considering how to group the business units into business areas. An important consideration is how to define responsibility for the staff and support units. In the end he decides to distribute the responsibility among the EVPs for these functions as depicted in Figure 8.7. For example, the head of IT will report to EVP 2, whereas the head of Group Credit & Risk Control will report to EVP 3. With this solution, one avoids the need for a separate Chief of Staff role. At the same time, the large and complex IT and Operations functions are placed within the same business area as the most IT-intensive businesses delivering retail, insurance and credit card services.

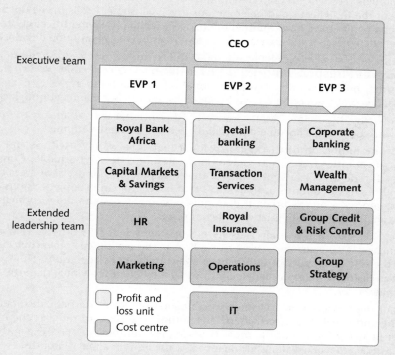

Figure 8.7 EVP responsibilities in Royal Bank

Discussion questions

1 What challenges do you think the proposed design would create?
2 How would you categorise these challenges in terms of the framework described in this chapter (cf. Table 8.17)?
3 How could these challenges be avoided?

Notes

1 The author was either the project manager or a project participant on these projects. The methodology that was followed was to document the situation that was observed during the consulting project. For example, one tool that was used was an 'issue log' where key observations, quotes from interviews and the like were noted down throughout the project. After the project was completed, this information was summarised and a meeting with the client manager was arranged where the client manager could provide feedback on draft descriptions of the cases. In order to protect the anonymity of the individuals and organisations involved, some details in the description of the companies have been omitted or changed, while preserving the basic structure of the challenge facing the managers and employees in the organisation described.

2 Since this project was completed (in 2004) the trend has reversed. At the time, the company described largely targeted large, international oil companies. Today, this and many other oil services firms target national oil companies to a greater extent, and national oil companies often do require suppliers to carry out manufacturing locally.

3 I acknowledge the help of Matt Grootveld (the internal consultant on the project team) who contributed documentation and discussed this case with me.

4 This is one limitation of the so-called RACI matrix, a widely used tool for defining responsibilities (RACI is an acronym for Responsible, Accountable, Consulted, Informed). The RACI is a simple matrix that lists processes or decision areas on one axis and the names of units or individuals that have a role in making decisions or performing a process on the other. It does not contain any design rules or principles for how to align the responsibilities with the processes.

5 We may add that such role reversals are not unique. Scherr (1993) noted that a client that engages a consulting or accounting firm is the paying customer, but also performs the role of supplier of information about the client's operations. However, the 'client-as-customer' role is usually performed by a different individual than the 'client-as-supplier' role.

6 Many of the services were delivered in collaboration with external consultancies or training and development providers. The author was asked to serve as the external project manager for one of the projects during the autumn of 2007. The author was given a desk and worked alongside members of the unit for about 5 months.

7 With a few exceptions, there was little overlap between the two product lines in terms of customers: Only rarely would the sales teams for both contract and multi-client target the same customer. If this had not been the case a more appropriate design would be a three-dimensional structure as discussed in Chapter 4.

References

Altshuller, G. S. (1985). *Creativity as an Exact Science*. New York: Gordon & Breach.

Ashkenas, R. (2007). Simplicity-minded management. *Harvard Business Review*, 85, 12, 101–9.

Goldenberg, J. and Mazursky, D. (2002). *Creativity in Product Innovation*. Cambridge: Cambridge University Press.

Kates, A. (2006). (Re) Designing the HR organization. *Human Resource Planning*, 29, 2, 22–30.

Scherr, A. L. (1993). A new approach to business processes. *IBM Systems Journal*, 32, 1, 80–98.

Suh, N. P. (2001). *Axiomatic Design: Advances and Applications*. New York: Oxford University Press.

Index